THE COMPLETE CHINESE Takeout COOKBOOK

KWOKLYN WAN

Over 200 Takeout
Favorites to Make at Home

Photography by Sam Folan and Gizem Kumbaraci

Hardie Grant

QUADRILLE

Publishing Director Sarah Lavelle
Editor Vicky Orchard
Assistant Editor Sofie Shearman
Series Designer Emily Lapworth
Designer Alicia House
Photographer Sam Folan,
except pages 4, 5, 7, 17, 19, 25, 30, 32, 38,
87, 88, 91, 93, 103, 109, 127, 129, 131, 132,
143, 146, 149, 159, 160, 169, 181, 190, 199,
203, 204, 215, 225, 245, 260, 269, 273, 276,
281, 286, 293 and 298 by Gizem Kumbaraci
Food Stylist Katie Marshall
Props Stylist Agathe Gits
Cover Typography Adam Hayes
Head of Production Stephen Lang
Production Controller Nikolaus Ginelli

Published in 2022 by Quadrille
an imprint of Hardie Grant Publishing

Quadrille
52–54 Southwark Street
London SE1 1UN
quadrille.com

Cataloguing in Publication Data: a catalogue record
for this book is available from the British Library.

Text © Kwoklyn Wan 2022
Photography © Quadrille 2022
Design © Quadrille 2022
Cover Typography © Adam Hayes 2022

ISBN 9781787137394

Printed in China

CONTENTS

BEEF & PORK

VEGETABLES

39.

89.

130.

161.

268.

287.

INTRODUCTION

I really can't quite believe that I'm actually writing the introduction to my FIFTH book. It's seriously mind-blowing, not to mention humbling to think that thanks to some higher force, it was little old me (well, not so little) who was chosen to not only share my father's and grandfather's legacy, but that of an entire nation.

I could never have predicted as a 5-year-old running up and down the stairs in my grandfather's restaurant that one day I'd be sharing so many of his recipes with so many people around the world.

If I'm brutally honest there were times I hated working in the restaurant. I mean, how many 14, 15 or even 16-year-old kids want to work on a Saturday night when their mates are out gadding around town? But this was my life, my reality, and look at me now (all smiles). So, what once drove me crazy I now thank, and with an open and loving heart can honestly say I would not change a thing.

My *Complete Chinese Takeout Cookbook* is a collection of favourites from Crispy Duck to Sweet Barbecue Ribs – you know the ones that literally fall off the bone – to sticky and gooey hot bananas in batter. When you think of comfort food and the dishes you ate growing up as a Friday or Saturday night treat, this book is the key to creating those dishes in your own kitchen.

For many, cooking these dishes will spark reminiscences of simpler times; flashbacks will flood their minds of family evenings sat around the coffee table watching *Dusty Bin* on the TV and then, in walk Mum and Dad with the TAKEOUT. Instantly the whole room would fill with the smells of crispy noodles, sweet sauces and Chinese chips. Oh my goodness, the smell of those chips would drive anyone crazy with hunger. The sounds of the rustle of the bag, the tearing of the chip paper and the unfolding of the aluminium containers revealing their hidden treasures: sweet and sour, curry, noodles, fried rice, satay chicken skewers, sweet BBQ ribs...

Now I've made you all hungry, the next step is simple, and I mean REALLY simple. Just flick through the pages of my super-duper book and as soon as you land on a recipe that you know will instantly transport you back to a 10-year-old you, go and cook it. I promise you that nothing gets the old grey matter pumping like the sights and smells of your childhood unfolding in front of your very eyes.

Happy wok'ing, you lovely, lovely people, you.

CHINESE ETIQUETTE AND FOOD FACTS

'The kitchen is the heart of the home.'

Chinese people have many customs and traditions, such as 'you must always respect your elders' and 'the littlest of actions have huge significant meanings'. Over the years I have not always got these right and have been told off by Grandma and Dad on many occasions. Even now (at the tender age of 48), Dad will correct me on the smallest of things, so much so it's now just expected and often laughed about.

CHINESE ETIQUETTE

After pouring tea, it is essential to never point the spout of the teapot at others because this gesture has the same meaning as using the finger to point, which in Chinese culture is considered rude. Therefore, the spout must be directed to where no one is sitting, usually outward from the table.

It is customary to serve fish at Chinese New Year, as it symbolises 'surplus and prosperity'. This dish is normally served with a pair of long, serving chopsticks.

When presented with a bowl of rice, receive it with both hands, as it marks a sign of respect. Receiving with only one hand signals laziness or disrespect.

Chinese meals are usually served on a lazy Susan to make family-style eating all the easier. When a dish is served, the most senior person gets first dibs and then it's rotated around the table. It is polite to only take a small portion to make sure everyone gets some.

Under no circumstances should chopsticks be placed upright in your bowl. This symbolises death.

FOOD FACTS

Be prepared for your Chinese host to place food in your bowl, usually without even asking. The host will often put chicken legs or other choice parts of the meal in the guests' bowls. Though Westerners may see this as interfering with one's independence and personal space, it is a sign of hospitality in China.

Chinese attach particular meanings to certain foods based on shapes, colours and legends. Superstition and tradition dictate that certain foods must be eaten for certain festivals or events to invoke a blessing. For example, ingot-shaped dumplings mean wealth at New Year, and round mooncakes represent family reunion at mid-autumn.

Noodles are an essential ingredient and a staple in Chinese cuisine, and one of the native ancient foods, with a history dating back to the Eastern Han Dynasty (206–220 BC). In ancient times, noodles were typically made from wheat dough but are now available in a wide variety of types, including rice noodles, ramen noodles, udon noodles, mung bean (glass) noodles and egg noodles, to suit all taste preferences and dietary requirements.

The invention of chopsticks reflects the wisdom of ancient Chinese people. A pair of chopsticks, though they look simple, can nip, pick, rip and stir food. Nowadays, chopsticks are considered to be lucky gifts for marriage and other important ceremonies.

CHINESE COOKING TECHNIQUES

Stir-frying

This is by far the most common method of cooking when using a wok. The wok was designed to sit above an open fire in a clay hole, the base and sides are very thin, so the heat is evenly distributed throughout the entire cooking surface. You must remember that once you begin cooking, you'll have to pay full attention to what is going on in the wok as you can easily burn the ingredients if you get distracted. With this in mind, it is important that all of your ingredients are prepared before you begin to cook.

Steaming

A traditional Chinese cooking method considered to be a healthy option as cooking requires very little to no oil. Food is often cooked within a bamboo basket and the moist heat enhances the foods' natural flavours and locks in their nutrients.

Deep-frying

Ensuring your oil is super-hot, this technique of cooking not only locks in the food's flavour and nutrients but adds a depth of texture that many other cooking methods cannot achieve. Many believe it's an unhealthy option but if cooked correctly the hot oil seals the outside of the ingredients, preventing excess oil being absorbed, and the high heat cooks the food super-fast.

Braising

Slow cooking in China has been perfected over thousands of years. There are many villages that are famous for their braising methods, cutting the ingredients into small pieces and braising them in small amounts of liquid, specialising in making the toughest of meats tender and juicy, where food melts in the mouth and slides off the bone.

Sautéing

This method uses less oil than deep-frying and a lower temperature. Meat is often cut into thin slices and coated in a cornflour (cornstarch) batter, cooked on one side and then flipped over to be cooked on the other side. Food is crisp on the outside and tender in the middle.

Tenderising

You've probably noticed that when you eat at a Chinese restaurant or takeaway, the meat or seafood always seems to be more tender, juicy and sometimes even has a silky-smooth texture as you eat it. This process is called tenderisation; the Chinese call it velveting. It's a very simple process, though it does take some forward planning, as ideally you want the meat tenderising for at least 2 hours before you cook it.

1 tbsp Chinese rice wine (Shaoxing wine) or water
1 tbsp cornflour (cornstarch)
1 tbsp dark soy sauce or oyster or Mushroom Stir-fry Sauce (page 343)
1 tbsp light soy sauce
1 tsp bicarbonate of soda (baking soda)

Put all the ingredients in a large bowl along with 350–600g (12oz–1lb 5oz) of your sliced meat, fish or king prawns (jumbo shrimp). Using your hands, mix everything together vigorously for around 30–45 seconds; there should be no liquid left sitting in the bottom of the bowl. Cover and set to one side for ideally 2 hours before cooking.

STORE CUPBOARD ESSENTIALS

'It's simple – great ingredients make great food.'

Quality and authenticity

As with all cooking, you will always get better results if you start with the best ingredients you can lay your hands on; not just for their flavour, but also for your own health, as you benefit from eating produce and meat that have been grown and raised in a higher welfare environment. Aim to pick up organic and free-range products where possible and consider using seasonal ingredients to make your food that much more flavoursome and nutritious, with the added bonus of being kinder on your wallet!

When shopping for specific Chinese ingredients, I would always, ALWAYS encourage you to find and explore your local Asian supermarket. You can find a world food aisle in almost all big supermarkets now, and they do offer a selection of soy sauces, sesame oil dressings, marinades and sauce mixes alongside dried noodles and rice. However, to achieve that truly authentic flavour, you really do need to use truly authentic ingredients. Plus, your budget will thank you for it, as most of these ingredients can be purchased for a fraction of the cost and in larger quantities by shopping local rather than in the 'speciality' aisle.

It's true that my kitchen cupboards are quite literally spilling with jars and cans of spices, sauces, dried herbs, oils and vinegars, but as a chef of many years, I'm always looking at recipe development, not to mention the simple fact that I completely lack the ability to leave my local Chinese supermarket or even the world food aisle of one of the big supermarkets carrying just the items on my shopping list! With so much variety of ingredients available in dried and preserved form, I love to keep my supplies well replenished.

Sesame oil

The tiniest amount of this oil added in marinades or at the very end of cooking can quite literally transform your dish from yum to OMG, nom, nom, nom. Extracted from the humble sesame seed it should be used sparingly as it's packed with flavour. Where possible buy pure sesame oil and not the blended variety.

Light soy sauce

The light variety is used to season your dish or as a dip. It's saltier than its darker sibling but still packed with that umami flavour that we all love. Made using fermented soya bean paste, grain and brine.

Dark soy sauce

Sweeter and thicker than its sibling, it's packed with that umami taste that brings a silky smoothness to our taste buds. Used to colour a dish and inject flavour. Made using fermented soya beans, molasses and sweetener agents, it is aged longer than light soy sauce.

Oyster sauce or Mushroom Stir-fry Sauce (page 343)

Used widely to inject some serious flavour into a dish. Made with either oysters or dried Chinese mushrooms, which have been slowly cooked down into a rich, dark velvety sauce.

Chinese five spice

Made by combining star anise, Sichuan peppercorns, cinnamon, fennel seeds and cloves, the ingredients are ground to a fine powder to create this well-loved and widely used seasoning. Used in many dishes but especially those that originate from Cantonese cuisine.

Sichuan pepper

Sichuan pepper's unique flavour is not spicy or pungent but lemony; its unique characteristic is the tingly buzzing numbness it produces in the mouth as you eat. It is often used in combination with fresh chillies and star anise in Sichuan cuisine.

Rice vinegar

Clear rice vinegar is made by fermenting rice, firstly into alcohol and then into acid. Compared with white distilled vinegar it is less acidic, delicate and sweeter in flavour. Black vinegar is made with glutinous rice and aged longer, which produces a woody, smoky malt flavour and is widely used in Southern Chinese cuisine.

Rice wine

Made from the fermentation of rice starch that has been converted into sugars. Typically it has an alcohol content of 18–25%. Consumed widely in Asian gastronomy and in cooking.

Fermented black beans

A widely used seasoning in Chinese cooking, fermented black beans are a must for the store cupboard. Soya beans are left to ferment, and as they mature they create a distinct pungent, salty flavour with a rich umami taste.

Cornflour (cornstarch)

Widely used in all Asian cooking, it's used to tenderise meats, thicken sauces and soups and coat ingredients before frying. Derived from corn grain.

Vegetable oil

The Chinese as a rule use an oil with a very high smoke point, which means it can get to a higher temperature before it begins to smoke. Groundnut oil is fantastic if you can find it, but if not, vegetable oil works just as well.

THE HOLY TRINITY

There are three main ingredients when cooking Cantonese food: garlic, ginger and spring onions (scallions). Sometimes used all together and sometimes on their own, you'll always find at least one when cooking traditional Cantonese cuisine.

Garlic

Though small, the little cloves pack a serious amount of flavour and are closely related to the onion, chive and leek. Originating in central Asia, garlic is widely used across the world for its pungent flavour as a seasoning.

Ginger

Ginger root has been used in China for millennia as a medicine and is closely related to turmeric and cardamom. It originates from the islands of Southeast Asia. Its flavour is hot and fragrant and it is prepared for consumption in many ways, including pickling, steeping in tea and candying, or used as an ingredient for cooking.

Spring onion (scallions)

Spring onions have a milder taste than their cousins onions, chives, shallots and garlic. The entire plant is edible, raw or cooked; the hollow leaves are used as a vegetable in many dishes around the world.

Tips when using these three Cantonese flavours: if you want a subtle hint of flavour, chop the ingredients into large pieces and as they cook, they will slowly infuse the dish with their aromatic yumminess. For a full-bodied 'kapow!' hit of flavour, finely chop or even mince the ingredients, this way every mouthful will be an aromatic explosion.

EQUIPMENT

The wok

The round-bottomed wok was designed to sit over a hollow above a roaring hot fire. Made from thinly beaten out carbon steel or cast iron, the entire surface of the wok reaches a high temperature, which makes it perfect for stir-frying. The wok builds up layers of oil each time it is used, which hardens to the surface, creating a non-stick layer often referred to as the seasoning of the wok. This means food literally glides across the surface as it cooks. You will probably find that when you buy a new wok food will stick to it, but over time it will get better. If you are using a seasoned wok, you must never use it for boiling or steaming as it will break down the seasoning and your wok will begin to stick again. For cooking on a home kitchen hob, you will often find that a good-quality non-stick wok will be more suitable, as home hobs can rarely achieve the high temperatures required for seasoning a carbon-steel wok.

Wok hei – 'Breath of the wok'

We've all seen the pictures or videos of huge fireballs billowing above a smoking-hot wok as the chef tosses the ingredients into the air; this is **wok hei**. The layer of oil built up over time helps create the charred flavour/aroma that briefly licks the ingredients as the flame engulfs the wok during seriously hot cooking; the intense heat and flames create a smoky flavour resulting in the caramelisation of the ingredients. A worldwide renowned method for Cantonese stir-frying.

How to season your wok

Only cast-iron and carbon-steel woks can be seasoned successfully.

1 When you buy a new unseasoned wok, the manufacturers will have coated the wok in oil to protect the metal. This needs to be removed by washing in hot soapy water, scrubbing with a scourer and then rinsing under hot water.

2 Thoroughly dry your wok by placing it over a low heat for 1–2 minutes to ensure all the water has evaporated.

3 Now heat your wok over a high heat. After 30–40 seconds, check the temperature by carefully flicking water into the wok, where little water beads should dance around and evaporate after 1–2 seconds.

4 Switch off the heat, add 2 tablespoons of either sunflower or groundnut oil and swirl the oil around so it coats the bottom and sides of your wok. (If the oil billows smoke immediately, the wok was too hot. Allow to cool and start again.)

5 Place your freshly oiled wok over a medium-low heat and add 6 spring onions (scallions), chopped into 4cm (1½in) pieces and 8 slices of ginger, each 3cm (1¼in) in length with skin on.

6 Stir-fry the aromatics for 15 minutes, smearing them around inside of the wok, fully coating the entire surface. If the aromatics become too dry, add another tablespoon of oil.

Your wok will begin to change to a yellow, blue, brown and maybe black colour and you'll notice a shine on the inside of the wok – this is the thin layer of oil building up.

7 Switch off the heat and allow your wok to cool. Once cooled, discard the spring onions and ginger and rinse out the wok with clean, warm water but DO NOT use soap and DO NOT scrub.

8 Wipe the wok and place over a low heat for 2 minutes until completely dry, then remove from the heat and allow to cool. Your wok should now have a warm subtle glow and is 'seasoned' or, in Cantonese, has **wok hei**.

IMPORTANT

1 Never use soap to wash your seasoned wok, rinse with hot water only.

2 Always ensure your wok is completely dry before storage, the best way is to wipe dry and place over a low heat for 2 minutes until no water is visible. Allow to cool and then store.

3 Use different woks for boiling and steaming. During your wok's infancy you'll damage the delicate seasoning layer you have just spent time developing. After time your wok will have built up a strong layer and be more resilient.

Chopping board

Nothing quite beats the feel of your knife or chopper on a wooden chopping board as you're slicing through vegetables. There's the confident grip you get as the blade bites into the wood after each chop, something you just don't get when using plastic boards. The larger the better in my opinion, as it gives you room to work and the weightier styles give your whole work surface a feeling of stability!

Chopsticks

Have you ever noticed that when you eat Chinese food everything is already cut into bite-sized pieces? For the Chinese, having to cut up food at the table is seen as uncivilised; this belief dates back over 2,000 years to the Zhou Dynasty. Chopsticks are eating utensils used in virtually all East Asian countries, held in the dominant hand they are of equal length, smooth and some are tapered at the end.

Spider strainer

Also known as the Chinese spider strainer, it is an invaluable piece of equipment when frying or boiling noodles or dumplings in a wok. The handle is often made of bamboo, while the strainer itself is metal and sometimes brass. Used in all of the Chinese restaurants and takeaways I've worked in, the Chinese kitchen just wouldn't work without one.

Knife or chopper

Over the years I have become an avid collector of Chinese kitchen knives, also known as the chopper. When choosing your chopper for everyday cooking, you want a thin, lightweight blade, something that will chop through vegetables evenly. If your chopper is too thick, you'll struggle to do the intricate slicing that many recipes require. Also, once you've invested in a good knife, look after it, sharpen it each time you use it and make sure it is completely dry after washing. A sharp knife really does make all the difference; nothing is quite so satisfying than feeling the blade glide through your ingredients as you prepare them for your meal.

Steamer

Steaming is just as commonplace in East Asian cooking as baking in the West, and a good steamer basket is well worth having to hand in your kitchen. Not particularly expensive and readily available from all Asian supermarkets or online, bamboo steamers are more effective than metal or glass versions, as the bamboo absorbs some of the excess moisture from the steam and prevents water dripping back on to the food. Simply placed over a pan or wok of boiling water, the gathered steam helps retain vital nutrients in your vegetables as well as steaming delicious buns, dumplings, fish and meat.

STARTERS
& SOUPS

CHINESE VEGETABLE SOUP

Chinese vegetable soup is incredibly light yet satisfying, packed with flavour, texture and those all-important nutrients retained in the crunch of the lightly simmered vegetables.

10 MINUTES   **10 MINUTES**   **SERVES 4**

1 tbsp vegetable oil

2 garlic cloves, peeled but left whole

5 thin slices of ginger

3 spring onions (scallions), roughly chopped

1.2 litres (5 cups) boiling water with 3 tsp chicken powder dissolved into it (can use vegetable stock cube if preferred)

2 tbsp light soy sauce

150g (1 cup) canned bamboo shoots, drained

150g (5oz) baby corn, cut in half and then quartered

150g (5oz) straw mushrooms, cut in half

200g (7oz) shredded Chinese leaf (Napa cabbage)

150g (5oz) carrots, peeled and thinly sliced

150g (5oz) broccoli florets

pinch of white pepper

pinch of salt to taste

dash of sesame oil

Pour the oil into a large saucepan over a medium heat and add the garlic, ginger and spring onions (scallions). Once softened and fragrant, add the chicken stock and soy sauce, bring to the boil and then allow to simmer for 10 minutes before adding the remaining ingredients, except the white pepper, salt and sesame oil. Simmer for a further 5 minutes, then check the seasoning and add white pepper and salt to taste. Finish off with a dash of sesame oil.

SEAWEED AND TOFU SOUP

This nourishing seaweed soup is packed with flavour, as well as being full of vitamins and minerals. Seaweed is a great source of umami and along with the crunch of bamboo shoots, the crisp snap of carrot batons and the subtle background heat from the pepper, this dish delivers on taste time and time again.

10 MINUTES   **10 MINUTES**   **SERVES 2-4**

1 litre (4 cups) vegetable stock

300g (10½oz) firm tofu, cubed

1 medium carrot, cut into matchsticks

60g (½ cup) canned bamboo shoots, drained and cut into matchsticks

3cm (1¼in) piece of ginger, cut into 3 slices

¼ tsp white pepper

2 tbsp light soy sauce

1 tbsp dark soy sauce

1 tbsp cornflour (cornstarch) mixed with 2 tbsp water

1 egg white, beaten (omit for vegan option)

4 nori seaweed sheets, cut into 2cm (¾in) squares

½ tbsp sesame oil

Put the vegetable stock into a large saucepan along with the tofu, carrot, bamboo shoots, ginger, white pepper and light and dark soy sauces. Bring to a gentle simmer and allow to cook for 5 minutes.

Gradually add the cornflour (cornstarch) mixture, stirring constantly until the mixture is smooth enough to coat the back of a spoon. Remove from the heat and quickly stir in the beaten egg white, if using. Finally, add the nori squares and sesame oil and stir through the soup. Check the seasoning before serving.

SPICE AND SOUR SOUP

This soup is rich, tangy and spicy, a complete mouth sensation that will satisfy any craving. Along with the crunchy carrots and soft tofu it really packs a punch in the flavour and texture departments.

15 MINUTES   **10 MINUTES**   **SERVES 2-4**

5g (¼ cup) dried wood ear mushrooms, cut into matchsticks
½ tbsp dark soy sauce
1 tbsp light soy sauce
8 tbsp rice vinegar
2 dried chillies, finely chopped
30g (1oz) firm tofu, cubed
1 medium carrot, cut into matchsticks
30g (¼ cup) canned bamboo shoots, drained and cut into matchsticks
30g (¼ cup) peas
4 eggs, beaten (omit for vegan option)
1.8 litres (7 cups) vegetable stock
½ tsp white pepper
1½ tsp salt
1 tbsp sugar
4 tbsp tomato ketchup
1 tbsp tomato purée (paste)
3 tbsp cornflour (cornstarch) mixed with 6 tbsp water
½ tbsp sesame oil

Soak the mushrooms in warm water for 10 minutes, then drain and transfer to a large wok or saucepan. Add the dark and light soy sauces, rice vinegar, dried chillies, tofu, carrot, bamboo shoots, peas, half the beaten eggs, vegetable stock, seasonings, sugar, ketchup and tomato purée (paste) to the pan with the mushrooms. Slowly bring to the boil, then reduce the heat and simmer for 3 minutes.

Give the cornflour (cornstarch) and water a good mix, then turn the heat up to medium and slowly add the mixture to the soup, stirring constantly until you reach the desired consistency. Remove from the heat and slowly pour in the remaining beaten eggs, stirring as you pour.

Finally, add the sesame oil and serve.

TOFU MISO SOUP

Not only is this soup utterly delicious, but it also delivers in the nutrition arena. A great source of protein and rich in a variety of nutrients and beneficial plant compounds, you can slurp away, comfortable in the knowledge that your body will be enjoying the benefits long after your taste buds have stopped singing!

5 MINUTES   **7 MINUTES**   **SERVES 2-4**

1 litre (4 cups) vegetable stock
3 nori sheets, cut into 3cm (1¼in) squares
3 spring onions (scallions), sliced into rings
3 tbsp miso paste
200g (7oz) silken tofu, cut into 2cm (¾in) cubes

Place a large saucepan over a medium-high heat, add the stock and the nori sheets and bring to the boil.

Add three-quarters of the chopped spring onions (scallions) and the miso paste and simmer for 5 minutes, adding the silken tofu for the last minute. Transfer to serving bowls and garnish with the remaining spring onions.

MOCK SHARK'S FIN SOUP

This is a very popular soup sold by street food hawkers in Hong Kong, often served at weddings or Chinese New Year. The long translucent strips of glass noodles imitate the appearance of a shark's fin.

10 MINUTES **25 MINUTES** **SERVES 3-4**

3 wood ear mushrooms
1 litre (4 cups) chicken stock
4 canned Chinese mushrooms, drained and cut into thin strips
1 cooked chicken breast, shredded
1 x 140g (5oz) can of crab meat, drained
1 tbsp dark soy sauce
1 tbsp Chinese rice wine (Shaoxing wine)
30g (1oz) dried mung bean (glass) noodles
pinch of salt
pinch of white pepper
2 tbsp cornflour (cornstarch) mixed with 4 tbsp cold water
2 eggs, beaten
dash of sesame oil

Soak the wood ear mushrooms in boiling water for 10 minutes. Drain and cut the mushrooms into thin strips, discarding the hard centres of the mushrooms.

Place a large pan or wok over a medium-high heat and bring the stock to the boil, then add the sliced Chinese and wood ear mushrooms, shredded chicken, crab meat, dark soy, rice wine and glass noodles. Bring to the boil, then add salt and white pepper to taste. Mix in the cornflour (cornstarch) mixture and slowly pour into the soup to thicken, stirring continuously. You may not need all of the cornflour mixture, so do this slowly and once the soup has thickened to your liking, stop. Switch off the heat, then swirl in the beaten eggs. Finally, add the sesame oil and serve.

TOM YUM SOUP

Although this dish originates from Thai cuisine, it has been widely served in many Chinese takeaways across the world. This is a deliciously nourishing soup that is spicy, sour and creamy, with a rich tang from the tomatoes and lime juice.

10 MINUTES   **30 MINUTES**   **SERVES 2-4**

2 lemongrass stalks
2 red bird's-eye chillies, finely chopped
3 garlic cloves, roughly chopped
1 tbsp grated ginger
1 tbsp oil (vegetable, groundnut or coconut)
1.5 litres (6 cups) vegetable stock
2–3 medium tomatoes, diced
1 x 400ml (14fl oz) can coconut milk
5 lime leaves (or use 1½ tbsp grated lime zest)
3 tbsp light soy sauce
220g (8oz) firm tofu, cubed
60g (1 cup) button mushrooms, sliced
¼ cup lime juice
1½ tbsp demerara sugar
½ tsp salt (or to taste)

Trim the top leaves of the lemongrass and, using the flat of your knife or a pestle, bruise the entire length of each stalk to get the most out of the citrusy flavour, then cut the stalks into quarters. Use a pestle and mortar to grind the chillies, garlic and ginger to a paste.

Heat the oil in a large saucepan over a medium heat and fry the lemongrass and chilli, garlic and ginger paste for about 3 minutes until fragrant. Add the vegetable stock, tomatoes, coconut milk, lime leaves and soy sauce and mix well, then bring to the boil. Reduce the heat to a simmer, cover and cook for 15 minutes.

Add the tofu and mushrooms to the pan and cook for a further 8 minutes before adding the lime juice and sugar, then seasoning with salt to taste. Serve and enjoy.

CHICKEN AND SWEETCORN SOUP

A big bowl of soup is sometimes all you really need. This recipe is quick, tasty and completely hassle-free. I'm sure once you give it a go it'll become your go-to dish when all you really want is a big bowl of satisfaction.

5 MINUTES   **8 MINUTES**   **SERVES 2-4**

800ml (3⅓ cups) chicken or vegetable stock
420g (15oz) can of creamed corn
170g (6oz) cooked chicken, shredded
¼ tsp white pepper
salt, to taste
30g (¼ cup) peas
2 tbsp cornflour (cornstarch) mixed with 4 tbsp water
1 egg, beaten
1 tsp sesame oil

In a non-stick wok or medium saucepan, combine the stock, creamed corn and chicken and bring to the boil. Reduce the heat, season with the pepper and add salt to taste, then add the peas and bring back to the boil.

Stir the cornflour (cornstarch) mixture and, while the soup is boiling, pour it in slowly, stirring the soup constantly until thickened to your desired consistency. Turn the heat down to low, slowly pour in the beaten egg, again stirring the soup at the same time. Switch off the heat, add the sesame oil, give it a quick stir and serve hot.

PEKING HOT AND SOUR SOUP

Developed in the Sichuan province of China, this soup is both spicy and sour. As soups go, this one is a must as it combines most of the elements you need to create a perfect mouthful: crunchy vegetables, succulent meats, a sharp twang from the vinegar and the subtle warmth of chilli.

5 MINUTES   **8 MINUTES**   **SERVES 4**

½ tbsp dark soy sauce

1 tbsp light soy sauce

6 tbsp rice vinegar

2 dried chillies, finely chopped

40g (1½oz) char siu pork (see page 193 or purchase from a Chinese supermarket), cut into matchsticks

30g (¼ cup) cooked and peeled prawns (shrimp)

15g (½oz) dried wood ear mushrooms, rehydrated in hot water, drained and cut into matchsticks

30g (1oz) firm tofu, cut into 1cm (½in) cubes

30g (1oz) canned bamboo shoots, cut into matchsticks

½ medium carrot, cut into matchsticks

30g (¼ cup) peas

1.8 litres (7½ cups) chicken stock

½ tsp white pepper

1½ tsp salt

2 tsp sugar

4 tbsp tomato ketchup

1 tsp tomato purée (paste)

6 tbsp cornflour (cornstarch) mixed with 12 tbsp water

2 eggs, beaten

½ tbsp sesame oil

Put all of the ingredients, except for the cornflour (cornstarch) mixture, eggs and sesame oil, into a large wok or saucepan. Slowly bring to the boil, then lower the heat and let the soup simmer for 3 minutes.

Give the cornflour mixture a good stir, turn the heat up to medium and slowly add the cornflour to the soup, stirring as you go, until thickened to your desired consistency. Turn off the heat and slowly pour in the beaten eggs, stirring as you pour.

Finally, add the sesame oil and serve.

MUSHROOM NOODLE SOUP

Slurpy noodles, earthy mushrooms and a hot, flavoursome broth: this has been a staple food in China since the Han Dynasty of 206 BC and is still much loved today by carnivores and veggies alike.

5 MINUTES **10 MINUTES** **SERVES 2-4**

300g (10½oz) medium noodles (you can use egg or rice noodles)

1 litre (4 cups) chicken or vegetable stock

200g (3½ cups) button mushrooms, thinly sliced

3 tbsp Mushroom Stir-fry Sauce (page 343 or use shop-bought)

2 tsp sugar

¼ tsp white pepper

3 spring onions (scallions), sliced into rings

salt, to taste

Place the dried noodle nests in a large bowl and cover with boiling water; allow to soak for 3 minutes, drain and set to one side.

Pour the stock into a medium saucepan and bring to the boil. Next, add the mushrooms along with the Mushroom Stir-fry Sauce, sugar and white pepper. Bring back to the boil and then turn down to a low simmer for 1 minute. Check the seasoning and add salt and a bit more white pepper, if needed.

Divide the noodles between 2 bowls (4 if this is a starter), pour over the soup and finally sprinkle with the spring onions (scallions).

VEGGIE WONTON SOUP

The Chinese describe wontons as 'little clouds', floating gently in a rich aromatic broth of ginger and spring onion (two of the Holy Trinity of Cantonese flavours).

30 MINUTES   **10 MINUTES**   **SERVES 2-4**

For the wontons

1 bag (approx. 260g/9¼oz) fresh spinach

10g (½ cup) dried wood ear mushrooms, soaked in warm water for 10 minutes

60g (2oz) medium firm tofu

3 spring onions (scallions), finely chopped

1 tbsp sesame oil

1 tbsp grated ginger

¼ tsp white pepper

1 tsp cornflour (cornstarch)

pinch of salt

16–20 wonton wrappers

For the soup

3cm (1¼in) piece of ginger, thinly sliced

1 tbsp soy sauce

800ml (3⅓ cups) vegetable stock

½ tsp white pepper

1 tsp salt

1 spring onion (scallion), finely chopped

1 tsp sesame oil

For the wontons, heat a wok over a medium heat, add the fresh spinach and cook until wilted. Transfer the wilted spinach to kitchen paper, squeeze out the excess water and then roughly chop and place in a large bowl. Finely chop the mushrooms and tofu into small pieces and add to the bowl, together with the remaining wonton ingredients, except the wrappers, and mix well.

To assemble the wontons, place a wonton wrapper in the palm of your hand and spoon ½ tablespoon of mixture into the centre. Carefully fold the sides of the wrapper, keeping the filling in the centre and pinch the wrapper just above the ball of mixture to seal. Continue with the remaining wrappers and filling until you have made all the wontons. Set to one side while you make the soup.

In a deep saucepan, add the ginger, soy sauce, stock, white pepper and salt and bring to the boil. Then turn down the heat and leave to simmer for 8–10 minutes.

While the soup simmers, bring a large saucepan of water to the boil, then carefully drop the wontons into the boiling water and cook for 2–3 minutes.

Divide the cooked wontons between bowls, sprinkle with the chopped spring onion (scallions) and drizzle over the sesame oil. Pour over the hot soup and serve.

NAPA CABBAGE AND TOFU SOUP

This is the Chinese version of a hearty vegetable soup. Presentation is key as this soup is served in its cooking pot – you want to see each ingredient in its own section of the pot; this not only looks amazing but as you eat you are able to identify the individual ingredients before they combine to create that perfect mouthful.

10 MINUTES   **20 MINUTES**   **SERVES 2-4**

1 litre (4 cups) vegetable stock
1cm (½in) piece of ginger, thinly sliced
½ tsp salt (or to taste)
¼ tsp white pepper (or to taste)
150g (5oz) daikon radish (mooli), cut into bite-sized pieces
3 spring onions (scallions), halved and thinly sliced lengthways
200g (7oz) Chinese leaf (Napa cabbage), cut into bite-sized pieces
handful of golden needle mushrooms (enoki), hard stalks removed
200g (7oz) firm tofu, cubed
1 nori seaweed sheet, ground to a powder

Pour the vegetable stock into a medium saucepan, add the sliced ginger and bring to the boil. Add the salt and white pepper and stir through the soup, then add the daikon radish and spring onions (scallions) and allow to simmer for 5 minutes.

Next, add the cabbage, mushrooms and tofu to the soup, each in its own part of the pan. Cook for another 8 minutes with the lid on. Turn off the heat, remove the lid and season to taste. Serve at the table in the pan, finally sprinkling with the powdered nori as you ladle into serving bowls.

CHICKEN CURRY SOUP

Whether you like to 'bring the heat' or just linger on the cusp of spiciness, you can tailor this soup to your own palate simply by choosing whichever curry sauce mix you prefer. Deliciously warming and so quick to make, this super-light soup is a midweek supper must-try!

5 MINUTES   **10 MINUTES**   **SERVES 2-4**

1 litre (4 cups) chicken stock
1 chicken breast, finely diced
2 squares of Chinese or Japanese curry sauce mix (bought in a block)
100g (2 cups) beansprouts
150g (2½ cups) button mushrooms, thinly sliced
pinch of salt
pinch of white pepper

Pour the chicken stock into a medium saucepan and bring to the boil over a medium-high heat. Add the diced chicken and bring back to the boil, then turn down to simmer for 3 minutes.

Break the curry sauce mix squares into the stock and mix well, ensuring they are completely dissolved. Add the beansprouts and mushrooms, then bring the soup back to the boil before reducing to a gentle simmer for another couple of minutes. Check the seasoning and adjust to taste with salt and white pepper. Serve and enjoy.

SPRING ONION PANCAKES

Cong you bing, or spring onion pancakes, are a very popular addition to many dim sum menus across China. Not dissimilar to the Indian paratha, this pan-fried unleavened bread is crispy on the outside, chewy on the inside and totally moreish.

1 HOUR   **20 MINUTES**   **SERVES 4**

For the pancakes
250g (2 cups) plain (all-purpose) flour, plus extra for dusting
500–750ml (2–3 cups) boiling water (this will vary slightly depending on the flour you use so adjust accordingly)

For the filling
4 tbsp coconut oil or vegetable lard, plus extra for brushing
6 spring onions (scallions), thinly sliced
½ tsp Chinese five spice
pinch of salt
pinch of white pepper
2 tbsp plain (all-purpose) flour
1 tbsp sesame seeds

To make the dough, put the flour into a large bowl and carefully pour over 500ml (2 cups) boiling water, then mix with a fork until no more water can be seen. You may need to add a little more water if the mixture is still too dry – you want the flour to come together to form a dough ball. Once cool enough to handle, knead the dough on a clean flat surface until it is smooth and not at all sticky. Set to one side and allow to rest for 45 minutes while you get started on the filling.

Heat 2 tablespoons of the coconut oil or vegetable lard in a wok, add the spring onions (scallions) and five spice and cook for 1 minute. Add a pinch of salt and pepper, then sprinkle over the flour and cook for 2 minutes over a medium-low heat. Set to one side and allow to cool.

Heat a dry wok over a medium-high heat, add the sesame seeds and toast until golden brown. Transfer to a plate to cool.

After your dough has rested for 45 minutes, knead for a further minute and then cut into 4 equal pieces. Take one piece and roll into a rectangle about 3mm (⅛in) thick. Brush with coconut oil, spread a thin layer of filling over the entire rectangle, then lightly sprinkle with toasted sesame seeds. Starting at one end, roll the full length of the dough into a long sausage shape, then coil into a pinwheel, tucking the loose end underneath. Using the palm of your hand, lightly roll to flatten each pinwheel to around 5mm (¼in) thick. Repeat with the remaining ingredients.

Heat the remaining coconut oil or vegetable lard in a flat-bottomed wok over a medium heat and fry each pancake for 2–3 minutes on each side, flipping a few times to ensure they do not burn. Drain on kitchen paper while you cook the rest. Cut into quarters and serve on their own or with your favourite dipping sauce.

SPICY WONTONS

Taking inspiration from the Sichuan province, my sweet, savoury, spicy and garlicky sauce is a deliciously rich and tingly dressing for these juicy and delicately flavoured dumplings.

20 MINUTES   **10 MINUTES**   **SERVES 2**

For the wontons
170g (6oz) minced (ground) pork
3 spring onions (scallions), finely chopped
1 tsp sesame oil
1 tbsp Chinese rice wine (Shaoxing wine)
pinch of salt
pinch of white pepper
1 tsp dark soy sauce
2 tsp light soy sauce
1 tsp cornflour (cornstarch)
20 wonton wrappers
1 egg, beaten

For the spicy sauce
1 tsp black rice vinegar
4 tbsp Chinese chilli oil
3 tbsp light soy sauce
3 garlic cloves, minced
1 tbsp honey
1 tsp sesame oil

Place all of the wonton ingredients (except the wonton wrappers and beaten egg) into a food processor and whizz for 30–45 seconds until everything is chopped finely and well mixed.

In another bowl, mix the sauce ingredients together and set to one side.

To assemble the dumplings, angle a wonton wrapper on your hand so that it faces you like a diamond. With your fingertips or a spoon, spread a thin layer of beaten egg along the top two edges of the wrapper. Place 1 teaspoon of the filling into the centre of the wrapper. Fold the bottom tip to the top tip to form a triangle and pinch along the edges, sealing the wonton and squeezing out the air to securely enclose the filling. Then fold the two corners together to create an ingot shape, brushing with a little more egg to help them stick together. Repeat until all of the filling has been used.

Bring a large saucepan of water to the boil, then drop your wontons into the water in batches of 6–8 and cook for 2–3 minutes. Drain and arrange on a serving plate. Pour over your spicy sauce and serve immediately.

TEMPURA VEG WITH DIPPING SAUCE

The trick to crispy tempura batter is to fold, not whisk, and yes, lumps are absolutely fine. Follow these tips and you'll soon be enjoying amazingly light, crispy-covered vegetables, which can be served with your favourite dipping sauces. An appetiser that looks, feels and tastes delicious.

3-5 HOURS   **10 MINUTES**   **SERVES 3-4**

1 litre (4 cups) oil, for deep-frying (ideally groundnut oil as it has a higher smoke point)
175g (1½ cups) plain (all-purpose) flour
1½ tbsp cornflour (cornstarch)
¼ tsp baking powder
½ tsp salt
750ml (3 cups) iced water or ice-cold soda water
selection of your favourite vegetables, cut into thin slices, such as courgette (zucchini), onion, pepper, carrot, sweet potato, baby corn

For the dipping sauce
2 sheets kombu seaweed flakes, crumbled
250ml (1 cup) water
4 tbsp mirin
4 tbsp light soy sauce
½ tbsp sugar

To make the dipping sauce, add the crumbled kombu sheets to a bowl and pour over the water. Allow to steep for 3–5 hours, then remove the kombu pieces from the water, keeping the used kombu water. Put the kombu water, mirin, soy sauce and sugar into a saucepan, bring to the boil and then turn off the heat and allow to cool. Transfer to a serving bowl.

Pour the oil for deep-frying into a large saucepan over a medium heat. Heat to 180°C (350°F) – any higher and the tempura may become too crispy and the veg not cooked; any lower and the batter will start to absorb the oil and become soggy.

Combine the plain (all-purpose) flour, cornflour (cornstarch), baking powder and salt in a large bowl. Pour in the water and use a fork to combine – it is perfectly fine to have small lumps of flour in your batter and it is important that you do not overwork the mixture, as this will build up the gluten in the flour and your batter will lose its lightness.

One at a time, dip the vegetables into the batter and then carefully lower into the oil, working in batches. Fry each vegetable for 3–5 minutes, turning them occasionally for even cooking and colour. Drain on kitchen paper and serve hot with the dipping sauce.

CRISPY SEAWEED

It's not seaweed at all! I'm not sure why Chinese seaweed is called seaweed when it's made from cabbage – all I know is how to make it and now I'm teaching you. In the restaurant we always served the seaweed with a sprinkle of dried fish powder (which just happens to taste lovely on top of vanilla ice cream!).

5 MINUTES   **10 MINUTES**   **SERVES 4**

300g (10½oz) Savoy cabbage, washed and thoroughly dried
groundnut oil, for deep-frying
½ tsp salt
½ tsp sugar

Separate the cabbage into individual leaves, then remove the centre stem from each one. Place 4 de-stemmed leaves on top of one another and tightly roll into a tube, then, using a very sharp knife, slice very thin discs until you have a pile of finely chopped cabbage leaves. Repeat with the remaining leaves.

Heat enough oil in a wok so the cabbage can be deep-fried. Heat to 180°C (350°F) and test with a small pinch of cabbage to ensure it sizzles before adding the first batch. Add about a quarter of the chopped cabbage and fry for about 1–2 minutes until crispy. Remove the cabbage with a slotted spoon or Chinese sieve and dry on kitchen paper. Repeat with the remaining sliced cabbage.

Evenly sprinkle over the salt and sugar. Toss well and transfer to a serving bowl. Serve straightaway.

VEGETARIAN MINI SPRING ROLLS

In Chinese cuisine, spring rolls are savoury rolls with Chinese leaf and other vegetable fillings inside a thinly wrapped cylindrical pastry. They are usually eaten during the Spring Festival (Chinese New Year), hence the name.

20 MINUTES   **15 MINUTES**   **SERVES 4**

20 spring roll wrappers (21.5cm/8¼in square), defrosted in the packet before separating
2 tbsp cornflour (cornstarch) mixed with 1 tbsp beaten egg
groundnut oil, for deep-frying
sweet chilli sauce, to serve

For the filling
1 tbsp groundnut oil
3 spring onions (scallions), sliced
2 garlic cloves, crushed
1 large carrot, peeled and finely shredded
½ Chinese leaf (Napa cabbage), shredded (1½ cups)
1 x 225g (8oz) can water chestnuts, drained and roughly chopped
1 x 227g (8oz) can bamboo shoots, drained and roughly chopped
50g (1 cup) beansprouts
1 tbsp light soy sauce
¼ tsp salt
¼ tsp white pepper
1 tsp sesame oil

Heat a wok over a high heat until hot. Add the 1 tablespoon of groundnut oil for the filling followed by the spring onions (scallions), garlic, carrot and Chinese leaf (Napa cabbage). Stir-fry for 2–3 minutes until soft. Add the water chestnuts, bamboo shoots, beansprouts, soy sauce and salt and pepper. Stir-fry for a further minute, turn off the heat and add the sesame oil. Transfer to a bowl and allow to cool.

Place a wrapper on a board with a corner pointing towards you and brush the edges with the cornflour (cornstarch) and egg mixture. Spoon a good tablespoon of the filling into the corner of the wrapper. Fold the tip of the corner over the filling, creating an 8cm (3¼in) sausage shape, then turn in the other two corners to enclose the filling and continue to roll. Repeat with the remaining wrappers and filling.

Pour enough oil into a wok so the spring rolls can float, heat to 160°C (325°F) and deep-fry the spring rolls in batches of four for 3–4 minutes, or until golden brown. Carefully lift from the oil and transfer to a wire rack or a plate lined with kitchen paper. Once all the spring rolls are cooked, serve hot with sweet chilli sauce for dipping.

SESAME SEED PRAWN TOAST

This was one of the dishes that needed to be batch-made in the restaurant. It would start with peeling cases of king prawns in freezing cold water, turning your hands blue (brrrrrr), then we had to devein each prawn one-by-one and push the prawns through a mincer. Next, we'd add the seasoning and cornflour and then beat the mixture for a good 20 minutes – this would stiffen it, making it denser and more springy. Finally we would spread the mixture on to pieces of white bread and then coat the prawn side in sesame seeds. It was an 'all-hands-on-deck' family affair. This recipe is much easier.

20 MINUTES   **5 MINUTES**   **SERVES 6-8**

280g (10oz) raw king prawns (jumbo shrimp), peeled and deveined
1 tbsp cornflour (cornstarch)
1 egg
½ tsp salt
4 slices of white bread
90g (⅔ cup) sesame seeds
groundnut oil, for shallow frying

Put the prawns, cornflour (cornstarch), egg and salt into a food processor and blend to a paste.

Spread the paste on to one side of each slice of bread (don't skimp). Tip the sesame seeds on to a plate or chopping board, then press the bread, paste-side down, into the seeds. (Only seed the paste side!)

Heat 5–8cm (2–3in) of oil in a large saucepan or wok until hot but not smoking. Lower each slice of bread, one or two at a time (depending on the size of your wok), into the oil and fry for 30–50 seconds on each side, or until golden brown. Remove the toasts and transfer to a plate lined with kitchen paper to drain the excess oil. Remove the crusts, slice into triangles and serve (on average, allow 2–3 triangles per person).

The beauty of these toasts is that they can be prepared a day in advance and kept in the fridge. Once your guests start to arrive, fire up the cooker, fry the coated bread and you'll be serving tasty, home-made prawn toast in minutes.

SATAY CHICKEN SKEWERS

This dish originates from Southeast Asia but has found its way on to most Chinese restaurant menus. Cook over an open BBQ and you'll be transported to the Far East with the smell of charcoal and smouldering spices.

2 HOURS   **5 MINUTES**   **15 MINUTES**   **SERVES 4**

450g (1lb) chicken thighs or breast fillet, cut into 2cm (¾in) cubes
1½ tsp salt
¼ tsp white pepper
1 tbsp groundnut oil
240ml (1 cup) water
5 tbsp crunchy peanut butter
2 tbsp dark soy sauce
1 tbsp brown sugar
2 garlic cloves, crushed
1 tbsp lime juice

You'll need 24 wooden skewers (pre-soaked in water).

In a large bowl, combine the chicken with 1 teaspoon of the salt, the white pepper and the groundnut oil. Cover and transfer to the fridge to marinate for 2 hours. If you don't have time, don't worry; it's not essential.

Pour the water into a small saucepan and add the peanut butter, soy sauce, sugar, garlic and remaining salt, stirring to mix well, then bring to the boil. Once boiling, remove from the heat and add the lime juice.

Thread the marinated chicken on to the soaked skewers, making sure you have equal amounts on each skewer. Put 3 tablespoons of the peanut sauce to one side in a small bowl and brush the remaining sauce over the skewered chicken.

Heat a large frying pan or large griddle pan over a medium-high heat, then cook the chicken skewers for 2–2½ minutes per side. Ensure the chicken is cooked thoroughly before serving (slice one of the cubes in half to check there is no pink meat).

Serve the skewers with the remaining peanut sauce for dipping.

CHAR SIU PUFFS

These moreish little morsels of succulently aromatic Chinese roast pork wrapped in puff pastry will be calling to you from the cooling rack. A word of caution however: hard as it may seem (and trust me, it's hard!) you should resist the overwhelming temptation to dive straight in, as their moist, rich centres will be like molten lava straight from the oven!

2 HOURS +   **40 MINUTES**   **3½ HOURS**   **MAKES 12-15**

1kg (2lb 4oz) pork shoulder
500ml (2 cups) Chinese BBQ Sauce (see page 344 or use shop-bought)
2 star anise
375g (13oz) ready-rolled puff pastry
1 egg, beaten with 1 tbsp water

Cut the pork into 2 equal pieces and place on a large baking tray along with the Chinese BBQ Sauce and star anise, massaging the sauce into the meat. Cover and leave to marinate for at least 2 hours or overnight in the fridge.

Remove the pork from the fridge at least 1–2 hours before you roast.

Preheat the oven to 200°C (400°F).

Uncover the pork, add 375ml (1½ cups) water and mix into the marinade that will have pooled in the tray. Place on the middle shelf of the oven to roast for 25 minutes, then turn the pork over and baste with the marinade – if it is looking a bit dry you can add more water to loosen it. Return to the oven for a further 20 minutes and repeat, returning to the oven for a final 10 minutes. The pork should be cooked all the way through and have a nice caramelised crust, which adds colour, flavour and texture. Set to one side and allow the meat to rest for 20 minutes, ensuring you reserve some of the marinade at the bottom of the baking tray. Discard the star anise.

Once the pork has rested, cut 250g (9oz) of the pork into 5mm (¼in) cubes. Put into a bowl, adding 3 tablespoons of the reserved marinade, and mix together well.

Preheat the oven again to 200°C (400°F). Unroll the pastry, leaving it on the paper it was rolled up in, and use a round cutter (about 8cm/3in in diameter) to cut out pastry circles. Place 1–2 tablespoons of the pork filling into the centre of each circle and carefully pull up the sides, pinching the pastry at the top to seal in the filling. Repeat until all of the pastry has been used.

Place your puffs on a baking tray and brush each puff with the egg-and-water wash. Bake in the oven for 15 minutes. Can be served hot or cold.

Kwoklyn's tip
There will be leftover pork, which can be stored, covered, in the fridge for 1 week; perfect for fried rice, chow mein or simply sliced and served over plain rice with some soy sauce.

STICKY AROMATIC RIBS

Chinese BBQ ribs: aromatic, tender, unctuous, sticky, sweet and oh so familiar to every Cantonese takeaway around!

2 HOURS +   **5 MINUTES**   **1 HOUR 15 MINS**   **SERVES 4**

1kg (2lb 4oz) ribs
3 star anise
2 cinnamon sticks
375ml (1½ cups) Chinese BBQ Sauce
  (page 344 or use shop-bought)
4 tbsp golden (light corn) syrup

Put the ribs in a large bowl with all the ingredients, except the golden (light corn) syrup. Massage into the meat, then cover and allow to marinate for at least 2 hours or overnight in the fridge.

Remove the ribs from the fridge and allow to come back up to room temperature; preheat the oven to 170°C (340°F).

Give the bowl a good toss and tip the ribs and any marinade that will have pooled in the bowl on to a large baking tray. Bake in the oven for 40 minutes, then increase the heat to 180°C (350°F), baste the ribs and return to the oven for another 10 minutes. Baste again and bake for a further 10 minutes, or until the ribs have begun to brown and even char a little. If you like your meat to literally fall off the bone, increase the first part of the cooking time to 1 hour before you start basting.

Remove the ribs from the oven and allow to rest for 15 minutes, then transfer to a serving plate and drizzle over the golden syrup.

CHICKEN YUK SUNG

Finely diced chicken stir-fried with classic Chinese aromatics, served in crisp iceberg lettuce leaves with crispy vermicelli (optional but highly recommended for added texture!) – deliciously light and tasty, creating the perfect mouthful.

10 MINUTES   **15 MINUTES**   **SERVES 2-4**

2 tbsp groundnut oil

2 garlic cloves, finely chopped

3cm (1¼in) piece of ginger, peeled and finely sliced

3 spring onions (scallions), finely sliced

500g (1lb 2oz) chicken, finely chopped

1½ tbsp dark soy sauce

3 tbsp oyster sauce

1 tbsp Chinese rice wine (Shaoxing wine)

1 tbsp granulated sugar

1 medium onion, finely chopped

1 large carrot, finely chopped

1 x 225g (8oz) can of water chestnuts, drained and finely chopped

1 tbsp sesame oil

1 iceberg lettuce, separated into individual leaves, washed and dried

For the vermicelli (optional)

60ml (¼ cup) vegetable oil, for frying

handful of dried rice vermicelli noodles

Gently heat 1 tablespoon of the groundnut oil in a wok. Add the garlic, ginger and spring onions (scallions) and fry until the ginger and garlic are aromatic, about 30 seconds. Add the chicken and cook for about 3–5 minutes until browned. Scrape everything into a bowl and set to one side.

In a small bowl, mix together the soy sauce, oyster sauce, rice wine and sugar and set to one side.

Heat the remaining groundnut oil in the wok over a medium heat, add the onion, carrot and water chestnuts and cook for 2–3 minutes, or until softened and browned. Add the soy sauce mixture and mix in well. Return the chicken to the wok and cook over a medium heat for about 2–3 minutes until the sauce has reduced – the mixture should be quite dry. Add the sesame oil and mix well.

If you're making the crispy vermicelli garnish, heat the vegetable oil in a frying pan over a medium heat and add the noodles – they will puff up FAST! Drain on kitchen paper ready for serving.

To serve, spoon some of the yuk sung and some fried vermicelli into a lettuce leaf, wrap and eat!

Kwoklyn's tip

The best way to separate lettuce leaves while keeping them intact is to hold the lettuce under a gently running cold tap – as the leaves fill with water, they peel (intact) away from the lettuce.

TOFU AND VEGETABLE SAMSA

So, who knew that East Asia had pyramids? These beautifully formed parcels were designed and created to replicate the Pyramid of Qin Shi Huang, the first emperor of China. A crispy outer shell representing the building itself is stuffed with creamy tofu, crunchy carrots, soft sweet potato and aromatic spices to represent the as-yet undiscovered riches hidden within.

45 MINUTES   **20 MINUTES**   **MAKES 12-14**

400g (14oz) sweet potato, cut into 2cm (¾in) cubes

1 large carrot, cut into 1cm (½in) dice

1 tbsp oil (vegetable, groundnut or coconut), plus extra for deep-frying

1 tbsp grated ginger, minced

1 medium onion, finely diced

2 tsp curry powder (use your favourite)

½ tsp ground turmeric

½ tsp ground cumin

½ tsp ground coriander

1 tsp salt

40g (⅓ cup) frozen peas

225g (8oz) firm tofu, drained and crumbled

5 spring onions (scallions), finely chopped

1 tbsp lemon juice

2 tbsp water

10–15 spring roll wrappers (25cm/10in square), each cut into 3 equal-sized rectangles

Place the sweet potato and carrot in a large saucepan, cover with water and bring to the boil. Cook for 5 minutes, then remove from the heat, drain and set to one side.

Heat the tablespoon of oil in a wok over a medium-high heat and fry the ginger for 20 seconds until fragrant. Add the onion and fry for about 2 minutes until translucent. Add the cooked sweet potato and carrots along with the curry powder, turmeric, cumin, coriander and salt and fry for 2 minutes, gently combining the ingredients. Carefully stir in the peas, tofu, spring onions (scallions), lemon juice and measured water. Cook for a further 5 minutes, then transfer to a bowl and allow to cool.

Taking a rectangle of spring roll wrapper, place a heaped teaspoon of the filling in the centre at the top of the wrapper. Brush the outer edges of the wrapper with water and then fold repeatedly from one edge to the other along the length of the strip to form a triangle. Pinch the edges and all the corners to make sure they are sealed tight (you don't want the filling to leak out). Repeat until the filling is used up.

Pour enough oil to deep-fry the samsa into a large saucepan and heat to 180°C (350°F). Fry the samsa in batches for 5 minutes each, turning a couple of times during cooking to achieve an even golden brown colour. Transfer to kitchen paper and serve warm or cold.

PANKO MUSHROOMS WITH OK DIPPING SAUCE

So, what's better than a mushroom starter? Mushrooms covered in a crispy panko crumb, of course. Crunchy on the outside and juicy on the inside, each mouthful is a taste sensation of juicy mushroom, oozing with garlic and cayenne pepper aromatics – and that's before you even get close to dipping into the silky, rich OK sauce.

10 MINUTES   **10 MINUTES**   **SERVES 3-4**

175ml (¾ cup) almond or soya milk
½ tsp garlic powder
¼ tsp cayenne pepper
½ tbsp cornflour (cornstarch)
½ tsp salt
100g (¾ cup) plain (all-purpose) flour
125g (1 cup) panko breadcrumbs
200g (7oz) baby button mushrooms, wiped clean
250ml (1 cup) oil (vegetable, groundnut or coconut), for shallow frying

For the dipping sauce
2 tsp light soy sauce
1 tsp Chinese five spice
250ml (1 cup) water
125ml (½ cup) tomato ketchup
4 tbsp brown table sauce
100g (½ cup) white or brown sugar
1½ tsp cornflour (cornstarch) mixed with 2 tbsp water

Put all the sauce ingredients, except the cornflour (cornstarch) mixture, into a wok. Heat gently and stir until the sauce starts to boil. Lower the heat and simmer for a few minutes. Gradually add the cornflour mixture, stirring constantly until thickened, then remove from the heat and set to one side.

In a large bowl, mix the almond or soya milk, garlic powder, cayenne pepper, cornflour and salt. Add the plain (all-purpose) flour and mix gently to create a smooth, pouring-consistency batter. Put the panko crumbs on a large plate.

To assemble the mushrooms you'll need some surface space. Place the mushrooms on one side, with the batter in the middle, followed by the breadcrumbs. Dip each mushroom into the batter and then coat evenly with panko breadcrumbs, trying not to drip too much wet batter into the breadcrumbs.

Heat enough oil to shallow-fry in a large frying pan and fry the breaded mushrooms in batches over a medium heat for 2 minutes, or until golden brown. Transfer to a wire rack or kitchen paper to drain.

Serve the mushrooms with your OK dipping sauce.

POTSTICKERS

The Chinese have a serious love affair with these succulent and juicy dumplings. Pan-fried and then steamed, every mouthful is sheer perfection.

1-2 HOURS   **30 MINUTES**   **MAKES 32**

For the dumpling wrappers

280g (2¼ cups) plain (all-purpose) flour, plus extra for rolling

175ml (¾ cup) just-boiled water

For the filling

3 tbsp oil (vegetable, groundnut or coconut), plus extra for frying

1 tbsp grated ginger

1 large onion, finely diced

1 large portobello mushroom, finely diced

20g (1 cup) dried Chinese mushrooms, soaked in warm water until soft, destalked and diced

150g (5oz) Chinese leaf (Napa cabbage), finely chopped

1 carrot, finely diced

5 spring onions (scallions), thinly sliced into rounds

2 tbsp light soy sauce

2 tbsp Chinese rice wine (Shaoxing wine)

2 tsp sugar

½ tsp white pepper

¾ tsp salt (or to taste)

2 tsp sesame oil

Put the flour into a large bowl and, using a wooden spoon, add the water in a steady stream, stirring as you go. Start to work the dough into a ball with your hands. Tip the ball out on to a clean un-floured surface and knead until the dough is smooth and not at all sticky.

Place the dough into a ziplock bag and squeeze the air out before sealing. Leave for at least 15 minutes (or up to 2 hours) at room temperature, while you prepare the filling. Add 2 tablespoons of the oil to a wok and place over a medium heat. Fry the ginger until fragrant, then add the onion and cook until it is translucent. Add the portobello and Chinese mushrooms and fry until the liquid in the wok has evaporated. Transfer to a bowl.

Wipe the wok and add another tablespoon of oil. Add the cabbage and carrot and fry over a medium heat until any liquid has evaporated. Add the cooked mushrooms, along with the spring onions (scallions), soy sauce, rice wine, sugar, white pepper and salt and mix well. Remove from the heat, stir through the sesame oil and transfer to a large bowl to cool.

Divide the dough into 32 equal pieces using a sharp knife. Roll each piece into a ball before flattening with the heel of your hand. Take a lightly floured rolling pin (to prevent sticking) and roll the dough into thin discs.

To assemble the potstickers, take a teaspoon of filling and place it in the centre of a wrapper, then fold one edge over to meet the other. Gently press the edges together, making sure that no filling escapes, and pinch the sealed edge to form ripples. Place on a sheet of greaseproof paper until you are ready to cook.

Heat 2 tablespoons of oil in a flat-bottomed wok over a medium-high heat. Add a batch of potstickers and allow to fry on one side only for 2 minutes, then add 5mm (¼in) water, reduce the heat to medium-low and cover with the lid. Allow to steam until the water has evaporated. Remove the lid, increase the heat to medium-high and fry until the potsticker bottoms are golden brown and crispy. Repeat with the next batch, adding more oil as necessary, until they are all cooked. Serve with your favourite dipping sauce.

CAULIFLOWER FRITTERS

I love to eat certain foods with my hands; it adds to the experience, evokes emotion and arguably makes food taste better, and these little savoury fritters are no exception. Golden brown and crispy on the outside, succulent and tender on the inside and punching well above their weight on taste. Use chopsticks for a less messy experience!

30 MINUTES   **15 MINUTES**   **SERVES 3-4**

1 large head of cauliflower, cut into florets
1 large courgette (zucchini), diced
60g (½ cup) plain (all-purpose) flour
2 eggs, beaten (vegan option: use ½ cup silken tofu, blended smooth)
3 garlic cloves, finely chopped
1 tbsp grated ginger
1 tsp Chinese five spice
½ tsp salt
¼ tsp white pepper
3 tbsp chopped spring onions (scallions)
2 tbsp oil (vegetable or groundnut)

Bring a large saucepan of water to the boil, add the cauliflower florets and cook for 2–3 minutes until tender. Drain and then cut into small pieces.

In a large bowl, mix the cauliflower and courgette (zucchini) with the flour, eggs (or tofu), garlic, ginger, Chinese five spice, salt, pepper and spring onions (scallions).

Heat the oil in a large non-stick frying pan over a medium-high heat. Add scoops of the mixture to the hot oil, ensuring you leave enough room for them to spread during cooking. Cook for 2–3 minutes on each side until cooked through, crispy and golden brown. Transfer to kitchen paper to drain. Serve warm.

TARO, SESAME AND LOTUS PUK PUKS

Nothing quite compares to the taste or aroma of fried sesame seeds, and these little puk puks are smothered with them. Each disc is a combination of soft yet chewy, sweet yet savoury, and the nutty flavour of taro (a tropical root vegetable used extensively in Asian cuisine) makes this even better. My mouth is quite literally watering at the very thought of these delicious treats.

1 HOUR　　**15 MINUTES**　　**MAKES 12**

450g (1lb) taro
70g (⅓ cup) sugar
220g (8oz) glutinous rice flour
4 tbsp lotus seed paste
140g (1 cup) sesame seeds
3 tbsp oil (vegetable, groundnut or coconut)

Bring a large saucepan of water to the boil. Peel and cut the taro into thumb-sized chunks, then boil for 10–15 minutes, or until tender. Drain and allow to cool for 15 minutes.

Place the cooked taro into a large bowl and add the sugar, then mash with a fork and mix well. Add the glutinous rice flour and knead to create a dough. Divide the mixture into 12 equal-sized balls, then flatten each ball into a disc on a clean flat surface. Add 1 teaspoon of sweet lotus paste to the centre of each disc and gather up the sides to form a ball, enclosing the paste within the dough. Gently flatten each ball to make a circular shape.

Pour the sesame seeds on to a large plate and coat each puk evenly in the seeds, pressing gently to ensure the seeds are sticking to the puks.

Heat the oil in a non-stick frying pan over a medium-high heat and fry each puk for 3 minutes on each side until golden brown and crispy. Transfer to a wire rack or kitchen paper to drain. Serve warm or cool.

HONEY-GLAZED CHILLI WINGS

Sweet and spicy, sticky and juicy – it is going to get messy but what's not to love about these wings. Forget the popcorn, these are the perfect 'movie night in' nibbles!

2 HOURS   **5 MINUTES**   **50 MINUTES**   **SERVES 4**

500g (1lb 2oz) chicken wings
8 tbsp sweet chilli sauce
4 tbsp runny honey
1 tbsp dark soy sauce
2 tbsp light soy sauce
2 tbsp oil (vegetable or groundnut)
¼ cup toasted sesame seeds

Put all the ingredients, except the toasted sesame seeds, into a large bowl. Use your hands to massage the marinade into the chicken, making sure everything is well coated. Cover and place in the fridge for 2 hours.

Preheat the oven to 170°C (340°F).

Toss the chicken again in the marinade before tipping the wings and sauce on to a baking tray. Bake in the oven for 20 minutes, then flip the wings over and baste in the marinade. Cook for a further 20 minutes, flip again and baste one last time. Increase the oven temperature to 200°C (400°F), then return the tray to the oven for a final 10 minutes.

Once the marinade has achieved its sticky caramelisation, remove the wings from the oven, transfer to a serving plate, sprinkle with the toasted sesame seeds and serve piping hot.

CHINESE BEER-BATTERED TEMPURA OYSTERS

Oysters, which were once plentiful and cheap, are now considered a luxury food – a delicacy even – and some would say, 'sophisticated'. Many shudder at the thought of eating these raw and I personally don't blame them. But lightly battered, deep-fried and served with a tasty dip, these work for me every time.

15 MINUTES   **5 MINUTES**   **SERVES 2**

12 raw oysters in their shells (see tip)
200ml (¾ cup) Chinese rice beer, chilled
85g (⅔ cup) plain (all-purpose) flour, plus a little extra for dusting
½ tsp salt
½ tsp sugar
oil (vegetable or groundnut), for deep-frying
1 lemon, cut into wedges
Wasabi Mayo (page 345) or your favourite dipping sauce

Remove the oysters from their shells and individually pat dry with kitchen paper. Wash and dry the empty shells and set both to one side.

Pour the beer into a large bowl, sift in the flour and carefully stir with a pair of chopsticks. It is very important that you do not over-whisk. It is fine to have small lumps of flour in the batter. Add the salt and sugar and gently stir into the batter.

Pour enough oil into a heavy-based saucepan to come at least 8cm (3in) up the sides and heat to 180°C (350°F).

Dust the oysters in some extra flour, bang off any excess, then dip into the beer batter and allow the excess to drip off. Carefully drop the oysters, in batches of 6 (so as to not overcrowd the pan), into the hot oil and fry for 2 minutes until crispy and golden brown. Drain on a wire rack or a plate lined with kitchen paper.

Place the drained oysters back into their shells and arrange on a serving plate along with the wedges of lemon and wasabi mayo.

Kwoklyn's tip
Ask your local fishmonger to shuck your oysters for you but remember to ask for the shells. If shucking at home, this can be done using a sharp knife or, for safety, a teaspoon handle, holding the oyster in a tea towel, as the shells can be sharp.

CRISPY WONTONS

You really can't beat the taste and texture sensation of these wontons with their savoury pork and prawn filling inside a crispy outer shell. Make time to enjoy the assembly and I promise the end result will be totally worth it!

---

1 HOUR   **40 MINUTES**   **15 MINUTES**   **SERVES 6**

225g (8oz) raw king prawns (jumbo shrimp), peeled and deveined
100g (½ cup) minced (ground) pork
1 bunch of spring onions (scallions), sliced into thin rings
30g (¼ cup) water chestnuts, finely diced
2 tsp light soy sauce
¼ tsp white pepper
½ tsp salt
1 tsp sugar
vegetable oil
1 packet of wonton wrappers

Dice the peeled prawns (shrimp) but not too finely – you still want some chunks.

Put the diced prawns, minced (ground) pork, chopped spring onions (scallions), water chestnuts, soy sauce, pepper, salt, sugar and 1 tablespoon of oil into a large bowl. Mix really well to combine all of the ingredients. Place in the fridge, uncovered, for at least 1 hour.

Angle a wonton wrapper on your hand so that it faces you like a diamond. With your fingertips or a spoon, spread a thin layer of water along the top two edges of the wrapper. Place 1 teaspoon of the filling into the centre of the wrapper. Fold the bottom corner to the top corner to form a triangle and pinch along the edges, sealing the wonton and squeezing out the air to securely enclose the filling. Then fold and pinch the two side corners together, brushing with a little more water to help them stick together. Repeat until all of the filling has been used.

Place a deep-sided wok or saucepan over a medium heat and add enough oil so that once the wontons are added they can float. Once the oil reaches 170°C (340°F), carefully lower the wontons into the oil in batches of five. Cook for 4–5 minutes, turning regularly to ensure even cooking and browning. Once cooked, drain the wontons over a wire rack while you cook the rest. Arrange on a plate and serve with your favourite dipping sauce.

SESAME SEED TEMPURA FRIED TOFU

Since around the eighth century, tofu has been much favoured by Zen Buddhist monks as a protein substitute for meat; over the centuries they have adapted and perfected recipes to create different textures. This recipe is one simple example of nutty sesame seeds in a crisp tempura batter enveloping firm yet creamy tofu.

25 MINUTES   **15 MINUTES**   **SERVES 2-3**

340g (12oz) firm tofu, cubed
85g (⅔ cup) plain (all-purpose) flour,
  plus extra for coating
½ tsp salt
½ tsp sugar
2 tbsp sesame seeds
200ml (¾ cup) chilled sparkling water
1 litre (4 cups) groundnut oil, for
  deep-frying

Pat the tofu pieces dry with kitchen paper and put to one side.

Put the flour, salt, sugar and sesame seeds into a large bowl and mix well. Using a balloon whisk, gradually stir in the sparkling water – it's OK to have small lumps of flour in the batter.

Pour the oil into a large heavy-based saucepan over a medium heat.

Coat the tofu in flour, dust off any excess and then dip into the batter, allowing the excess to drip off. Carefully place the tofu into the hot oil and fry for 2–3 minutes until crispy and golden brown. Drain on a wire rack or kitchen paper. Serve with your favourite dipping sauce – hoisin sauce (page 342) for me please.

SWEET LOTUS BAO

These Chinese steamed buns are light and fluffy, and stuffed with a sweet lotus paste (which can be bought in any Chinese supermarket). These would usually be served at the beginning of the meal as part of a dim sum menu to whet your appetite for the main courses, but to be honest, any time is a good time. Bao and tea in the morning; bao and coffee mid-morning; bao for lunch or even a bao and hot chocolate supper – simply delicious.

2½ HOURS   **10 MINUTES**   **MAKES 12**

560g (4¾ cups) plain (all-purpose) flour, plus extra for dusting
11g (⅓oz) instant dried yeast
½ tsp salt
1 tsp baking powder
30g (1oz) caster (superfine) sugar
2 tbsp vegetable oil, plus extra for greasing
320ml (1¼ cups) whole milk (for a vegan option use soy or almond milk)
12 tbsp lotus seed paste

To make the dough, mix all of the ingredients, except the lotus paste, together in a large bowl.

Turn out on to a clean lightly floured surface and knead for 6 minutes until the dough is soft, springy and not at all sticky. Bring the mixture together to form a ball, then place into a lightly greased bowl, cover and leave for 2 hours until the dough has doubled in size.

Turn out the dough on to a lightly floured worktop, lightly flatten and roll into a long sausage shape. Divide into 12 equal pieces and flatten each piece into a 12cm (5in) round.

Place 1 tablespoon of lotus paste into the centre of each bao and carefully bring the edges together to form a round parcel, twisting the top to form a seal. Repeat with the remaining dough.

Place the sealed dough balls on to a sheet of perforated baking paper in a bamboo steamer with a lid, leaving about 2cm (¾in) between each one, as they will grow as they steam. Steam over a high heat for 10 minutes. Be careful when you remove the lid as the escaping steam will billow around your hand. Remove from the basket and enjoy warm.

Note
You can also steam the bao without any filling – once you have cut the dough into equal pieces, simply roll into balls, place on non-stick paper and steam for 8–10 minutes.

CRISPY AROMATIC DUCK WITH HOISIN SAUCE AND PANCAKES

Everyone, and I do mean everyone, LOVES this dish; it's the perfect sharing plate to be enjoyed with friends and family.

10 MINUTES   2 HOURS +   1-2 HOURS   SERVES 4-6

4 spring onions (scallions), halved

thumb-sized piece of fresh unpeeled ginger, sliced

1 litre (4 cups) chicken stock

120ml (½ cup) Chinese rice wine (Shaoxing wine)

120ml (½ cup) dark soy sauce

100g (½ cup) demerara sugar

1½ tbsp Chinese five spice

2 star anise

1 tsp cloves

3 cinnamon sticks

½ tbsp salt

4 duck legs (or you can use a whole duck cut into quarters)

To assemble

1 pack of Chinese pancakes (average 10 pancakes per pack)

2 spring onions (scallions), cut into matchsticks

1 cucumber, cut into matchsticks

60ml (¼ cup) hoisin sauce (page 342 or use shop-bought)

Put the spring onions (scallions), ginger, stock, rice wine, soy sauce, sugar, spices and salt into a large, lidded saucepan and stir well to combine. Add the duck legs and massage the marinade into the skin. Pop the lid on, put the pan in the fridge and leave to marinate for at least 2 hours or ideally overnight.

At the end of the marinating time, take the lid off the pan and set it over a high heat, bring to the boil, then turn down to a simmer. Cover and cook for 1–2 hours, keeping an eye on the liquid to ensure it doesn't boil dry – add water if needed. Remove the duck legs from the liquid and place on a wire rack to cool. Preheat the oven to 220°C (425°F).

Arrange the duck legs on a baking tray and cook in the oven for around 15–20 minutes, or until the skin has turned lovely and crispy.

Towards the end of the duck's cooking time, steam the pancakes for 6 minutes (or according to the packet instructions). Remove the duck from the oven and shred the meat from the bones using two forks. Serve straightaway with the warm pancakes, spring onions, cucumber and hoisin sauce and let everyone fill and roll their own pancakes.

HO CHI MINH
FRIED SPRING ROLLS

These Pan-Asian rolls were my all-time favourite dish growing up in my parents' restaurant. Crispy rice paper spring rolls stuffed with crunchy peppers, crisp beansprouts and noodles, all wrapped up in an ice-cold lettuce leaf and then dipped in a sweet, tangy chilli sauce – sheer heaven.

45 MINUTES   **45 MINUTES**   **SERVES 3-5**

2 nests of mung bean (glass) noodles
1 tbsp sesame seeds
1 tbsp oil (vegetable, groundnut or coconut), plus extra for shallow-frying
1 tbsp light soy sauce
1 tbsp dark soy sauce
2 tbsp Sriracha chilli sauce
1 tsp Chinese five spice
1 tsp ground Sichuan pepper
½ tsp salt
225g (8oz) firm tofu, cut into 5mm (¼in) slices
10 rice paper rounds, 22cm (9in) in diameter
½ red (bell) pepper, deseeded and thinly sliced into strips
1 carrot, thinly sliced into strips
3 spring onions (scallions), halved and thinly sliced into strips
small handful of beansprouts
1 round lettuce, leaves separated, washed and drained, to serve

For the sweet chilli vinegar dip
125ml (½ cup) water
125ml (½ cup) rice vinegar
50g (½ cup) sugar
4 tbsp honey (or use agave or maple syrup)
1 tsp grated ginger
½ tsp grated garlic
1 red bird's-eye chilli, finely chopped
1 tsp tomato ketchup

Put the mung bean (glass) noodles into a large bowl, cover with boiling water and leave to soak for 3–5 minutes. Once the noodles are soft, drain and set to one side.

To make the sweet chilli vinegar dip, combine all the ingredients in a saucepan, bring to the boil and then simmer for 3–5 minutes until slightly reduced and sticky. Pour into a bowl and set to one side.

Place a wok over a medium-low heat. Add the sesame seeds and slowly toast for 2–3 minutes until they have turned golden brown. Transfer to a plate and allow to cool.

Put the oil, soy sauces, Sriracha, Chinese five spice, Sichuan pepper and salt into a large bowl and mix well. Arrange the tofu slices on a shallow plate, then evenly coat the top of the tofu slices with the marinade, keeping some of the marinade for later. Set to one side and leave for 20 minutes.

Preheat the oven to 180°C (350°F). Lay the marinated tofu pieces on a baking tray and bake for 10–15 minutes. Turn the tofu over, cover with the remaining marinade and bake for a further 10–12 minutes. Remove from the oven and allow to cool. Once cooled, cut the tofu into 5mm (¼in) strips.

To assemble the rolls, soak a rice paper round in warm water for 20–30 seconds. Shake off any excess water and lay flat on a clean worktop. Add strips of vegetables and tofu, some beansprouts, a sprinkle of toasted sesame seeds and some noodles. Fold both sides over the filling, then roll up the rice paper to form a sausage shape.

Heat 250ml (1 cup) oil in a deep-sided frying pan over a medium heat. Carefully fry the rolls, turning them frequently so that they cook evenly, until golden brown all over. Drain on kitchen paper. To eat, take a round lettuce leaf and place one crispy roll in the centre, wrapping the leaf snugly around the roll. Then dip!

STEAMED SCALLOPS WITH GLASS NOODLES

These gloriously decadent, tender scallops sit on a nest of mung bean noodles and are oozing with an aromatic steaming liquor that simply must be drunk from the shell.

---

10 MINUTES   **5 MINUTES**   **SERVES 2-4**

2 nests of mung bean (glass) noodles
8 fresh scallops in their shells
2 garlic cloves, finely chopped or grated
3cm (1¼in) piece of ginger, cut into thin matchsticks
light soy sauce or Hot Chilli Dragon Sauce (page 342)

Put the noodle nests in a large bowl and pour over enough boiling water to cover; allow to soak for 5 minutes. Drain and set to one side.

Preheat your steamer. If using a bamboo steamer, fill a saucepan with water, bring to a rolling boil and set the steamer over the pan.

Open the scallops and remove from the shells (you can ask your fishmonger to do this for you), keeping the shells for cooking and serving on. Wash the scallops and shells in cold water, then place each shell on a steady worktop. Add a fork twirl of noodles and lay a scallop on top. Season each with a tiny pinch of garlic and 2–3 ginger matchsticks. Once all of the scallops are prepared, carefully place them on their shells into the steamer and steam for 3–5 minutes, depending on the size of your scallops.

Transfer the scallops in their shells to serving plates and season with 1 teaspoon of soy sauce or Hot Chilli Dragon Sauce. Serve hot.

SWEET CHINESE BBQ RIBS

Sticky, juicy and aromatic and a firm favourite for most carnivores, these ribs will tantalise your taste buds! They're so tender, the meat literally falls off the bones.

10 MINUTES **1 HOUR** **SERVES 4**

1kg (2lb 4oz) pork ribs, cut into 8cm (3¼in) lengths
3 garlic cloves, finely chopped
5cm (2in) piece of ginger, peeled and finely chopped
1 spring onion (scallion), halved
2 tbsp Chinese five spice
8 tbsp hoisin sauce (page 342 or use shop-bought)
8 tbsp yellow bean sauce
50g (¼ cup) sugar
4 tbsp rice wine
2 tsp salt
1 litre (4 cups) chicken stock
2 tbsp cornflour (cornstarch) mixed with 4 tbsp water
2 tbsp groundnut oil
3 tbsp runny honey (optional)

In a large saucepan with a lid, place the ribs and all of the ingredients, except the stock, cornflour (cornstarch) mixture, oil and honey, and massage them into the meat. Now add enough stock so the ribs are almost completely submerged under the liquid. Bring the pan to the boil, turn down to a simmer and place the lid on the pan. Cook over a low heat for 30 minutes (keep an eye on the sauce and add more stock if necessary). Remove the ribs from the sauce and place on a wire rack set over a bowl to drain.

Preheat the oven to 200°C (400°F). Strain the remaining sauce through a sieve into a clean saucepan and bring back to the boil. Slowly add the cornflour mixture, stirring to thicken the sauce to your desired consistency, ideally so that the sauce coats the back of a spoon. Turn off the heat and set to one side.

Arrange the ribs on a baking tray, lightly brush with the oil and place in the hot oven for 10 minutes (make sure they do not burn). Remove from the oven and brush the ribs with the thickened BBQ sauce or, if you like, some honey, and put back into the oven for another 5 minutes. Serve on a large plate with the remaining BBQ sauce.

Tip
If you're looking to achieve the 'red glow' that you see on restaurant ribs, you can always add a dash of red food colouring to the sauce mixture at the start of the cooking process.

GRIDDLED SWEET POTATO PANCAKES

Served hot, warm or even cold, these ever-so-sweet pancakes are chewy, savoury and perfect at any time of the day. My own memories of these pancakes are when my auntie would bring over a batch for my dad and, like any cheeky child, I'd eagerly sneak a couple to savour in front of the TV.

1½ HOURS   **10 MINUTES**   **MAKES 12**

450g (1lb) sweet potatoes
70g (⅓ cup) sugar
220g (8oz) glutinous rice flour
2–3 tbsp vegetable or sunflower oil

Preheat the oven to 200°C (400°F). Bake the sweet potatoes in their skins in the oven for 1 hour, or until tender. Remove and allow to cool for 15 minutes.

Remove the skins from the sweet potatoes and set to one side, then place the flesh into a large bowl. Combine the potato flesh and sugar with a fork. Add the glutinous rice flour and knead together to create a dough. Divide the mixture into 12 equal-sized balls and then flatten each ball into a 10cm (4in) disc.

Pour the oil into a hot wok and gently fry the cakes for 2–3 minutes on each side until golden brown. Transfer to a wire rack or kitchen paper to drain.

Kwoklyn's tip
Sprinkle the discarded skins with a little salt and Chinese five spice and lay out on a baking tray. Bake in the oven on a low heat until crisp. These are delicious snacks to be eaten with your favourite home-made Chinese dipping sauces.

CHINESE BEER-BATTERED PAKODA

Who doesn't love fried finger food as a perfect weekend treat? Also known as Manchurian balls, these Indo-Chinese savoury bites are made using Chinese rice beer, which gives each pakoda a unique fermented rice flavour.

10 MINUTES **15 MINUTES** **SERVES 3-4**

150g (1¼ cups) buckwheat flour

75g (generous ½ cup) plain (all-purpose) flour

½ tsp chilli powder

1 tsp garlic powder

2 tsp onion powder

2 tsp Chinese five spice

½ tsp ground Sichuan pepper

¼ tsp baking powder

1 tsp salt

200ml (¾ cup) Chinese beer (Buddha or Tsing Tao)

180g (6oz) sweet potato, peeled and cut into small dice

1 onion, finely diced

1 green (bell) pepper, deseeded and finely diced

5 spring onions (scallions), cut into thin rounds

1 tsp grated ginger

1 litre (4 cups) oil (vegetable, groundnut or coconut), for deep-frying

In a large bowl, mix the flours, spices, baking powder and salt. Slowly pour in the beer, whisking the batter to a smooth, thick consistency. Stir in the sweet potato, onion, green pepper, spring onions (scallions) and ginger.

Pour the oil for deep-frying into a large saucepan, adding enough oil to come no higher than a third of the way up the sides, and place over a medium-high heat. Working in batches of three or four fritters, drop spoonfuls of the mixture into the oil and fry for 5 minutes, or until golden brown, remembering to keep turning them as they cook to get an even colour. Drain on kitchen paper.

Serve the pakoda with your favourite dipping sauce and a bottle of chilled Chinese beer.

CHINESE-STYLE BUFFALO WINGS

We've all heard of and probably tasted the American-style buffalo wing, smothered in its rich, spicy and very tangy sauce. Well, these Chinese-style wings deliver just as much mouth-watering action; they're crispy and juicy with a spicy tang thanks to the fermented chilli beans. Set your taste buds on high alert because there's going to be a lot going on with each bite.

10 MINUTES **30 MINUTES** **SERVES 4**

500g (1lb 2oz) chicken wings
750ml (3 cups) vegetable oil, for deep-frying
50g (½ cup) cornflour (cornstarch)
2 tbsp chilli bean sauce
5 tbsp rice vinegar or apple cider vinegar
1½ tbsp tomato purée (paste)
2 tbsp light soy sauce
2 tbsp sugar

Use kitchen scissors to remove the tips from the wings and then carefully separate each wing into the drumette (the upper part of the wing that resembles a small drumstick) and the flat (the middle part of the chicken wing that connects the drumette and the tip). Pat each piece dry with kitchen paper and set to one side.

Pour the oil into a large saucepan and heat to 175°C (347°F).

Put the cornflour (cornstarch) into a large bowl and dredge each wing, banging off the excess flour. Carefully fry the wings, in batches so as not to overcrowd the pan, for 8–10 minutes, or until the chicken is completely cooked. Drain on a wire rack or a plate lined with kitchen paper and set to one side.

Once all of the wings have been fried, place a wok over a medium heat and add the cooked wings with the chilli bean sauce, rice vinegar, tomato purée (paste), soy sauce and sugar. Stir gently until all the pieces are well coated in the sauce, then transfer to a serving plate.

PANCAKE ROLLS

Chinese pancake rolls are very popular in Chinese fish and chip shops, takeaways and restaurants. Eaten alone or dipped in your favourite sauce, these large cylindrical parcels are packed full of beansprouts and ooze as you bite into them.

30 MINUTES **25 MINUTES** **SERVES 4-6**

oil (vegetable or groundnut), for frying
300g (6 cups) beansprouts
6 baby corn, quartered lengthways
30g (¼ cup) bamboo shoots, roughly chopped
1 cup shredded char siu pork (see Char Siu Puffs, page 49)
3 tbsp light soy sauce
1 tsp salt
½ tsp white pepper
2 tsp sugar
8 x 22cm (8½in) spring roll wrappers, defrosted

Place a wok over a high heat until hot. Add 1 tablespoon of oil along with the beansprouts and stir-fry for 1 minute before adding the baby corn and bamboo shoots. Stir-fry for a further 1 minute and then add the shredded pork, soy sauce, salt, pepper and sugar. Continue to stir-fry for a few more minutes until everything is well combined and cooked all the way through. Place a colander over a large bowl and tip the mixture in to cool and drain.

Once the mixture has fully cooled, place a spring roll wrapper on a board with one corner pointing towards you and brush the edges with water. Spoon 2–3 generous tablespoons of mixture into the centre of the wrapper. Fold the bottom corner up over the filling, fold the side corners in to enclose the filling and create a large fat sausage shape, and then roll towards the final corner. Use a little more water to help seal the wrapper. Repeat with the remaining wrappers and filling.

Pour enough oil into a deep-sided wok so that once the pancake rolls are added they can float. Heat the oil to 170°C (340°F) and cook the spring rolls two at a time for 7–9 minutes, or until golden brown. Remove the rolls from the oil and place on a wire rack or a plate lined with kitchen paper. Once all of the pancake rolls are cooked, serve hot.

Kwoklyn's tip
If you're making ahead, the unfried rolls can be frozen for up to a month in a sealed container. Uneaten fried rolls can also be stored in a sealed container in the fridge for up to 3 days and enjoyed as a cold snack. The cooked rolls may lose some of their crispness in the fridge but can be refreshed with a second flash in the wok or baked in the oven on a wire rack; however, please make sure the contents are fully reheated before eating if using either method.

CHICKEN DUMPLINGS

More than just tasty parcels, dumplings represent abundance and wealth and are eaten throughout the Chinese New Year as a symbol of good luck. Whole families get together to make these yummy pouches, which can be filled with meat, vegetables and seafood.

1½ HOURS   **1 HOUR**   **SERVES 6-8**

280g (2¼ cups) plain (all-purpose) flour, plus extra for dusting
180ml (¾ cup) just-boiled water
250g (generous 1 cup) minced (ground) chicken
200g (scant 1 cup) minced (ground) pork shoulder (needs to be quite fatty)
1 bunch of spring onions (scallions), sliced into rings
3 tbsp oyster sauce
¼ tsp salt
¼ tsp white pepper
1 tbsp light soy sauce
1 tsp sugar
oil (vegetable or groundnut), for frying

To make the dumpling wrappers, put the flour into a bowl and gradually pour in the just-boiled water in a steady stream, stirring with a wooden spoon until all of the flour is damp. Pull the mixture together with one hand and form it into a ball; the dough will still be fairly lumpy at this stage.

Tip the ball out on to a smooth un-floured surface and knead with the heel of your hand for about 2 minutes until the dough is silky and slightly elastic.

Put the dough into a ziplock bag and squeeze the air out before sealing. Leave for at least 15 minutes at room temperature (or up to 2 hours), while you prepare the filling. The dough will create condensation in the bag and will feel soft when it is ready.

Mix the remaining ingredients together in a large bowl, reserving the oil for frying. Mix well as you want an even distribution of ingredients.

Divide the dough into 32 equal pieces using a sharp knife. Taking one piece at a time, roll into a ball before flattening with the heel of your hand. Take a lightly floured rolling pin (to prevent sticking) and roll the dough until very thin but not too fragile to handle.

Place a teaspoon of filling into the centre of the wrapper, then fold one edge over to meet the other side and gently press the edges together, making sure that no filling escapes or is caught in the edge. Gather the sealed side of the parcel to form ripples around the edge of the dumpling. Place on a sheet of greaseproof paper until you are ready to cook.

Heat 2 tablespoons of oil in a flat-bottomed wok, or frying pan with a lid, over a medium-high heat. Cook the dumplings in batches of 8–10 to avoid overcrowding, adding more oil as necessary. Fry on one side only for 2 minutes, then add 1cm (½in) water, reduce the heat to medium-low and cover with the lid, allowing the dumplings to steam until the water has evaporated. Remove the lid, increase the heat to medium-high and fry until all the bottoms are golden brown and crispy. Drain on kitchen paper and enjoy hot.

PLAIN RICE ROLL

Originally from the Guangdong province of China, the rice roll or Cheung Fun is a delicate mix of soft, slippery and chewy, with a little bit of bounce. The mild and neutral flavour of the rolls make them the perfect vessels to carry a variety of meat and seafood fillings and they are most commonly served as a dim sum dish drizzled in a sweet soy sauce.

10 MINUTES **5 MINUTES** **SERVES 2–4**

For the rice rolls
250ml (1 cup) water
6 tbsp rice flour
2 tbsp wheat starch
2 tbsp cornflour (cornstarch)
2 tbsp mung bean starch
pinch of salt
2 spring onions (scallions), finely chopped (optional)
spray oil

For the sweet soy sauce
3 tbsp light soy sauce
½ tbsp dark soy sauce
3 tbsp water
½ tbsp sugar
1 tsp sesame oil

Place all of the sauce ingredients together in a bowl, mix well and set to one side.

Put all the rice roll ingredients except the spray oil together in a bowl, mix well and set to one side to rest for 10 minutes.

Spray a non-stick baking tray with a couple of squirts of spray oil, just enough to cover the base, and place into a steamer for 1 minute to heat up. Gently give the rice roll batter a mix and ladle a thin layer into the baking tray. Cover and steam for 3 minutes.

Once steamed, remove the baking tray and, using a spatula, carefully roll the rice roll sheet into a cylinder. If you are using a wide baking tray, you can chop your rice roll in half to make it easier to remove from the tray. Transfer to a serving plate and then cut each roll into roughly 7.5cm (3in) pieces, lightly drizzle over your sweet soy sauce and serve.

Repeat the process until all of the batter has been used.

Kwoklyn's tip
If you have a rice roll steamer in your equipment arsenal, fantastic! If not, fear not; these delicious rolls can be steamed just as perfectly in a standard steamer over boiling water using a baking tray or foil tray chosen to fit the steamer basket. When choosing your tray, ensure it is slightly smaller than the steamer basket to allow adequate steam flow and to enable you to lift it out to remove the rolls once they are cooked. To avoid water dripping on to your rice roll, you can wrap the lid of the steamer in a large tea towel before placing over the steamer.

CHICKEN & DUCK

CANTONESE-STYLE ORANGE CHICKEN

A variation of a Cantonese takeaway favourite, these light and crispy battered balls of chicken are tossed in a luxurious sauce that carefully balances a little bit of sweet yin from the orange and sugar, with a little bit of sour yang from the rice vinegar. One or two bites will just never be enough!

10 MINUTES   **15 MINUTES**   **SERVES 2**

125ml (½ cup) orange cordial/concentrate/squash
250ml (1 cup) water
½ tbsp minced ginger
½ orange, cut into half-moons
2 tbsp rice vinegar
1 tbsp Chinese rice wine (Shaoxing wine)
2 tbsp sugar (if you like it sweeter you can add more sugar)
2 tbsp cornflour (cornstarch) mixed with 4 tbsp water, plus 50g (½ cup) cornflour for coating
1 litre (4 cups) vegetable oil
300g (10½oz) chicken breast, cut into thick strips
1 egg, beaten
¼ tsp salt

Place a large saucepan over a medium heat and add the orange cordial, water, ginger, orange slices, rice vinegar, rice wine and sugar. Bring to the boil, then reduce the heat and simmer for 1–2 minutes. Give your cornflour (cornstarch) mixture a mix and slowly stir it into the sauce, a little at a time, until thickened to your desired consistency. Switch off the heat and leave to one side.

Place the oil in a large saucepan and heat to 170–180°C (340–350°F).

Place the chicken in a large bowl, add the beaten egg and salt and mix well. Add the cornflour to another large bowl, then dust each piece of chicken in the cornflour and bang off any excess. Gently drop the coated chicken into the oil and fry for around 5 minutes or until completely cooked and golden brown (if you have a food thermometer probe, the internal temperature should be 75–80°C/167–176°F). Remove the cooked chicken and drain over a wire rack. Arrange the chicken on a plate, spoon over the orange sauce and serve.

CHINESE POPCORN CHICKEN

A game changer in the snacking arena! Battered cubes of succulent chicken breast, marinated in rich Chinese aromats and finished with a seasoning that will deliver a slam dunk on your taste buds. Perfect served with chips and a cold Chinese beer!

2 HOURS +   **30 MINUTES**   **20-30 MINUTES**   **SERVES 4**

450g (1lb) chicken breast, cut into bite-sized cubes
3 garlic cloves, minced
1 tbsp light soy sauce
2 tbsp oyster sauce
2 tbsp Chinese rice wine (Shaoxing wine)
1 tbsp Chinese five spice
250g (2½ cups) cornflour (cornstarch)
1 egg, beaten
1 litre (4 cups) vegetable oil

For the seasoning
½ tsp paprika
1 tsp Chinese five spice
1 tsp garlic powder
½ tsp salt
pinch of ground black pepper

Add the cubed chicken, garlic, soy sauce, oyster sauce, rice wine, five spice and 1 tablespoon of the cornflour (cornstarch) to a large bowl. Using your hands, vigorously massage the marinade into the chicken for at least 30–40 seconds. Cover and place in the fridge overnight or for at least 2–3 hours if you can't wait that long!

Remove the marinated chicken from the fridge and add the beaten egg along with another tablespoon of cornflour and this time carefully massage the chicken to ensure it is evenly coated.

Place the oil in a large saucepan and heat to 170–180°C (340–350°F).

Place the remaining cornflour on a large plate or baking tray to give you more room to work. Coat the chicken in the flour, one piece at a time, so it is all fully covered. Bang off any excess and carefully lower into the hot oil. Working in batches to avoid overcrowding the pan, cook the chicken pieces for 5–6 minutes per batch or until golden brown, crispy and cooked all the way through. Drain on a wire rack or kitchen paper.

While your chicken is draining, mix the seasoning ingredients together in a small bowl.

Transfer the cooked chicken to a serving plate and evenly sprinkle over the seasoning.

SMOKED CHILLI CHICKEN

This recipe was only just recently introduced to me by fellow chef David Wong, and boy what a recipe. It has all the classic Chinese takeaway flavours and textures combined with proper home comfort yumminess.

---

10 MINUTES   **10 MINUTES**

SERVES 2

1 litre (4 cups) vegetable oil

300g (10½oz) chicken breast, cut into bite-sized pieces

3 tbsp hoisin sauce (page 342 or use shop-bought)

1 egg, beaten

50g (½ cup) cornflour (cornstarch)

3 tbsp chilli bean sauce

½ tbsp sugar

Place the oil in a large saucepan and heat to 170–180°C (340–350°F).

Place the chopped chicken breast into a large bowl along with the hoisin sauce and massage into the meat. Add the beaten egg and mix well. In another large bowl, dust each piece of chicken in the cornflour (cornstarch) and bang off any excess. Gently drop the coated chicken into the oil and fry for around 5 minutes or until completely cooked and golden brown (if you have a food thermometer probe, the internal temperature should be 75–80°C/167–176°F). Remove the cooked chicken and drain over a wire rack or on kitchen paper.

Place a wok over a medium-high heat and add the chilli bean sauce, sugar and enough water to just loosen the mixture, then bring to a gentle boil. Toss in your cooked chicken, and once completely coated, transfer to a serving plate and enjoy.

MARINATED CHICKEN SKEWERS

Don't limit this chicken to barbecues and picnics – these tasty skewers make a great starter dish or easy snack, eaten straight from the stick or eased away and stuffed into a fresh wrap with a mound of salad and dollop of mayo!

2 HOURS +   **10 MINUTES**   **40 MINUTES**   **SERVES 4**

340g (12oz) chicken breast, cut into 3cm (1¼in) cubes
80ml (⅓ cup) honey
3 garlic cloves, finely chopped or grated
4 juice of 1 lemon
250ml (1 cup) light soy sauce

If you are using wooden or bamboo skewers, soak them in water for at least 1 hour before using.

Put all the ingredients in a large bowl and mix well, making sure the chicken is well coated. Cover and allow to marinate for at least 2 hours.

Preheat the oven to 180°C (350°F). Thread 3 cubes of chicken on to each skewer, then place on a foil-lined baking tray. I'd recommend 2 skewers per person. Once all of the chicken has been threaded on to your skewers, spoon over the remaining marinade. Bake in the oven for 40 minutes, basting and turning the skewers every 15 minutes.

Once you are happy that the chicken is cooked through, transfer to a serving plate. These are best eaten warm but are also tasty as a cold snack or filling for baguettes, wraps or pittas.

CHICKEN WITH SWEET GINGER AND PINEAPPLE

'The Chinese do not draw any distinction between food and medicine.'
The Importance of Living, Lin Yutang

Ginger has many medicinal uses and is used in its many forms – fresh, dried, preserved, powdered, ground and candied – in hundreds of Chinese recipes.

Way back when, in my parents' Chinese restaurant, there were jars and jars of sweet ginger on the storeroom shelves ready to prepare this sweetly fragrant and aromatic dish.

10 MINUTES   **10 MINUTES**   **SERVES 2**

1 tbsp groundnut oil

300g (10½oz) chicken breast fillet, thinly sliced

1 garlic clove, finely chopped

1 onion, roughly chopped

1 carrot, cut into thin thumb-sized slices (slice the carrot diagonally)

8 slices of Chinese sweet pickled ginger

100g (3½oz) drained canned pineapple chunks

1 tbsp rice vinegar

½ tsp salt

1 tbsp granulated sugar

120ml (½ cup) chicken stock

1 tbsp tomato ketchup

1 tbsp cornflour (cornstarch) mixed with 2 tbsp water

1 tsp sesame oil

Heat the groundnut oil in a wok over a medium heat. Add the chicken and stir-fry for 2–3 minutes, then add the garlic and stir-fry for a further 15 seconds, followed by the onion and carrot. Stir-fry for a further minute before adding the sweet ginger and pineapple, stirring to combine well.

Add the vinegar, salt, sugar, stock and ketchup, bring to the boil, then reduce the heat and simmer for 1 minute. Slowly add the cornflour (cornstarch) mixture, stirring the sauce continuously. Remove from the heat, stir in the sesame oil and serve straightaway with a bowl of steaming Egg Fried Rice (see page 275).

SOY-BRAISED WINGS

The dark soy sauce mixed with light soy is what gives these wings their distinct dark colouring and, combined with the muscovado sugar for stickiness, they are finger-licking good! Usually, I prefer the flats to simply slurp off the bone but the succulent drumettes really do come into their own in this luscious sticky sauce.

10 MINUTES　　**1 HOUR 20 MINS**　　**SERVES 4**

16 whole chicken wings, separated into
　flats and drumettes

For the braising stock
1 litre (4 cups) chicken stock
2 star anise
1 cinnamon stick
2 bay leaves
125ml (½ cup) light soy sauce
125ml (½ cup) dark soy sauce
150g (¾ cup) muscovado sugar

Place all the braising stock ingredients in a saucepan and bring to the boil. Once boiling, turn down the heat to a simmer and reduce by half. Pick out the star anise, cinnamon stick and bay leaves and discard.

While the stock is simmering, place the wings in a large saucepan of boiling water and cook for 2–3 minutes, then rinse under cold water for 1–2 minutes, drain and leave to one side.

Bring your reduced soy sauce stock back up to the boil, then place the wings into the pan, ensuring they are completely submerged, and wait for the stock to return to the boil. Turn down to a simmer, place a tight lid on the pan and cook for 10 minutes, then switch off the heat and allow to cool in the liquid for at least 45 minutes.

Remove the cooked wings and set to one side.

Heat a wok or a non-stick frying pan over a medium heat and, once hot, place the wings into the wok and allow to caramelise before turning. Once you've turned the wings, pour in 125ml (½ cup) of the braising stock and allow to reduce into a sticky sauce. You will want to gently move the wings around in the sauce as it is reducing to prevent any burning. Transfer to a serving plate and tuck in.

DRUNKEN CHICKEN SOUP

Potently aromatic and definitely one for a 'quiet night in' ... don't eat and drive, folks! Instead stay home and bask in the internal warmth of this hearty broth.

10 MINUTES   **40 MINUTES**   **SERVES 4-6**

400g (14oz) chicken thigh fillets, skinned and boneless, if preferred
3 tbsp vegetable oil
2 thumb-sized pieces of ginger, roughly sliced
1.5 litres (6 cups) Chinese rice wine (Shaoxing wine)
2 tbsp brandy
875ml (3¾ cups) water
1 tsp salt, plus extra to taste
¼ tsp white pepper, plus extra to taste
1 tsp sugar
2 tbsp pure sesame oil

Cut the chicken into bite-sized pieces, removing any excess fat.

Heat a large saucepan or deep-sided wok over a medium-high heat, add the vegetable oil and ginger and fry for 45 seconds, or until fragrant. Add the chicken pieces and cook for 8–10 minutes until gently browned.

Pour in the rice wine and brandy and bring to the boil. Allow to boil for a couple of minutes, then add the water along with the salt, white pepper and sugar. Bring back to the boil and then turn down to simmer for 30 minutes. During the cooking process you may find that a scum forms on the top of the soup; skim this off and discard it.

Once the chicken is fully cooked, have a final taste and adjust the seasoning to your liking. Drizzle with the sesame oil and serve.

SWEET SOY PULLED CHICKEN

Perfect served in a freshly steamed bao or even a freshly baked baguette, with soy-pickled cucumber and shredded lettuce; close your eyes and with a mouthful of this sweet, succulent chicken, let the flavours transport you to the bustling street markets of Hong Kong.

5 MINUTES   **1 HOUR**   **SERVES 4**

2 skinless and boneless chicken breasts
80ml (⅓ cup) rice vinegar
160g (½ cup) blackberry jam
1 tsp celery salt
1 tbsp chilli flakes
120ml (½ cup) light soy sauce
50g (¼ cup) sugar
375ml (1½ cups) water

Put all the ingredients into a saucepan that has a tight-fitting lid. Bring to the boil and then turn down to a low simmer and place the lid firmly on.

After 45 minutes remove the lid and bring back up to the boil. Once the liquid has reduced by two-thirds, remove from the heat and allow to cool for 15 minutes.

Carefully shred the chicken, then mix with the remaining cooking liquid and serve.

SHREDDED CHICKEN IN PEKING SAUCE

Crispy coated shreds of chicken, lavishly tossed in a rich, sweetly tangy sauce. Perfect heaped on top of boiled rice or chow mein but even better snaffled straight from the wok before serving!

10 MINUTES　　**15 MINUTES**　　**SERVES 2**

1 litre (4 cups) vegetable oil, plus 1 tbsp

300g (10½oz) chicken breast, cut into thin strips

1 egg, beaten

¼ tsp salt

50g (½ cup) cornflour (cornstarch), plus 1 tsp cornflour mixed with 2 tsp water

1 small onion, sliced

½ green (bell) pepper, deseeded and sliced

1 tbsp Worcestershire sauce

1 tbsp hoisin sauce (page 342 or use shop-bought)

2 tbsp honey

3 tbsp tomato ketchup

1 tbsp brown sauce

2 tbsp muscovado sugar

60ml (¼ cup) chicken stock

Place the oil in a large saucepan and heat to 170–180°C (340–350°F).

Place the chicken into a large bowl, add the beaten egg and salt and mix well. In another large bowl, dust each piece of chicken in the cornflour (cornstarch) and bang off any excess. Gently drop the coated chicken into the oil and fry for around 2–3 minutes or until completely cooked and golden brown (if you have a food thermometer probe, the internal temperature should be 75–80°C/167–176°F). Remove the cooked chicken and drain over a wire rack or on kitchen paper.

Place a wok over a medium-high heat, add the 1 tablespoon of oil along with the onion and pepper and fry for 1 minute. Next, add the Worcestershire sauce, hoisin sauce, honey, tomato ketchup, brown sauce, sugar and chicken stock and bring to the boil. Give your cornflour mixture a mix and slowly stir into the sauce, a little at a time, until thickened to your desired consistency. Once the sauce has thickened, turn off the heat and toss in your fried chicken. Transfer to a serving plate and enjoy.

ROASTED CHICKEN THIGHS IN OYSTER SAUCE

Over the centuries, the Chinese, and especially the Hakka people, have perfected the art of roasting meats. Following this tradition and the knowledge passed down to me from my dad and his father before him, my roasted chicken thighs are first caramelised in a pan with classic Cantonese flavours of ginger and spring onion, before being placed in the oven to continue cooking in a rich, aromatic gravy.

10 MINUTES   **40 MINUTES**   **SERVES 2**

3 tbsp Chinese rice wine (Shaoxing wine)
3 tbsp oyster sauce
1 tbsp vegetable oil
4 spring onions (scallions), cut into 5cm (2in) lengths
2 tbsp grated ginger
4 chicken thighs
pinch of salt
pinch of white pepper

Stir the rice wine and oyster sauce together in a small bowl and set to one side.

Preheat the oven to 180°C (350°F).

Place a non-stick wok or frying pan over a medium-high heat. Once hot, add the oil, spring onions (scallions) and ginger and fry for 45 seconds until fragrant.

Season each chicken thigh with a pinch of salt and pepper and place skin-side down into the hot pan, then turn the heat down to medium and cook for 2–3 minutes. Once the chicken skin has browned, flip it over so it can brown for a further 2–3 minutes on the other side.

Transfer to a small baking tray and pour over the oyster sauce mixture, then bake in the oven for 30 minutes, basting the chicken with the sauce halfway through the cooking time.

Serve with your favourite noodles or steamed rice and vegetables.

CHICKEN AND MUSHROOMS

This dish will work with any type of edible mushroom you can get your hands on. Experiment – the kitchen is your playground!

5 MINUTES   **7 MINUTES**   **SERVES 2**

200g (7oz) portobello mushrooms
1 tbsp groundnut oil
3 garlic cloves, crushed
½ tsp finely chopped ginger
2 chicken breast fillets, thinly sliced
2 tbsp oyster sauce
1 tbsp dark soy sauce
¼ tsp salt
¼ tsp white pepper
1 tsp granulated sugar
80ml (⅓ cup) chicken stock
1 tbsp cornflour (cornstarch) mixed with
   2 tbsp water
1 tsp sesame oil

Cut the mushrooms into bite-sized pieces if necessary. Place a wok over a medium-high heat, add the groundnut oil, garlic and ginger and fry for about 30 seconds until fragrant. Add the chicken and stir-fry for 2 minutes, then add the mushrooms and stir-fry for a further minute.

Add the oyster sauce, soy sauce, salt, white pepper, sugar and chicken stock and mix well. Bring the sauce to the boil and allow to reduce by a third – this will take about 2 minutes. Pour in the cornflour (cornstarch) mixture to thicken the sauce, stirring constantly, then remove from the heat and add the sesame oil. Transfer to a serving dish and enjoy with rice.

PAPER BAG CHICKEN

Don't quote me on it but I'm pretty confident my dad invented this dish. I have fond memories of stapling the bags together after they had been filled with a mixture of mouth-watering ingredients. Cooked in their own little parcels they are, in my opinion, the tastiest thighs you'll ever eat.

2 HOURS +   **10 MINUTES**   **30 MINUTES**   **SERVES 2-3**

450g (1lb) bone-in chicken thighs
5 spring onions (scallions), cut into 5cm (2in) lengths
thumb-sized piece of ginger, peeled and cut into matchsticks
vegetable or sunflower oil, for deep-frying

For the marinade
3 star anise
1 cinnamon stick
2 tbsp honey
2 tsp Chinese five spice
1 tbsp light soy sauce
1 tsp dark soy sauce
1 tbsp oyster sauce
2 tsp sesame oil

Combine all the marinade ingredients in a large bowl, add the chicken thighs and massage well. Allow to marinate in the fridge for at least 2–3 hours or ideally overnight.

Once the chicken has marinated, place one chicken thigh into a 20cm (8in) square greaseproof paper bag along with a few strips of the spring onions (scallions) and ginger. (These bags can be bought from catering suppliers or constructed from greaseproof paper.) Fold the top of each bag over twice to create a lip and then, using a stapler, staple the lip together. Once all of the thighs are bagged, heat enough oil for deep-frying the bags in a large saucepan. Heat to around 180°C (350°F), then carefully place 2–3 bags into the oil and fry for 12–15 minutes, depending on the size of the thighs. Serve in the bags, being careful as you open them as they should have filled with a dramatic steam during cooking.

Kwoklyn's tip
Chicken thighs do vary in size from one shop to another, so to check that they are cooked all the way through after the allotted cooking time, I always sacrifice the dramatic plume of steam on the largest thigh in the batch and pierce the bag with a probe to ensure the internal temperature of the meat is between 75–80°C (167–176°F). If my test thigh is cooked, I can be confident the rest are good to go!

HONEY AND LEMON CHICKEN

This was a firm favourite in my dad's Cantonese restaurant – delicate, battered crispy chicken served on a bed of pineapple and drenched in a sweet yet tangy lemon sauce.

20 MINUTES   **15 MINUTES**   **SERVES 4**

For the chicken
groundnut oil, for deep-frying
2 large chicken breast fillets
½ tsp salt
80g (⅔ cup) cornflour (cornstarch)
1 egg
200g (7oz) drained canned pineapple
  chunks, to serve
½ lemon, cut into slices, to garnish

For the honey and lemon sauce
120ml (½ cup) lemon cordial
3 tbsp runny honey
1 tbsp custard powder (instant vanilla
  pudding mix)

First, start to make the sauce. Pour the cordial and honey into a wok and add the custard powder (instant vanilla pudding mix). Stir over a medium heat until the sauce starts to boil. Lower the heat and stir continuously until you reach the desired consistency. Remove from the heat and set to one side.

Heat a large saucepan or wok over a medium-high heat and fill with enough oil so it's deep enough for the chicken to float. Heat to 170°C (340°F).

Meanwhile, butterfly each chicken breast (slice through the breast horizontally but not all the way through, then open it out so it resembles a butterfly). Season with the salt. Tip the cornflour (cornstarch) on to a large plate, break the egg into a wide shallow bowl and beat. Coat the chicken in the cornflour, brushing off any excess, then dip the floured chicken into the beaten egg. Coat the chicken with cornflour for a second time, brushing off excess flour.

Carefully lower the chicken into the hot oil and deep-fry for 6–8 minutes, or until the chicken is golden brown, crispy and cooked all the way through. If you have a food probe thermometer, the internal temperature of the chicken should be at least 78°C (175°F). Transfer to a wire rack to drain or on to a plate lined with kitchen paper.

Reheat the sauce and arrange the pineapple on a serving plate. Slice the chicken into bite-sized pieces, place on top of the pineapple and garnish with the sliced lemon. Pour the sauce over the top and serve straightaway.

CANTONESE-STYLE PAN-FRIED CHICKEN

Lightly fried chicken morsels dressed in the classic Cantonese 'Holy Trinity' that is garlic, ginger and spring onion. Add a little red chilli heat and these tasty bites will be the perfect topping for any rice or noodle dish.

2 HOURS +   **10 MINUTES**   **15 MINUTES**   **SERVES 2**

450g (1lb) boneless chicken thighs, cut into bite-sized pieces
1 tbsp vegetable oil
1 garlic clove, roughly chopped
3 slices of ginger
1 red sweet pointed (Romano) pepper, deseeded and cut into bite-sized pieces
1 red chilli, thinly sliced
½ onion, cut into cubes
2 spring onions (scallions), cut into 5cm (2in) lengths and shredded
¼ tsp salt
⅛ tsp or a pinch of white pepper

For the marinade
1 tsp chicken powder
¼ tsp white pepper
pinch of sugar
2 tsp ginger, minced
1 tsp cornflour (cornstarch)
1 tbsp vegetable oil
½ tbsp light soy sauce

Place the chicken and all of the marinade ingredients in a large bowl and massage the marinade into the chicken. Set to one side for at least 2 hours or ideally overnight in the fridge.

Place a non-stick frying pan over a medium-high heat and once smoking hot, add the oil along with your marinated chicken. Fan the chicken out so that there is a single layer of chicken in direct contact with the pan. If your pan is larger than the gas/electric ring beneath, move the pan over the centre of the heat source to ensure that all of the chicken receives direct heat for a few seconds – this will help it to brown, but try not to be tempted to stir or move the chicken. After 2–3 minutes, turn the heat down to low, cover the pan with a lid and allow to cook covered for a further 3–4 minutes. Uncover the chicken, turn the heat back up to high and, using a pair of tongs or chopsticks, flip the chicken over so it can brown on the other side. Continue to pan-fry for a further minute or two, then add the roughly chopped garlic and ginger and stir. After a further 30 seconds, add the red pepper, chilli, onion and spring onions (scallions) along with the salt and white pepper. Stir-fry for a further 2 minutes, then transfer to a serving plate and enjoy with a bowl of steamed rice or atop your favourite chow mein.

SWEET AND SOUR CHICKEN BALLS

Friday nights just wouldn't be the same without these balls of chicken loveliness.

10 MINUTES   **15 MINUTES**   **SERVES 4**

125g (1 cup) plain (all-purpose) flour
2 tsp baking powder
1 tsp salt
2 eggs
160ml (⅔ cup) semi-skimmed milk
1 tbsp groundnut oil, plus extra for deep-frying
4 chicken breast fillets, cut into 3cm (1¼in) cubes

For the sweet and sour sauce
240ml (1 cup) orange juice
3 tbsp sugar
1 tbsp tomato purée (paste)
1 tbsp tomato ketchup
3 tbsp white wine vinegar
3 tbsp cornflour (cornstarch) mixed with 6 tbsp water

First, make the sauce. Put all the ingredients, except the cornflour (cornstarch) mixture, into a large saucepan over a medium heat. Bring to the boil and then simmer for 5 minutes. Slowly pour the cornflour mixture into the sauce a little at a time, stirring continuously, until thickened to your desired consistency, then take off the heat and set to one side.

Mix the flour, baking powder and salt in a large bowl. In a separate bowl, beat the eggs, milk and the 1 tablespoon of oil together. Pour the wet mixture into the flour and mix well to create a smooth paste. Add the chicken and mix, making sure each piece is thoroughly coated.

Heat some oil to 170°C (340°F) in a deep-sided saucepan or wok, ensuring you have enough oil in the wok so that the chicken will fry without touching the bottom. Carefully lower the chicken into the oil one piece at a time and fry in batches of 5 pieces for about 5–6 minutes until golden brown and cooked through. If you have a food probe thermometer, the internal temperature should reach 78°C (175°F). Remove the chicken from the oil and drain on a wire rack or on a plate lined with kitchen paper. Repeat until you've fried all the chicken, then serve with the sweet and sour dipping sauce.

CHINESE CHICKEN CURRY

Introduced into China from Malaysia by the Cantonese, this signature sauce is often also served with fish balls and beef brisket.

---

5 MINUTES **25 MINUTES** **SERVES 2**

1 tbsp groundnut oil
2 chicken breast fillets, sliced into thin strips
1 onion, roughly chopped
4 button mushrooms, sliced
¼ tsp salt
¼ tsp sugar
40g (¼ cup) peas

For the curry sauce
1 tbsp groundnut oil
2 onions, sliced into strips
5 garlic cloves, crushed
2 carrots, sliced into small discs
2 tbsp plain (all-purpose) flour
4 tsp curry powder (use your favourite: mild, medium or hot)
600ml (2½ cups) chicken stock
2 tsp honey
4 tsp light soy sauce
1 bay leaf
1 tsp garam masala

First, make the curry sauce. Heat the oil in a wok or non-stick saucepan, add the onions and garlic and cook until softened. Stir in the carrots and cook over a low heat for 10–12 minutes.

Add the flour and curry powder and cook for 1 minute. Gradually stir in the stock until combined, then add the honey, soy sauce and bay leaf. Slowly bring to the boil, then reduce the heat and simmer for 15 minutes or until the sauce thickens but is still a pouring consistency. Stir in the garam masala, then strain the curry sauce through a sieve and set to one side, discarding the veg and bay leaf.

Heat the oil in a wok over a medium heat and, when hot, add the chicken and stir-fry for 2 minutes. Add the onion and mushrooms and fry for a further 2–3 minutes, ensuring the chicken is cooked through. Now add the salt and sugar, mix well, then pour in the strained curry sauce and add the peas. Bring to the boil, then reduce the heat to a simmer for 3 minutes, allowing the curry sauce to thicken again. If the curry sauce is too thick, add a splash of water to loosen it. Serve with Perfect Steamed Rice (page 274).

CHICKEN AND CASHEW NUTS

When cooking Chinese food, it's always important to think about the flavours and textures of the ingredients. Juicy chicken combined with succulent baby corn and salty, crunchy cashew nuts come together beautifully in this dish.

5 MINUTES   **7 MINUTES**   **SERVES 2**

1 tbsp groundnut oil
3 garlic cloves, crushed
½ tsp finely chopped ginger
2 chicken breast fillets, sliced
1 onion, roughly chopped
1 carrot, finely diced
40g (¼ cup) canned water chestnuts, sliced into bite-sized discs
30g (¼ cup) canned bamboo shoots
3 baby corn cobs, cut into bite-sized pieces
2 tbsp oyster sauce
1 tbsp dark soy sauce
80ml (⅓ cup) chicken stock
¼ tsp salt
¼ tsp white pepper
1 tbsp cornflour (cornstarch) mixed with 2 tbsp water
30g (1oz) salted, roasted cashew nuts
1 tsp sesame oil

Place a wok over a medium-high heat, add the groundnut oil, garlic and ginger and fry for about 30 seconds until fragrant. Add the chicken and stir-fry for 2 minutes. Add the onion, carrot, water chestnuts, bamboo shoots and baby corn and stir-fry for a further 2 minutes. Spoon in the oyster sauce and soy sauce, pour in the stock and add the salt and pepper. Stir well, bring to the boil and then turn down to a simmer for 2 minutes.

Pour in the cornflour (cornstarch) mixture to thicken the sauce, stirring as you do, then remove from the heat, add the cashew nuts and sesame oil and mix well. Transfer to a serving dish and enjoy.

CANTONESE CHICKEN THIGHS ON SPRING ONION FRIED RICE

Nothing screams Cantonese cuisine like the aromatic combination of garlic, ginger and spring onions. This recipe embraces all three flavours, and when mixed with the perfect textures of crispy chicken skin wrapped around juicy thigh meat and served on top of lightly seasoned fried rice, it is in my opinion an all-singing, all-dancing mouth sensation.

1 HOUR +   **10 MINUTES**   **50 MINUTES**   **SERVES 2**

1 bunch of spring onions (scallions)
4 skin-on chicken thighs
2 garlic cloves, thinly sliced
4 thumb-sized pieces of ginger, peeled and cut into thin matchsticks
3 tbsp vegetable oil
1 packet of pre-cooked basmati rice
½ tbsp light soy sauce
salt
white pepper

Prepare the spring onions (scallions) by slicing the green ends into 5cm (2in) lengths and the white parts into fine rings.

Put the chicken thighs in a large bowl with the garlic, ginger and the spring onion greens along with 2 tablespoons of the oil and a pinch of salt and pepper. Massage the mixture into the meat, then cover and leave to marinate for at least 1 hour (or leave in the fridge overnight).

Preheat the oven to 180°C (350°F). Put the marinated chicken on to a baking tray and roast for 30–40 minutes, or until cooked and the juices run clear. Remove from the oven and allow to rest.

Heat a non-stick frying pan or wok with the remaining tablespoon of oil. Once the oil begins to smoke, add half the spring onion whites and fry for about 30 seconds until fragrant. Add the rice and use the back of a wooden spoon to break up any rice clumps. Continue to fry for 3–5 minutes, seasoning with salt and pepper. Once the rice is fully heated, add the soy sauce and mix well.

Divide the rice between 2 plates, top with the cooked chicken thighs, garnish with the remaining spring onion whites and enjoy.

WANDERING DRAGON

The mythical Chinese Dragon has long been a symbol of happiness and prosperity, which for me describes this dish perfectly: rich in ingredients and delivering happiness to all who eat it.

5 MINUTES   **7 MINUTES**   **SERVES 2**

1 tbsp groundnut oil
1 onion, diced
1 garlic clove, crushed
1 chicken breast fillet, thinly sliced
30g (¼ cup) drained canned Chinese
   straw mushrooms
30g (¼ cup) canned bamboo shoots
3 baby corn cobs, halved lengthways
1 carrot, thinly sliced
10 raw king prawns (jumbo shrimp),
   shelled and deveined
2 tbsp Chinese rice wine (Shaoxing
   wine)
1 tbsp light soy sauce
½ tbsp dark soy sauce
2 tbsp oyster sauce
½ tsp salt (or to taste)
½ tsp sugar
½ tsp white pepper
120ml (½ cup) chicken stock
1 tbsp cornflour (cornstarch) mixed with
   2 tbsp water
1 tsp sesame oil

Heat the groundnut oil in a large wok or deep-sided frying pan over a medium-high heat. Add the onion and garlic and fry for 1 minute. Add chicken and stir-fry for 2 minutes, then add the mushrooms, bamboo shoots, corn and carrot and fry for another minute.

Next, add the prawns (shrimp) and rice wine and stir-fry for 1 minute.

Add the remaining ingredients, except for the cornflour (cornstarch) mixture and the sesame oil, stir and bring to the boil. Once the sauce is boiling, slowly add the cornflour mixture as you stir to thicken the sauce. Remove from the heat, add the sesame oil and serve immediately.

ASIAN-STYLE CRISPY DUCK SALAD

I'm really not sure that anything beats crispy duck on flavour, especially crispy duck seasoned with Chinese five spice and served with sweet, juicy orange segments, crunchy salad and hoisin sauce. The flavour and texture profile of this dish is quite simply magical.

5 MINUTES   **12 MINUTES**   **SERVES 2**

1 large duck breast
1 tsp Chinese five spice
2 tbsp hoisin sauce (page 342 or use shop-bought)
1 bag of mixed salad leaves
1 orange, peeled and cut into 2cm (¾in) cubes (you can also use pear, mango, lychee or pomegranate)
salt
white pepper

Season the duck breast on both sides with a pinch of salt and pepper and ½ teaspoon of the Chinese five spice. Heat a dry non-stick wok over a medium-high heat, then place the breast into the hot wok, skin-side down. Turn down the heat to medium and cook for 2–3 minutes, or until the skin is golden brown, then turn the breast over and cook for a further 3–5 minutes. Remove from the pan and allow to rest for 5 minutes, then cut into thin slices.

Wipe your wok clean and reheat over a medium-high heat. Add the sliced duck and cook until crispy, seasoning again with a pinch of salt and pepper and the remaining five spice. Mix well and transfer to a plate lined with kitchen paper to drain.

In a small bowl, combine the hoisin sauce with 2 tablespoons of water.

Arrange your salad leaves on a large plate and top with the cooled drained duck and orange cubes. Drizzle with the hoisin dressing and toss together. Serve and enjoy.

ROAST DUCK WITH BEANSPROUTS AND CHINESE BBQ SAUCE

This dish is a spin on the classic chop suey dish we all know and love. Finished with crisp duck breasts, lavishly drizzled in a rich aromatic BBQ sauce, this dish is something else. A must-try if you are craving a taste explosion.

5 MINUTES   **20 MINUTES**   **SERVES 2**

2 boneless Peking Roast Duck breasts (see page 126)
1 tbsp groundnut oil
2 spring onions (scallions), halved lengthways and thinly sliced
1 garlic clove, crushed
1 small onion, thinly sliced
1 small carrot, thinly sliced
3 handfuls of beansprouts
½ tbsp dark soy sauce
¼ tsp salt
½ tsp sugar
½ tsp white pepper
120ml (½ cup) chicken stock
1 tbsp cornflour (cornstarch) mixed with 2 tbsp water
1 tsp sesame oil

For the BBQ sauce
2 tbsp Chinese five spice
240ml (1 cup) chicken stock
2 tbsp rice wine
120ml (½ cup) hoisin sauce (page 342 or use shop-bought)
120ml (½ cup) yellow bean sauce
2 star anise
1 cinnamon stick
50g (¼ cup) sugar
3 tbsp cornflour (cornstarch) mixed with 6 tbsp water

If you're short of time, pre-cooked duck from the supermarket will be fine for this recipe. However, the dish won't have the same authentic taste, so it is well worth taking the time to source and prepare the full ingredients.

Place the duck breasts in a medium-low oven (160°C/325°F) to reheat for 20 minutes, remove from the oven and slice into bite-sized pieces.

Meanwhile, make the BBQ sauce. Place all the ingredients, except the cornflour (cornstarch) mixture, in a saucepan and gently bring to the boil. Turn down the heat and simmer for 15 minutes. Slowly stir the cornflour mixture into the sauce until it has thickened and coats the back of a spoon. Remove the star anise and cinnamon stick and set the sauce to one side.

Heat a non-stick wok over a medium heat, add the oil, the spring onions (scallions) and garlic and fry for about 30 seconds, until fragrant. Add the onion and carrot and stir-fry for a further minute. Add the beansprouts and fry for another minute, then season with the dark soy, salt, sugar and white pepper and mix well.

Add the stock, bring to the boil, then thicken with the cornflour mixture, slowly pouring it into the pan while stirring. Remove from the heat, add the sesame oil and transfer to a serving plate. Arrange the sliced duck over the top of the chop suey, drizzle with the BBQ sauce and serve.

STUFFED CANTONESE DUCK WITH CRAB MEAT SAUCE

When asked what my favourite Chinese dish is, the answer will nine times out of ten be classic Roast Duck and Rice, but if King Prawn-stuffed Cantonese Duck is on the menu, then I simply have no choice but to indulge! And indulge you will as this dish is rich and luxurious in its ingredients and texture, from the plump, springy king prawn stuffing to the moist meat of the duck, wrapped in the crispy skin and dressed in the aromatic crab sauce.

40 MINUTES   **10 MINUTES**   **SERVES 4-6**

¼ Peking Roast Duck (see page 126, or use shop-bought), deboned
½–1 litre (2–4 cups) vegetable oil
1 tsp chicken powder dissolved in 250ml (1 cup) hot water
70g (2½oz) cooked crab meat
pinch of white pepper
½ tbsp cornflour (cornstarch) mixed with 1 tbsp water, plus extra for dusting
1 egg white, beaten
drizzle of sesame oil

For the stuffing
250g (9oz) large raw king prawns (jumbo shrimp), peeled and deveined
1 tbsp cornflour (cornstarch) mixed with 2 tbsp water
2 spring onions (scallions), finely chopped
½ tsp salt
½ tsp sugar
⅛ tsp or a pinch of white pepper

Begin by chopping your king prawns (jumbo shrimp), roughly to begin with and then continue chopping them finer until you have a chunky paste. This does take a little while, but I find this method much better than using a food processor, as you will retain a slightly chunkier texture. Transfer your minced prawn paste to a large bowl and begin to mix vigorously with a pair of chopsticks, keep mixing for at least 3 minutes until the paste becomes sticky. Give the cornflour (cornstarch) mixture a stir and add it little by little to the paste, mixing constantly; this will help to firm the paste. Once you have a sticky, firm prawn paste, scoop it into a ball in your hand and then with a little force throw it back into the bowl. You want to do this around 10 times; this will help give the filling a springy texture when cooked.

Now add the chopped spring onions (scallions), salt, sugar and pepper, stir them evenly through the paste and set to one side.

Lay the deboned duck on its back on a clean plate or chopping board, dust the inside with a little cornflour, bang off any excess and, using a knife or a teaspoon, fill the inside of the duck with your prawn paste. Leave the duck paste-side up until you are ready to cook.

Place a wok over a medium-high heat, add the oil and, once hot, carefully place your filled piece of duck paste-side down in the hot oil. Cook for at least 2 minutes or until the paste has turned golden brown and is a little crispy, then carefully flip the duck over and fry for another minute or two. Transfer to a wire rack to drain, skin side up.

In a clean wok, add your chicken stock, crab meat and white pepper. Bring to a simmer, then give the cornflour mixture a stir and slowly add to the sauce, stirring constantly. Once thickened, switch off the heat and slowly pour in the egg white, stirring continuously. Finally, add a drizzle of sesame oil.

Cut your stuffed duck into bite-sized slices, arrange on a serving plate and pour over your sauce.

ROAST DUCK WITH PLUM SAUCE

The sweet, tangy plum sauce perfectly cuts through the richness of the duck and is delicious served on freshly boiled rice or crispy chow mein.

If you're short of time, pre-cooked duck from the supermarket will be fine for this recipe. However, the dish won't have the same authentic taste, so it is well worth taking the time to source and prepare the full ingredients.

5 MINUTES   **35 MINUTES**   **SERVES 2**

2 boneless Peking Roast Duck breasts (see page 126)
150g (1 cup) drained canned pineapple chunks

For the plum sauce
2 tbsp sugar
2cm (¾in) piece of ginger, finely chopped
3 shallots, finely diced
6 tbsp dark soy sauce
2 tbsp rice vinegar
1 tbsp rice wine
450g (1lb) fresh plums, stoned and chopped into small cubes
150ml (⅔ cup) purple grape juice
2½ tbsp ready-made Chinese plum sauce
¼ tsp salt

First, make the plum sauce. Gently dissolve the sugar in a wok over a medium-low heat. Once the sugar has caramelised and turned brown, add the ginger and shallots and cook for a further 30 seconds. Add the remaining sauce ingredients, bring to the boil and then reduce the heat and simmer for 30 minutes. The sauce should coat the back of a spoon. Strain the sauce through a fine sieve into a bowl and set to one side.

Place the duck breasts on a baking tray in a medium-low oven (160°C/325°F) to reheat for 20 minutes. Remove from the oven and cut into slices.

Spoon the pineapple on to a serving plate and carefully arrange the slices of duck on top. Pour the plum sauce into a small saucepan and reheat it for a few minutes, then spoon over the duck. Serve and enjoy.

PEKING ROAST DUCK

Revered for its glistening red, crispy skin, Peking Duck dates back to the Ming Dynasty when cooks from all over China travelled to the capital to cook for the Emperor. Traditionally served in thin slices and eaten with pancakes, spring onions, cucumber and a sweet plum or hoisin sauce.

1½ HOURS PLUS 2 HOURS RESTING   **1 HOUR 20 MINS**   **SERVES 6**   **24 HOURS +**

1.5–2kg (3lb 5oz–4lb 8oz) whole duck
½ tbsp salt
¼ tbsp white pepper
1 tbsp Chinese five spice
½ tbsp white granulated sugar
2 litres (8 cups) water
125ml (½ cup) Chinese rice wine (Shaoxing wine)
125ml (½ cup) Chinese red vinegar (to help colour the skin)
120ml (½ cup) runny honey
plum sauce, to serve

For the marinade
1 tbsp light soy sauce
1 tbsp oyster sauce
1 tbsp hoisin sauce (page 342 or use shop-bought)
½ tbsp Chinese five spice
½ tbsp white granulated sugar
5 spring onions (scallions), cut into 5cm (2in) lengths
3 thin slices of ginger
3 garlic cloves, crushed

Remove and discard any excess fat from the cavity of the duck, then wash in lukewarm water and pat dry with a clean tea towel. Inspect the skin and remove any remaining feathers with tweezers, or you can use a kitchen blowtorch to singe them off but be careful not to scorch the skin.

In a bowl, combine the salt, white pepper, five spice powder and sugar, mix well and rub all over the duck and inside the cavity. Place the duck on a tray and leave, uncovered, in the fridge for at least 2 hours.

Mix all of the marinade ingredients together in a bowl. Stuff the marinade into the cavity of the duck and, using a metal skewer, lace the cavity together until fully sealed so the marinade won't fall out during cooking.

Using your hand or a small wooden spoon, gently loosen the skin from the meat of the duck, being very careful not to tear it. Secure an S-shaped hook into the duck's neck so that you can hang the bird or, alternatively, you can use butcher's string tied securely under the wings. Carefully lift the duck with the hook or string to ensure it is secure and isn't going to fall off.

Fill your largest saucepan or wok with the water and bring to the boil; the wider the pan, the better, as it will give you more space to work without too much splashing. Holding the duck over the pan, ladle over the boiling water. You want to do this for at least 2 minutes, ensuring you don't miss any part, as this process will tighten the skin and add to the crispiness. Place the freshly bathed duck on a wire rack, pat dry and allow to cool.

Discard the water from the saucepan or wok, wipe clean and then add the rice wine, red vinegar and honey and gently bring to the boil. Turn the heat down to low and then, again holding the duck over the hot liquor, ladle over the duck for at least 2 minutes. Lay the basted duck on a wire rack, breast side up, remove the hook or string, then place, uncovered, in the fridge for at least 24 hours and up to 48 hours to air dry.

Remove the duck from the fridge to come up to room temperature, this will take 20–30 minutes. Wrap the wings and legs in foil as this will prevent them from burning and preheat your oven to 220°C (425°F).

Place the duck on its wire rack over a large roasting tray and roast for 10 minutes, then turn the oven down to 180°C (350°F) and roast for a further 25 minutes. Remove the duck from the oven and carefully flip it over so that it is laying breast side down. Return to the oven for 25 minutes, then discard the foil and carefully flip the duck so it is breast side up and roast for a final 20 minutes. Remove from the oven and leave to rest for 15 minutes. Remove the metal skewer and discard the marinade from the cavity. Chop into small pieces or slice thinly and serve with plum sauce.

SEAFOOD

CANTONESE LOBSTER WITH GLASS NOODLES

There really is no easy way to say this but, a lobster will be harmed in the making of this dish... However, I truly do believe that through the personal act of dispatching the creature in the most humanely possible way while offering a muttered thanks for its sacrifice, we can fully appreciate the majesty of the dish we are about to enjoy.

45 MINUTES   15 MINUTES   SERVES 4

1 live lobster (around 750–900g/ 1lb 10oz–2lb)
150g (5oz) dried mung bean (glass) noodles
100g (1 cup) cornflour (cornstarch)
2 eggs, beaten
pinch of salt
500ml (2 cups) vegetable oil

For the sauce
6 slices of ginger
3 garlic cloves, roughly chopped
5 spring onions (scallions), cut into 3cm (1¼in) lengths, whites and greens separated
1 tbsp light soy sauce
2 tbsp Chinese rice wine (Shaoxing wine)
1 tbsp oyster sauce
250ml (1 cup) chicken stock
pinch of white pepper
1 tsp sugar
pinch of salt, to taste
1 tbsp cornflour (cornstarch) mixed with 2 tbsp water

Begin by placing your lobster in the freezer for 15–20 minutes – this will sedate the lobster without freezing the meat.

Meanwhile, place the noodles into a pan of boiling water for 2–3 minutes and, once softened, drain and set to one side.

Remove the lobster from the freezer and place on a chopping board with its head facing towards your dominant hand. Take a sharp knife and place it point down at the base of the lobster's head, just behind the eyes, then carefully and quickly plunge the knife through the shell and cut down towards the top of the head.

Remove and discard the feathery gills, the green innards and the digestive tract/vein. Cut the lobster in half from head to tail, then remove the claws, and elbow section. Carefully crack the shell on the claws, as you want them to stay intact. Cut the body from the tail and then cut the tail into 3 or 4 equal pieces on each half.

Rinse the prepared lobster under cold water, drain and pat dry with a clean tea towel. Mix 1 tablespoon of the cornflour (cornstarch) with the beaten eggs and salt, dip the lobster pieces in the batter and then dust in the remaining cornflour to coat completely, banging off any excess.

Place a wok over a medium-high heat, add the oil and, once hot, flash-fry the lobster pieces in batches for 20–30 seconds per batch. Transfer to a wire rack or kitchen paper and allow to drain.

Pour the excess oil into a heatproof bowl but do not wipe the wok clean and place it back over a medium-high heat. Add the ginger, garlic and the whites of the spring onions (scallions). Fry for 20 seconds and then add your drained lobster pieces, continuing to stir-fry for a further 2 minutes. Next, add the light soy sauce, rice wine, oyster sauce, chicken stock, white pepper and sugar. Bring to the boil, check the seasoning and, if required, add a pinch of salt to taste. Now add the spring onion greens, then give the cornflour mixture a stir and pour into the sauce, stirring constantly until thickened to your desired consistency. Once thickened, switch off the heat and stir in the drained noodles. Transfer to a serving plate and enjoy.

Kwoklyn's tip
If you can't face the thought of dispatching a lobster, a good-quality fishmonger can supply a ready-prepared lobster, but ensure that you store it at a constant chilled temperature and cook it on the same day.

FANTAIL KING PRAWNS

Yes, you could serve a prawn cocktail at your next shindig... I'd suggest you don't but, hey, it's your party, so you go rock that 80s vibe...

Or you could serve my fantail King Prawns in their lightly spiced crispy coats that are just begging to be dipped in your favourite dipping sauce.

---

20 MINUTES   15 MINUTES   SERVES 6 AS A PARTY SNACK

450g (1lb) large raw king prawns
    (jumbo shrimp), unpeeled
50g (½ cup) plain (all-purpose) flour,
    plus extra for dusting
25g (¼ cup) cornflour (cornstarch)
1 tsp paprika
1 tsp chilli powder (optional)
1 tsp baking powder
½ tsp onion powder
½ tsp garlic powder
750ml (3 cups) ice-cold water
1 litre (4 cups) vegetable oil

Firstly, you'll need to prepare the king prawns (jumbo shrimp). Remove the heads by simply gripping the body of a prawn with one hand and the head in the other and pulling. The head should come away in one piece, then remove the legs by pulling them off too. Carefully peel the shell off the prawns but leave the tail on. Once the prawns are peeled, carefully lay them flat on a chopping board and run a sharp knife across their backs, ensuring you don't cut all the way through but deep enough so you can fan the prawns out to remove and discard the black vein (digestive tract). Once this process is complete, pat the prawns dry with kitchen paper.

In a large bowl, combine the plain (all-purpose) flour, cornflour (cornstarch), paprika, chilli powder (if using), baking powder, onion powder and garlic powder. Once these are mixed, using a whisk or a pair of chopsticks, slowly pour in the ice-cold water, mixing the flour mixture at the same time to create a batter.

Place the oil in a large saucepan and heat to around 180–200°C (350–400°F).

Dust the prepared prawns in the extra flour and bang off the excess, then dip them in the batter and carefully lower them into the hot oil. Fry in batches until golden brown, this will take around 2–3 minutes per batch. Transfer to a wire rack or kitchen paper to drain.

Arrange on your serving plate and serve with your favourite dipping sauce.

Kwoklyn's tip
Don't discard the king prawn heads or shells, as they make the most amazing fish stock. Simply add the prawn shells and heads to a large saucepan filled with water and bring to the boil. Turn down to a simmer and, using a large spoon, skim off any scum and then reduce the liquid by a third. Pour through a sieve, reserving the liquid, and use to make delicious broths and sauces.

CHILLI AND SALT SQUID WITH PEPPERS AND ONIONS

I order this dish every time I head to a Cantonese restaurant; it evokes so many memories of my days working in Mum and Dad's restaurant. As soon as I smell it, I'm instantly transported back into the kitchen, to the sound of the Chinese range roaring away and the woks clanging as ingredients are tossed into the air, the flashes of flames as the fire meets the sizzle and spit of hot oil.

10 MINUTES   **10 MINUTES**   **SERVES 2**

300g (10½oz) fresh squid, a mixture of cleaned tubes and tentacles
½ tbsp salt
½ tbsp Chinese five spice
1 tsp freshly ground black pepper
groundnut oil, for deep-frying, plus 1 tbsp
50g (½ cup) cornflour (cornstarch)
1 egg, beaten
1 small onion, finely diced
½ green (bell) pepper, deseeded and finely diced
2 bird's-eye chillies, finely chopped
1 garlic clove, crushed
2 tbsp water
1 tsp sesame oil

Slice the squid into bite-sized pieces and gently score the back of each tube piece with a criss-cross pattern. This will help the squid cook evenly and stop it from curling up too much.

In a separate bowl, mix the salt, five spice and black pepper and set aside.

Pour enough oil to deep-fry the squid into a large wok or deep-sided saucepan and heat to 180°C (350°F). Spread the cornflour (cornstarch) on a plate and put the beaten egg in a shallow bowl. Coat each piece of squid in the cornflour, shaking off the excess, then dip into the egg and then back into the cornflour.

Gently lower the squid in batches into the hot oil and deep-fry for around 3 minutes, turning once or twice to allow each piece to brown evenly. Remove the squid and place on a wire rack or a plate lined with kitchen paper to drain.

Heat the 1 tablespoon of oil in a wok or frying pan until the oil just begins to smoke. Add the onion, green pepper and chillies. Stir-fry for 30 seconds over a high heat, then add the garlic and mix thoroughly. Add the deep-fried squid and evenly sprinkle in the five-spice mixture. Quickly toss the ingredients together, pour in the water and quickly toss again, coating each piece. Turn off the heat, add the sesame oil and serve immediately.

KING PRAWNS AND TOMATOES

The first time I ever cooked this dish was at my nan's house. My nan LOVES king prawns as a treat, and even as a young child I cooked this for her. Served on top of freshly steamed sticky rice, this dish is hard to beat as a comfort food.

8 MINUTES   **10 MINUTES**   **SERVES 2**

1 tbsp groundnut oil

1 garlic clove, crushed

12 raw king prawns (jumbo shrimp), shelled and deveined

6 tomatoes, each cut into 8 wedges

120ml (½ cup) fish stock

3 tbsp tomato ketchup

1 tbsp tomato purée (paste)

1 tsp salt

1 tsp sugar

1 tbsp Chinese rice wine (Shaoxing wine)

1 tbsp light soy sauce

1 tbsp cornflour (cornstarch) mixed with 2 tbsp water

Heat the oil in a wok over a high heat. Add the garlic, quickly tossing to avoid burning, then carefully (to avoid the oil spitting) add the king prawns (jumbo shrimp) and tomatoes. Stir constantly over a medium heat until the prawns begin to turn pink.

Now, add the fish stock, tomato ketchup, tomato purée (paste), salt, sugar, rice wine and soy sauce and mix well. Once everything is bubbling away, slowly add the cornflour (cornstarch) mixture, stirring constantly. Turn off the heat and serve straightaway.

KUNG PO KING PRAWNS

Succulent king prawns coated in a crispy cornflour batter, smothered in a rich, tangy spicy sauce, served with crunchy vegetables and milky cashew nuts, this dish originates from the Sichuan province of China, dating to around 1820–60, and is named after a Palace Guardian whose title was Gongbao.

10 MINUTES   **15 MINUTES**   **SERVES 2**

1 tbsp groundnut oil, plus extra for frying
14 raw king prawns (jumbo shrimp), shelled and deveined
1 egg, beaten
¼ tsp salt
50g (½ cup) cornflour (cornstarch)
1 garlic clove, crushed
½ small onion, roughly chopped
½ red (bell) pepper, deseeded and roughly chopped
30g (¼ cup) canned bamboo shoots, finely chopped
40g (¼ cup) canned water chestnuts, sliced
1 green bird's-eye chilli, finely chopped
30g (¼ cup) roasted cashew nuts

For the kung po sauce
120ml (½ cup) water
2 tbsp hoisin sauce (page 342 or use shop-bought)
2 tbsp granulated sugar
½ tbsp tomato purée (paste)
1 tbsp tomato ketchup
2 tbsp rice vinegar
2 tbsp cornflour (cornstarch) mixed with 4 tbsp water

First make the kung po sauce – place a medium saucepan over a medium heat and add all the sauce ingredients, except the cornflour (cornstarch) mixture. Bring to the boil and then simmer for 5 minutes. Slowly pour the cornflour mix into the sauce a little at a time, stirring continuously, until thickened to your desired consistency, ideally to coat the back of a spoon. Take off the heat and leave to one side.

Pour enough oil into a wok or a large saucepan to deep-fry the prawns (shrimp) so they can float without touching the bottom of the pan and heat to 170°C (340°F).

Place the prawns into a large bowl, add the beaten egg and salt and mix well to coat each prawn. Tip the cornflour into another large bowl and coat each prawn in the cornflour, shaking off the excess. Gently drop the prawns into the oil and fry for around 2–3 minutes, or until completely cooked. Remove the prawns and drain on a wire rack.

Place a wok over a medium-high heat, add the 1 tablespoon of oil and the garlic and fry for 15 seconds. Add the onion and red pepper and fry for a further minute. Add the bamboo shoots, water chestnuts and chilli and stir-fry for 1 more minute. Now add the kung po sauce and heat through thoroughly, before turning off the heat and adding the cooked prawns and the cashew nuts. Stir to coat everything in the sauce and serve straightaway.

BLACK BEAN MUSSELS

These mussels take flavour and texture to a whole different level, hitting your senses from every angle. Salty, sweet, aromatic, juicy and soft.

---

10 MINUTES   **12 MINUTES**   **SERVES 4**

4 tbsp fermented Chinese black beans
120ml (½ cup) warm water
2 tbsp vegetable oil
1 onion, finely diced
2 garlic cloves, finely chopped or grated
1 green (bell) pepper, deseeded and
    finely diced
½ tsp salt
¼ tsp white pepper
1 tsp sugar
2 tbsp light soy sauce
500g (1lb 2oz) live fresh mussels

Soak the fermented black beans in the warm water for 10 minutes, then drain through a sieve and set to one side.

Place a wok over a medium-high heat. Once smoking, add the oil and swirl around the wok, then add the onion and garlic and fry for 1 minute. Next, add the green pepper and cook for another minute, then add the drained black beans, salt, pepper, sugar and soy sauce and mix well. Now add the mussels along with 4 tablespoons of water, mix well again and cover with a lid to keep in the steam (use another large frying pan if your wok doesn't have a lid).

After 2 minutes shake the pan, keeping the lid on, and continue to cook for another 2 minutes. Uncover and stir well to ensure all of the ingredients are fully combined. The mussels should now be open (discard any that remain closed) and coated in the black bean sauce. Remove from the heat and serve.

KING PRAWN FOO YUNG

Egg foo yung or, as I like to call it, Chinese scrambled eggs, is a dish derived from a Guangdong recipe in China. It is difficult to translate into English word for word, but it basically means 'lightly cooked eggs'. The dish was popularised in Western countries, where it was served as a well-folded omelette, but it is actually supposed to be served as a chunky scrambled egg.

5 MINUTES **5 MINUTES** **SERVES 2**

1 tbsp groundnut oil
1 small onion, cut into strips
1 carrot, thinly sliced
30g (½ cup) sliced button mushrooms
12 raw king prawns (jumbo shrimp), shelled and deveined
½ tsp salt
¼ tsp white pepper
4 eggs, beaten
30g (¼ cup) peas
1 tsp sesame oil

Heat the oil in a wok over a high heat. Once your wok is really hot, add the onion, carrot and mushrooms and stir-fry for 1 minute. Add the king prawns (jumbo shrimp) and stir-fry for a further 40 seconds, then add the salt and pepper and toss the ingredients together. Lower the heat to medium, add the beaten eggs and peas and slowly and gently move the ingredients around the wok, allowing the eggs to cook. Once the eggs are cooked to your liking, turn off the heat, add the sesame oil, stir and serve at once.

CHINESE MUSHROOMS
IN SCALLOP SAUCE

My mum's favourite 'meaty' mushrooms dressed in a delicate yet luxurious scallop sauce.

35 MINUTES   **5 MINUTES**   **SERVES 2**

12–15 whole dried Chinese mushrooms
50g (2oz) dried scallops
1 tbsp vegetable oil
2 garlic cloves, minced
3 slices of ginger
2 tbsp oyster sauce
1 tbsp Chinese rice wine (Shaoxing wine)
1 tsp sugar
2 tsp dark soy sauce
60ml (¼ cup) chicken or fish stock
1 tsp cornflour (cornstarch) mixed with 2 tsp water
dash of sesame oil

Place the dried mushrooms in a bowl of just-boiled water and allow to soak for 30 minutes to rehydrate, then remove and discard the stalks. At the same time, place the dried scallops in another bowl of just-boiled water, allow to soak for 15 minutes, then drain.

Slice the mushrooms into bite-sized pieces.

Heat the vegetable oil in a wok over a medium heat, add the garlic and ginger and stir-fry for 20 seconds, then add the mushrooms and fry for 2 minutes. Next, add the scallops, oyster sauce, rice wine, sugar, dark soy sauce and stock. Stir all of the ingredients together in the wok, then give the cornflour (cornstarch) mixture a quick mix and slowly add to the sauce, stirring constantly until thickened to your desired consistency. Once thickened, turn off the heat, add a dash of sesame oil and serve.

SICHUAN KING PRAWNS

A king prawn dish that packs a punch on flavour, smells divine and tastes amazing! Chilli bean sauce, or doubanjiang, is a spicy, salty paste made from fermented soya beans, salt, rice and spices and is used extensively in Sichuan cooking.

8 MINUTES **10 MINUTES** **SERVES 2**

1 tbsp groundnut oil
2 garlic cloves, crushed
½ tsp finely chopped ginger
1 spring onion (scallion), finely sliced
1 onion, finely chopped
1 carrot, finely chopped
½ red (bell) pepper, deseeded and diced
14 raw king prawns (jumbo shrimp), shelled and deveined
1 tbsp Chinese rice wine (Shaoxing wine)
1 tsp rice vinegar
1½ tbsp chilli bean sauce
2 tbsp tomato ketchup
1 tbsp hoisin sauce (page 342 or use shop-bought)
30g (¼ cup) water chestnuts, diced
¼ tsp salt
¼ tsp sugar
¼ tsp white pepper
240ml (1 cup) chicken stock
1 tbsp cornflour (cornstarch) mixed with 2 tbsp water
1 tsp sesame oil

Place a wok over a medium-high heat, add the groundnut oil, garlic, ginger and half of the spring onion (scallion) and fry for 30 seconds. Add the onion, carrot and red pepper and stir-fry for a further 2 minutes. Add the king prawns (jumbo shrimp), along with the rice wine, vinegar, chilli bean sauce, ketchup, hoisin sauce, water chestnuts, salt, sugar and pepper. Stir-fry for a further minute, then pour in the chicken stock and bring to the boil. Lower the heat and simmer for 2 minutes.

Add the cornflour (cornstarch) mixture, stirring to prevent lumps, then turn off the heat. Add the sesame oil and mix well. Transfer to a serving plate and garnish with the remaining spring onion.

KING PRAWNS, GINGER AND SPRING ONION

This dish screams Cantonese cuisine at its finest. Using all three of the 'Holy Trinity' ingredients, it's a taste sensation. Aromatic notes tickle your nose and the subtle yet ever so flavoursome heat from the ginger tickles your tongue.

10 MINUTES   **5 MINUTES**   **SERVES 2**

1 tbsp groundnut oil
1 garlic clove, crushed
3 spring onions (scallions), halved, then halved again lengthways
3cm (1¼in) cube of ginger, peeled and thinly sliced
1 small onion, thinly sliced
1 carrot, thinly sliced
6 baby corn cobs, halved lengthways
12 raw king prawns (jumbo shrimp), shelled and deveined
½ tsp salt (or to taste)
¼ tsp white pepper
½ tsp sugar
1 tbsp oyster sauce
2 tbsp white wine (optional)
60ml (¼ cup) fish stock
1 tbsp cornflour (cornstarch) mixed with 2 tbsp water
1 tsp sesame oil

Heat the oil in a wok or deep-sided frying pan, add the garlic, spring onions (scallions) and ginger and stir thoroughly. After about 1 minute, once you can smell the aromatics filling the air, add the onion, carrot and baby corn and stir-fry for 30 seconds. Add the king prawns (jumbo shrimp), along with the salt, pepper and sugar.

After 1 minute add the oyster sauce and the wine, if using. Mix thoroughly and add the stock to create a sauce. Once the ingredients are bubbling away, slowly add the cornflour (cornstarch) mixture, constantly stirring as you pour. Turn off the heat, add the sesame oil and serve immediately.

CANTONESE-STYLE SOFT-SHELLED CRAB

The season of the soft-shelled crab is relatively short, traditionally marked by the first full moon in May and ending around September each year. With their crispy battered shells tossed in a classic Cantonese sauce packed full of aromatic flavours, what better dish to celebrate the summer with.

10 MINUTES   **15 MINUTES**   **SERVES 2**

4–6 soft-shelled crabs (300–350g/ 10–12oz)
500ml–1 litre (2–4 cups) vegetable oil
50g (½ cup) cornflour (cornstarch)
50g (½ cup) rice flour
1 tsp white pepper
1 tsp Chinese five spice
1–2 tsp garlic powder
1 tsp chicken stock powder
2 eggs, beaten

For the sauce
1 tbsp vegetable oil
1 garlic clove, minced
3 slices of ginger
1 onion, thinly sliced
1 carrot, cleaned or peeled and thinly sliced
splash of Chinese rice wine (Shaoxing wine)
2 spring onions (scallions), cut into 5cm (2in) lengths
2 tbsp oyster sauce
125ml (½ cup) fish or chicken stock
½ tsp sugar
½ tbsp cornflour (cornstarch) mixed with 1 tbsp water
salt, to taste (optional)
1 tsp sesame oil

To clean the crabs, lift the shell on each side of the body and scrape out the feather-type gills. Snip off the eyes and mouth. Give the crabs a quick rinse and then pat dry with kitchen paper.

Add enough vegetable oil to deep-fry the crabs to a wok or deep saucepan and heat to 180°C (350°F).

In a large bowl, add the cornflour (cornstarch), rice flour, white pepper, five spice, garlic powder and chicken powder and mix well. Dip each crab into the mixed flour, then into the beaten eggs. Dust the dipped crabs in the flour mixture again and then bang off any excess. Carefully place the crabs into the hot oil in batches of 2 or 3 and fry for 3–4 minutes, turning frequently to ensure even cooking. Once golden brown and crispy, remove and drain on a wire rack or kitchen paper.

To make the sauce, heat the oil in a wok, add the garlic and ginger and stir-fry for about 15–20 seconds. Add the onion and carrot and stir through. Add a splash of rice wine, mix for 30 seconds, then add the spring onions (scallions), oyster sauce, stock and sugar. Slowly add the cornflour mixture, stirring constantly until thickened to your desired consistency. Check the seasoning and, if needed, add salt to taste. Toss the drained crabs quickly in the sauce, remove from the heat and drizzle with the sesame oil.

Delicious served with Fried Potato Birds' Nests (page 261) and a side of Chinese Pickled Vegetables (page 270).

STUFFED PEPPERS

Supremely popular on the southern Chinese street-food scene, these delectable stuffed peppers are equally worthy of a place on any banquet menu.

20 MINUTES   **10 MINUTES**   **SERVES 2-4**

2 green (bell) peppers, deseeded and cut into 3–4cm (1¼–1½in) cubes
½ tbsp cornflour (cornstarch) mixed with 1 tbsp water, plus extra for dusting
3 tbsp fermented black beans
2 tbsp vegetable oil
2 garlic cloves, minced
1 tsp chicken powder dissolved in 250ml (1 cup) hot water
½ tbsp light soy sauce
1 tsp dark soy sauce
1 tsp sugar
1 tbsp Chinese rice wine (Shaoxing wine)
drizzle of sesame oil

For the fish paste
150g (5oz) large raw king prawns (jumbo shrimp), peeled and deveined
200g (7oz) white fish, such as tilapia or sea bass, deboned and skinned
1 tbsp cornflour (cornstarch) mixed with 2 tbsp water
2 spring onions (scallions), finely chopped
1 tsp salt
½ tsp sugar
⅛ tsp or a pinch of white pepper

Begin by chopping the king prawns (jumbo shrimp) and fish. Roughly chop to start and then continue chopping until you have a smooth-ish paste. This does take a little while, but I find this process much better than using a food processor. Transfer the fish and prawn paste to a large bowl and begin to mix with a pair of chopsticks. Keep mixing for at least 3 minutes until the paste becomes sticky. Give the cornflour (cornstarch) mixture a stir and, little by little, add to the fish and prawn paste, mixing constantly; this will help firm the paste. Once you have a sticky firm paste, gather the paste into a ball in your hands and then with a little force throw it back into the bowl. You want to do this around 10 times. This will help the paste become springy.

Now add your chopped spring onions (scallions), salt, sugar and white pepper and combine evenly.

Dust the inside of your cut peppers with a little cornflour, bang off any excess and, using a knife or a teaspoon, fill each piece of pepper with enough paste so it slightly mounds. Place on a plate, paste-side up, until you are ready to cook.

Prepare the fermented black beans by firstly rinsing in warm water to remove any grit, then in a small bowl, add 1 tablespoon of warm water to the beans and, using your fingers or the back of a spoon, mush the beans to break them up slightly.

Place a wok over a medium-high heat, add the oil and, once hot, carefully place the filled peppers, paste-side down, into the hot oil. Cook for at least 2 minutes or until the paste has turned golden brown and is a little crispy. Now add the garlic and stir-fry for 20 seconds, being careful not to break the filling away from the peppers, then add the black beans and stir in gently. Add the chicken powder water, light soy sauce, dark soy sauce and sugar, combine gently into the liquid and allow to simmer for 2–3 minutes. Stir in the rice wine, then give the cornflour mixture a stir and slowly add to the sauce, stirring constantly to thicken. Switch off the heat and finally drizzle with sesame oil.

FIRECRACKER KING PRAWNS

In Chinese tradition, letting off firecrackers at Chinese New Year was believed to ward off evil spirits and bring joyfulness and good luck for the coming year, so whether you go for hot sauce or sweet chilli, with every crack of these crispy wrappers, you'll be sure to feel a deep sense of explosive joy!

20 MINUTES   **8 MINUTES**   **SERVES 5-6 AS A PARTY SNACK**

1 tbsp hoisin sauce (page 342 or use shop-bought)
2 tbsp chilli sauce (use your favourite)
pinch of black pepper
1 tsp garlic paste
20 large raw king prawns (jumbo shrimp), peeled and deveined
10 small spring roll wrappers
1 egg, beaten
750ml (3 cups) vegetable oil

In a bowl, combine the hoisin sauce, chilli sauce, black pepper and garlic paste to make a marinade.

Carefully cut the king prawns (jumbo shrimp) horizontally along the sides 3–4 times, ensuring you do not cut all the way through. This will help the prawns to lay flat rather than curled. Add the king prawns to the marinade, mix well and set to one side.

Cut the spring roll wrappers in half diagonally, creating 2 stacks of triangles. Carefully separate one of the triangle sheets and lay a king prawn a quarter of the way along the long edge, so the tail remains sticking out. Fold the side point of the wrapper over the prawn and roll towards the centre, creating a cylinder. At the halfway point, fold over the top of the wrapper to enclose the prawn and continue to roll, egg washing the last quarter and rolling to the other point to seal the wrapper.

Heat the oil to 180°C (350°F) in a wok or deep-sided saucepan. Carefully lower the prawns into the oil and cook in batches for around 3–4 minutes until golden brown. Transfer to a wire rack or kitchen paper to drain.

Serve with your favourite dipping sauce.

XO KING PRAWNS

Hong Kong shorthand for high quality and luxury, XO sauce is made from dried shrimps and scallops and literally oozes depth of flavour and umami deliciousness. Absolutely worth the high price tag and totally addictive!

5 MINUTES   **7 MINUTES**   **SERVES 2**

1–2 tbsp vegetable oil
3 thin slices of ginger
1 tbsp minced garlic
280–320g (10–11¼oz) large raw king prawns (jumbo shrimp), peeled and deveined
100g (3½oz) mangetout (snowpeas)
5 spring onions (scallions), cut into 5cm (2in) lengths
3 tbsp XO sauce
1 tbsp light soy sauce
1 tsp sugar
60ml (¼ cup) chicken or fish stock
1 tbsp Chinese rice wine (Shaoxing wine)
1 tsp cornflour (cornstarch) combined with 2 tsp water
pinch of salt, to taste

Heat the oil in a non-stick wok over a high heat, add the ginger and garlic and cook for 20 seconds to release their aromas. Add the king prawns (jumbo shrimp) and cook for 1–2 minutes, stirring regularly to ensure even cooking.

Next, add the mangetout (snowpeas) and spring onions (scallions) and cook for a further 30 seconds, stirring to combine the ingredients. Stir in the XO sauce, light soy sauce, sugar and stock and, once all of the ingredients are piping hot, add the Chinese rice wine.

Give the cornflour (cornstarch) mixture a mix and pour into the sauce, stirring constantly until thickened to your desired consistency. Check for seasoning and add salt to taste if required.

SEA BASS ROLLS

Sharing plates have become one of the world's biggest food trends; not only is this dish great for sharing but it is also a fantastic conversation starter, as everyone around the table builds their very own perfect mouthful.

10 MINUTES   **6 MINUTES**   **SERVES 2-4**

300g (10½oz) straight-to-wok medium noodles (you can use egg or rice noodles)
2 sea bass fillets
pinch of salt
pinch of white pepper
1 tbsp oil (vegetable, groundnut or coconut)
¼ cucumber, deseeded and cut into 5cm (2in) batons
1 carrot, cut into 5cm (2in) matchsticks
8 x 22cm (8½in) rice paper rounds

Fill a medium saucepan with water and bring to the boil. Once boiling, add the noodles and cook for 2 minutes until loosened and soft. Drain and set to one side.

Season both sides of the sea bass fillets with a sprinkle of salt and pepper. Heat a non-stick wok or frying pan over a medium–high heat and add the oil. Once the oil is hot and smoking, place the fillets skin-side down into the pan. Cook for 3–4 minutes, trying your best not to move the fillets, as you want to build up some caramelisation on the skin so that it becomes crispy. Flip the fillets over and cook for a further 2 minutes, then remove from the pan and set to one side to rest for a couple of minutes, skin-side up to preserve the crispiness.

Cut the fillets into strips. On a large platter if you have one, or individual smaller plates, arrange your cooked sea bass, drained noodles, cucumber and carrots in separate piles.

Take a rice paper round and moisten with a little water on both sides to soften, this will take about 30 seconds. Once the rice paper round is pliable, lay it flat on a clean plate and arrange your filling of fish (including some of the crispy skin), cucumber, noodles and carrot in a heaped line on the bottom third of the rice paper round. Fold the bottom third of the wrapper over the filling and then fold the loose side edges over into the centre, continuing to roll the tasty bundle forwards on to the rest of the wrapper until you have a tightly wrapped parcel.

Serve with your favourite dipping sauce.

SHELL-ON CANTONESE GARLIC KING PRAWNS

Mum and Dad bought the Panda Restaurant in the mid-80s; I was 11 years old and worked as a pot washer in the kitchen before moving on to the range and starting my training as a chef. It's strange how some memories remain so clear, like my fondness for the smell of this dish. I think it's the amazing combination of garlic and butter being cooked together that always tickled my nose and made my mouth water.

10 MINUTES **7 MINUTES** **SERVES 2**

16 large raw king prawns (jumbo shrimp), left whole and unpeeled
2 tbsp vegetable oil
1 medium white onion, finely diced
5 garlic cloves, finely chopped or grated
1 green (bell) pepper, deseeded and finely diced
4 tbsp salted butter
1 tsp sugar
½ tsp salt
¼ tsp white pepper

Carefully cut a slit along the back of each prawn (shrimp) and remove the digestive tract. Rinse under cold water, drain and set to one side.

Place your wok over a medium-high heat. Once hot, add the oil and swirl around the pan to warm, then add the diced onion and fry for 30 seconds, followed by the garlic; continue to fry for 20 seconds. Next, add the green pepper, and after 30 seconds add the drained whole king prawns. Continue stir-frying for 2 minutes, by which time the prawns should have started to turn pink.

Add the butter and evenly sprinkle in the sugar, salt and pepper. Mix well and fry for a further 2–3 minutes until the prawns are cooked through. Serve and enjoy.

CRISPY SEA BASS FILLETS WITH BOK CHOY

After a long day these pan-fried sea bass fillets with freshly boiled rice, juicy veg and a sweet soy sauce are the perfect recipe to unwind with when you really don't want the fuss of cooking a complicated meal. Well balanced and delicious, it's a dish to feed the mind, body and soul.

10 MINUTES   **12 MINUTES**   **SERVES 2**

2 tbsp dark soy sauce
3 tbsp light soy sauce
1 tbsp sugar
4 tbsp oil (vegetable, groundnut or coconut)
2 sea bass fillets
pinch of salt
pinch of white pepper
200g (7oz) bok choy, quartered lengthways
250g (9oz) Perfect Steamed Rice (page 274)

First, make the sweet soy sauce. Combine both soy sauces in a heatproof bowl along with the sugar. Heat 3 tablespoons of the oil in a small saucepan over a medium-high heat until smoking. Carefully pour the oil over the soy sauce mixture, mixing at the same time – it will sizzle and spit! Set to one side.

Season both sides of the sea bass fillets with a sprinkle of salt and white pepper. Heat the remaining tablespoon of oil in a non-stick wok or frying pan over a medium-high heat and place the fillets, skin-side down, into the pan. Cook for 3–4 minutes, trying your best not to move the fillets, as you want to build up some caramelisation on the skin so that it becomes crispy. Flip the fillets over and cook for a further 2 minutes. Remove from the pan and set to one side to rest.

In the same pan as you cooked the fish, add the quartered bok choy and fry for 2 minutes. Add a pinch of salt and pepper and continue to fry for a further 1–2 minutes until tender.

Spoon a bed of rice on to 2 warmed plates, then carefully lay a fish fillet on top followed by the bok choy. Finally, spoon over the sweet soy sauce mixture and serve.

KING PRAWNS IN YELLOW BEAN SAUCE WITH CASHEW NUTS

Juicy king prawns smothered in a sweet yellow bean sunshine sauce, with tender broccoli and creamy cashews. Juicy, crunchy and creamy, all in one saucy mouthful!

---

10 MINUTES　　**10 MINUTES**　　**SERVES 2**

1 tbsp vegetable oil
1 garlic clove, minced
3 thin slices of ginger
14 large raw king prawns (jumbo shrimp), peeled and deveined
290g (9¾oz) tenderstem broccoli
3 spring onions (scallions), cut into 5cm (2in) lengths
2 tbsp yellow bean sauce
1 tbsp light soy sauce
½ tbsp rice vinegar
125ml (½ cup) chicken or fish stock
1 tsp cornflour (cornstarch) mixed with 2 tsp water
handful of salted cashew nuts

Place a wok over a medium-high heat and add the oil along with the garlic and ginger and fry for 20 seconds until aromatic. Next, add the prawns (shrimp) and fry for 1 minute, flipping over as they start to turn pink, then add the broccoli and spring onions (scallions). Cook for a further minute, then add the yellow bean sauce, soy sauce, rice vinegar and stock. Bring the sauce to the boil, give your cornflour (cornstarch) mixture a quick mix and pour into the sauce, stirring constantly until thickened to your desired consistency. Once thickened to your liking, turn off the heat, mix in the cashew nuts and serve.

BEEF
& PORK

BRAISED BLACK PEPPER SHORT RIBS

Saucier than their steamed counterparts, which you'll find on many dim sum restaurant menus, these black pepper short ribs are deliciously tender with a deep fiery heat from the abundant helping of black pepper.

2 HOURS +   **10 MINUTES**   **45 MINUTES**   **SERVES 2-4**

450g (1lb) beef short ribs, cut into bite-sized pieces
2 tbsp vegetable oil
500ml (2 cups) chicken or beef stock
3 tbsp oyster sauce
½ tsp dark soy sauce
2 tbsp Chinese rice wine (Shaoxing wine)
2 tsp freshly ground black pepper
1 tbsp cornflour (cornstarch) mixed with 2 tbsp water

For the marinade
1 tbsp oyster sauce
1 tbsp Chinese rice wine (Shaoxing wine)
½ tsp freshly ground black pepper
2 tsp cornflour (cornstarch)
1 tsp sesame oil
½ tbsp light soy sauce

Combine the short ribs with all the marinade ingredients, massaging the marinade thoroughly into the meat. Set to one side in the fridge for at least 2 hours but ideally overnight.

When you're ready to start cooking, if the short ribs are in the fridge, place on the kitchen worktop and allow to come back up to room temperature for around 30 minutes–1 hour.

Heat the oil in a wok over a medium-high heat, add the marinated short ribs and turn the heat down to medium, turning the ribs to brown on all sides. Next, add the stock, oyster sauce, dark soy sauce, rice wine and half the black pepper. Mix everything together until well combined, bring to the boil, then turn down to a simmer, cover with a lid and cook gently for 30 minutes. Remove the lid, turn the heat back up to high, give the cornflour (cornstarch) mixture a stir and slowly pour it into the sauce, stirring continuously until thickened to your desired consistency. Once the sauce has thickened to your liking, remove from the heat, transfer to a serving plate and sprinkle over the remaining black pepper.

SHREDDED CRISPY CHILLI BEEF

Sweet, spicy, aromatic, sticky and crispy all rolled into one dish. Could you really ask for anything more?

10 MINUTES   **15 MINUTES**   **SERVES 4**

100g (1 cup) cornflour (cornstarch)
2 eggs
450g (1lb) beef fillet, sliced into strips
groundnut oil for deep-frying,
    plus 1 tbsp
thumb-sized piece of ginger, finely
    chopped
4 garlic cloves, crushed
1 carrot, cut into thick matchsticks
½ onion, cut into strips
3 tbsp light soy sauce
4 tbsp rice vinegar
1 tbsp granulated sugar
2 tbsp honey
2 spring onions (scallions), finely sliced
3 tsp chilli flakes
½ tbsp sesame oil
1 green chilli, sliced, to serve

Tip the cornflour (cornstarch) into a large bowl and beat the eggs in another. Add the beef strips to the beaten eggs and mix thoroughly, then transfer the beef strips to the cornflour, coating each piece and shaking off any excess.

Pour enough oil to deep-fry the beef into a wok and heat to 180°C (350°F). Carefully drop the beef slices into the oil in batches and fry for 2–3 minutes until crispy. Remove and leave to drain on a wire rack or a plate lined with kitchen paper.

Heat the 1 tablespoon of oil in a non-stick wok, add the ginger and garlic and fry for 20 seconds. Add the carrot and onion and continue to fry for a further minute. Now add the soy sauce, vinegar, sugar, honey, spring onions (scallions) and chilli flakes and bring to the boil. Add the crispy beef and stir to coat evenly. Take off the heat, stir in the sesame oil and serve straightaway with the green chilli scattered on top.

BLACK PEPPER BEEF WITH ONIONS AND GREEN PEPPERS

This dish was always served on a sizzling platter in the restaurant. We had ox-shaped, heavy cast-iron platters that we'd heat until they nearly glowed red. They were then placed on to their wooden serving boards and billows of smoke would fill the kitchen. We'd pour the beef covered with its rich sauce on to the platter and it would sizzle and spit, filling the air with an aromatic cloud of smoke that smelled simply amazing.

2 HOURS +   **10 MINUTES**   **5 MINUTES**   **SERVES 4**

2 tsp whole black peppercorns
450g (1lb) beef fillet, sliced into bite-sized pieces
2 tbsp oyster sauce
1 tbsp Chinese rice wine (Shaoxing wine)
2 tsp light soy sauce
splash of sesame oil
2 tsp cornflour (cornstarch), plus 1 tbsp mixed with 2 tbsp water
1½ tbsp groundnut oil
2 garlic cloves, thinly sliced
1 small green (bell) pepper, deseeded and diced
1 small onion, diced
120ml (½ cup) chicken or vegetable stock

Coarsely grind the peppercorns in a pestle and mortar – not too fine but you don't want any whole corns. Put the beef strips, three-quarters of the ground pepper, the oyster sauce, rice wine, soy sauce, sesame oil and the 2 teaspoons of cornflour (cornstarch) into a large bowl. Mix thoroughly to coat the meat and leave to tenderise and marinate for 2 hours or overnight. (This isn't essential but it does make a huge difference.)

When you're ready to cook, heat your wok over a high heat. As soon as the wok starts to smoke, add the oil and the marinated beef, leaving any marinade in the bowl for later. Stir-fry until the outside of the beef has browned, then add the garlic, green pepper and onion and continue stir-frying for 2 minutes. Add the remaining marinade and the stock. Once boiling, drizzle the cornflour mixture into the sauce, stirring continuously, until the sauce thickens. Transfer immediately to a plate, sprinkle over the remaining ground black pepper and serve.

CHINESE BEEF CURRY PUFFS

Back in my early days as a chef working at Cheng's Garden Chinese takeaway in Leicester, we would spend hours making these parcels of curry yumminess and, of course, quality control taste testing was an essential part of the job...

20 MINUTES   **20 MINUTES**   **SERVES 4-6**

1 tbsp vegetable oil
1 large onion, finely diced
3 garlic cloves, minced
450g (1lb) lean minced (ground) beef
2 tbsp curry powder (use your favourite)
1 tbsp ground turmeric
1 tsp ground cumin
1 tsp sugar
pinch of white pepper
1 tsp salt
1 tbsp cornflour (cornstarch)
125ml (½ cup) beef (or chicken) stock
3 sheets of ready-rolled puff pastry
    (approx. 980g/2lb 3oz)
2 eggs, beaten

Heat the oil in a non-stick wok over a medium-high heat and add the onion and garlic. Stir-fry for 1–1½ minutes until translucent, then add the minced (ground) beef and continue to cook for 3–4 minutes until browned. Next, add the curry powder, turmeric, cumin, sugar, white pepper and salt, combine well and cook for a further 2 minutes, then sprinkle in the cornflour (cornstarch), mixing it evenly through the ingredients. Add the stock and continue to cook for a further minute, allowing the mixture to thicken. Switch off the heat, transfer to a bowl and allow to cool.

Once the filling has cooled, unroll the puff pastry sheets and cut each sheet into 6 equal squares. Spoon 1–2 tablespoons of the beef filling on to each square, brush 2 edges of each square with beaten egg and then fold in half diagonally (corner to corner) creating a triangle. Press the edges together and use a fork to crimp and seal them. Transfer to a baking tray lined with baking paper and brush the tops with the beaten eggs.

Preheat the oven to 180°C (350°F) and cook the puffs in the oven for 15–20 minutes or until golden brown. Remove from the oven and allow to cool slightly before diving in. Delicious served warm or cold.

BEEF AND ONION

Tender strips of beef tossed with melt-in-the-mouth onions in a rich Chinese 'gravy'. Take the time to marinate the beef and this dish will be forever foolproof!

2 HOURS +   **10 MINUTES**   **7 MINUTES**   **SERVES 2**

250g (9oz) beef, such as flank, sirloin or skirt, thinly sliced
250ml (1 cup) vegetable oil
1 large onion, thinly sliced
3 spring onions (scallions), cut into 5cm (2in) lengths
1 tsp chicken powder dissolved in 60ml (¼ cup) hot water
1 tsp dark soy sauce
½ tbsp light soy sauce
½ tbsp oyster sauce
1 tsp cornflour (cornstarch) mixed with 2 tsp water

For the marinade
½ tbsp Chinese rice wine (Shaoxing wine)
1 tsp dark soy sauce
½ tbsp oyster sauce
1 tsp cornflour (cornstarch)

Place the sliced beef into a bowl along with all the marinade ingredients. Massage the marinade into the meat and set to one side for 2 hours or ideally overnight in the fridge.

Heat the oil to 180°C (350°F) in a wok over a medium–high heat, add the marinated beef and shallow-fry for 1 minute. Drain on a wire rack or kitchen paper and set to one side.

Carefully pour the oil from the wok into a heatproof bowl or pan but do not wipe the wok clean. Place back over a high heat, add the onion and fry until translucent and the edges have just begun to caramelise. Add the beef, spring onions (scallions), chicken powder water, soy sauces and oyster sauce. Bring to the boil, give the cornflour (cornstarch) mixture a stir and pour into the sauce, stirring constantly until thickened to your desired consistency. Once thickened to your liking, remove from the heat and serve.

Delicious heaped over steamed rice.

SWEET AROMATIC BEEF

Mini ribs simmered to tender perfection and tossed in sticky sweet and sour sauce.

---

2 HOURS +   **10 MINUTES**   **5 MINUTES**   **SERVES 2**

250g (9oz) beef, such as flank, sirloin or skirt, thinly sliced

250ml (1 cup) vegetable oil

3 spring onions (scallions), cut into 5cm (2in) lengths

1 onion, cut into thin slices

½ green (bell) pepper, deseeded and thinly sliced

1 sweet red pointed (Romano) pepper, deseeded and thinly sliced

2 tbsp hoisin sauce (page 342 or use shop-bought)

3 tbsp tomato ketchup

½ tbsp rice vinegar

1 tsp dark soy sauce

2 tsp sugar

For the marinade

½ tbsp Chinese rice wine (Shaoxing wine)

1 tbsp hoisin sauce (page 342 or use shop-bought)

½ tsp dark soy sauce

1 tsp cornflour (cornstarch)

Place the sliced beef in a bowl with the marinade ingredients. Massage the marinade into the meat and set to one side to marinate for 2 hours or ideally overnight in the fridge.

Heat the oil to 180°C (350°F) in a wok over a medium-high heat, add the marinated beef and shallow-fry for 1 minute. Drain and set to one side.

Drain the excess oil from the wok but do not wipe it clean and place it back over a medium-high heat. Add the spring onions (scallions) and onion and fry for 1 minute, then add the green and red peppers and the drained beef. Stir-fry for a further 1–2 minutes and then add the hoisin sauce, tomato ketchup, rice vinegar, dark soy sauce and sugar. Toss to coat all the ingredients with the sauce and then transfer to a serving plate.

OK BEEF

I have many fond memories of this dish from my youth. One of my closest friends lived a few streets away from our restaurant and without fail he would order OK Beef and fried rice every night, which meant we always had time for a quick catch-up. Although this recipe was developed in the UK for Western taste buds, it is enjoyed throughout the world and has become a firm favourite on the menu in many Cantonese restaurants.

5 MINUTES   **10 MINUTES**   **SERVES 4**

groundnut oil, for deep-frying,
    plus ½ tbsp
1 egg, beaten
340g (12oz) beef fillet, thinly sliced
100g (1 cup) cornflour (cornstarch)
1 onion, thinly sliced

For the OK sauce
2 tsp light soy sauce
1 tsp Chinese five spice
250ml (1 cup) water
125ml (½ cup) tomato ketchup
4 tbsp brown sauce
100g (½ cup) white or brown sugar
1½ tsp cornflour (cornstarch) mixed with
    2 tbsp water

Place all the sauce ingredients, except the cornflour (cornstarch) mixture, in a wok and heat gently, stirring until it starts to boil. Lower the heat and simmer for a few minutes. Pour in the cornflour mixture, stirring until thickened, then remove from the heat and set to one side.

Pour enough oil to deep-fry the beef into a large saucepan or wok and heat to 180°C (350°F).

In a large bowl, massage the egg into the beef slices. Tip the cornflour on to a large plate and coat the beef strips a few at a time, making sure each piece is covered and shaking off any excess.

Carefully lower the coated beef in batches into the hot oil and deep-fry for 2–3 minutes, or until the beef is golden brown and crispy. Transfer to a wire rack or a plate lined with kitchen paper to drain.

Heat the ½ tablespoon of oil in a non-stick wok and fry the onion until tender, then add the fried beef and the sauce. Mix thoroughly to coat each piece, then transfer to a serving plate and serve.

MISO STEAK ON STIR-FRIED VEGETABLES

Miso paste is a fantastic way of injecting flavour into soups and rice dishes and for marinating meats. The umami flavouring creates a smooth and silky texture in the mouth, and this, mixed with the charred yet juicy pieces of steak, results in an amazing taste and texture combination.

2 HOURS   **5 MINUTES**   **12 MINUTES**   **SERVES 2**

3 tsp sugar
3 tbsp Chinese rice wine (Shaoxing wine)
2 tbsp red miso paste
1 garlic clove, finely chopped or grated
2 x 150g (5oz) steaks (fillet or sirloin)
2 tbsp oil (vegetable or groundnut)
1 x 320g (11oz) bag of stir-fry vegetables
½ tsp salt
¼ tsp white pepper
2 tbsp light soy sauce

In a large bowl, mix together 2 teaspoons of the sugar, 2 tablespoons of the rice wine, the miso paste and the garlic. Add the steak and massage the marinade thoroughly into the meat. Cover and set aside for 2 hours.

Place a non-stick wok over a medium-high heat, add 1 tablespoon of the oil and fry the steaks for 3 minutes on each side for medium rare or cook a little longer if you prefer your steak well done. Transfer to a plate and allow to rest for a couple of minutes.

Add the remaining oil to the wok followed by the stir-fry vegetables. After 3–5 minutes, season with the salt, pepper, light soy sauce and the remaining rice wine and sugar. Mix well and stir-fry for 2–3 minutes, then transfer to a serving plate.

Slice your cooked steak into bite-sized slices and arrange over the top of the vegetables.

BEEF WITH OYSTER SAUCE

Tender pieces of beef served in a rich dark gravy/sauce. Serve this dish over steamed rice (see page 274) and watch the sauce seep through the grains, flavouring the entire bowl.

5 MINUTES **8 MINUTES** **SERVES 4**

1 tbsp groundnut oil
1 garlic clove, crushed
1 onion, diced
1 carrot, thinly sliced
8 button or chestnut mushrooms, quartered
30g (¼ cup) canned bamboo shoots
340g (12oz) beef fillet, cut into bite-sized slices
1 tbsp light soy sauce
½ tbsp dark soy sauce
3 tbsp oyster sauce
½ tsp salt (or to taste)
½ tsp sugar
½ tsp white pepper
60ml (¼ cup) chicken stock
1 tbsp cornflour (cornstarch) mixed with 2 tbsp water
1 tsp sesame oil

Place a wok over a medium-high heat, add the oil and garlic and stir-fry for 15 seconds. Add the onion and carrot and fry for a further 1 minute, then add the mushrooms and bamboo shoots and fry for another minute. Add the beef and stir-fry for 2 minutes.

Add the remaining ingredients, except the cornflour (cornstarch) mixture and sesame oil, and bring to the boil. Slowly pour in the cornflour mixture, stirring as you do to thicken the sauce, then remove from the heat. Stir in the sesame oil and serve.

FILLET STEAK CANTON

This dish is as close to a Chinese/American BBQ sauce as it gets – rich, dark, sticky and with that perfect twang, it really gets those juices flowing as you bite into a piece of tender steak and crisp onion. Although not essential, marinating your beef to tenderise it really does make a huge difference.

2 HOURS +   **5 MINUTES**   **8 MINUTES**   **SERVES 4**

500g (1lb 2oz) beef fillet, cut into slices across the grain
2 tbsp groundnut oil
1 tbsp Chinese rice wine (Shaoxing wine)
1 tbsp light soy sauce
2 tsp sesame oil
1 tbsp cornflour (cornstarch), plus 1 tbsp mixed with 2 tbsp water
1 garlic clove, crushed
1 onion, sliced into strips

For the sauce
1 tbsp oyster sauce
6 tbsp tomato ketchup
3 tbsp brown sauce
1 tbsp Worcestershire sauce
2 tbsp granulated sugar
120ml (½ cup) chicken stock
¼ tsp white pepper

Put the beef strips, 1 tablespoon of the groundnut oil, the rice wine, soy sauce, 1 teaspoon of the sesame oil and the 1 tablespoon of cornflour (cornstarch) in a large bowl. Mix thoroughly and leave to marinate for 2 hours or overnight.

When you're ready to cook, put all the sauce ingredients into a saucepan and slowly bring to the boil, then lower the heat and simmer for 3 minutes. Remove from the heat and set to one side.

Place a wok over a medium-high heat, add the remaining groundnut oil and the garlic and stir-fry for 15 seconds. Add the onion and fry for a further minute. Add the marinated beef and stir-fry for 2 minutes, then pour in the sauce and bring to the boil. Slowly pour in the cornflour mixture, stirring constantly, to thicken the sauce. Remove from the heat, stir in the remaining sesame oil and serve straightaway.

BEEF, GREEN PEPPER AND BLACK BEAN SAUCE

This easy stir-fry is a great midweek supper. Just make sure you make enough, as you'll be going back for seconds and maybe even thirds.

10 MINUTES　　**8 MINUTES**　　**SERVES 4**

1 tbsp groundnut oil
1 onion, diced
1 green bird's-eye chilli (optional)
1 garlic clove, finely chopped
1 green (bell) pepper, deseeded
　and diced
1 carrot, thinly sliced
340g (12oz) beef fillet, cut into
　bite-sized slices
1 tbsp light soy sauce
2 tbsp Chinese fermented black beans
½ tsp salt (or to taste)
½ tsp sugar
½ tsp white pepper
60ml (¼ cup) chicken or beef stock
½ tbsp dark soy sauce
1 tbsp cornflour (cornstarch) mixed with
　2 tbsp water
1 tsp sesame oil

Heat the groundnut oil in a large wok or deep-sided frying pan over a medium heat. Add the onion, chilli (if using) and garlic and stir-fry for 1 minute, or until the onion becomes translucent. Add the green pepper and carrot and stir-fry for a further 2 minutes.

Add the beef and stir-fry for 1 minute, then add the light soy sauce, black beans, salt, sugar and pepper and stir-fry for another minute.

Pour in the stock and dark soy sauce and bring to the boil. Slowly add the cornflour (cornstarch) mixture, stirring as you pour it in, until thickened to your desired consistency. The sauce should be thick enough to coat the back of a spoon. Remove from the heat, stir in the sesame oil and serve straightaway.

HAPPY FAMILY

A mixture of char siu pork, chicken, beef and seafood served with mixed vegetables in a rich, aromatic gravy, this is an American-Chinese recipe created in Chinatown, San Francisco, by Chinese immigrants who had moved to the USA to work in the mines and on the railways.

5 MINUTES   **7 MINUTES**   **SERVES 4**

2 tbsp groundnut oil
1 garlic clove, crushed
1 onion, diced
40g (1½oz) chicken breast fillet, sliced
1 red (bell) pepper, deseeded and diced
1 carrot, sliced
40g (½ cup) small broccoli florets
40g (½ cup) sugarsnap peas, cut into bite-sized pieces
30g (¼ cup) canned bamboo shoots
3 baby corn cobs, halved lengthways
40g (¼ cup) canned water chestnuts, cut into bite-sized slices
8 king prawns (jumbo shrimp), shelled and deveined
40g (1½oz) Chinese Roast BBQ Pork (see page 193), cut into bite-sized slices
40g (1½oz) fillet steak, sliced
1 tbsp light soy sauce
½ tbsp dark soy sauce
2 tbsp oyster sauce
1 tsp granulated sugar
¼ tsp salt
¼ tsp white pepper
120ml (½ cup) chicken stock
1 tbsp cornflour (cornstarch) mixed with 2 tbsp water
1 tsp sesame oil

Heat the groundnut oil in a wok over a medium-high heat, add the garlic and onion and fry for 1 minute. Add the chicken and fry for 2 minutes, then add the remaining vegetables and stir-fry for 2 minutes.

Add the prawns (shrimp), pork and the beef, stir-fry for a minute and then add the soy sauces, oyster sauce, sugar, salt, pepper and stock. Bring to the boil, turn down the heat and simmer for 2 minutes.

Stir in the cornflour (cornstarch) mixture to thicken the sauce, then remove from the heat, stir in the sesame oil and serve.

CHILLI AND SALT MINI RIBS

The ultimate in spicy rib simplicity! Crispy yet tender pork ribs heavily dusted with the unmistakeable Chinese takeaway-style chilli and salt seasoning.

2 HOURS +   **10 MINUTES**   **30 MINUTES**   **SERVES 2-4**

350g (12oz) pork ribs, cut into 2.5cm (1in) pieces
1 litre (4 cups) vegetable oil, plus 1 tbsp
1 onion, finely diced
2 garlic cloves, roughly chopped
½ green or red (bell) pepper, deseeded and finely diced
1 tsp Chinese five spice
2 tsp salt
1 tsp coarsely ground black pepper
2 tsp chilli flakes

For the marinade
2 eggs, beaten
1 tbsp Chinese five spice
2 tsp chilli powder
2 tbsp cornflour (cornstarch)

Wash the ribs in cold water, drain and then pat dry with kitchen paper or a clean tea towel. Place the ribs in a bowl along with the marinade ingredients. Massage the marinade into the ribs and set to one side to marinate for at least 2 hours or ideally overnight in the fridge.

First fry: Heat the oil in a saucepan or wok to around 160–170°C (320–340°F) and cook the marinated ribs in batches until cooked through, this should take around 5–6 minutes per batch. Transfer to a wire rack or kitchen paper and allow to drain thoroughly.

Second fry: Heat the same oil to 200°C (400°F) and re-fry the ribs until golden brown and crispy. Transfer to a wire rack or kitchen paper and drain again.

Place a clean wok over a medium-high heat and add the 1 tablespoon of oil along with the onion and garlic and stir-fry for 1–1½ minutes until softened. Add the diced peppers and continue to cook for a further 1–2 minutes, then add the cooked ribs and sprinkle over the five spice, salt, black pepper and chilli flakes. Give everything a good mix and serve immediately.

STICKY HOISIN GLAZED PORK

The Chinese learnt thousands of years ago that when you marinate meat, it not only imparts it with flavour but also tenderises it. These pork chops are marinated in an aromatic sweet sauce; once cooked they remain juicy and succulent with the unmistakeable flavours of Cantonese roast meats.

1 HOUR 10 MINS   **16 MINUTES**   **SERVES 4**

6 tbsp hoisin sauce (page 342 or use shop-bought)
3 tbsp light soy sauce
1 tsp sugar
5 tbsp water
3 tbsp vegetable oil
2 garlic cloves, finely chopped or grated
4 pork chops

In a small bowl, mix together the hoisin sauce, soy sauce, sugar and water and set to one side.

Preheat a saucepan over a medium heat, add 1 tablespoon of the oil and fry the garlic for 30 seconds until fragrant. Add the sauce mix and bring to the boil, then turn down to a simmer and reduce by a third. Remove from the heat and allow it to cool.

Place the pork chops into a ziplock bag, pour in the sauce mix and seal, squeezing out any excess air. Marinate for at least 1 hour.

Remove the chops from the bag. Shake off any excess marinade and reserve for later. Place a frying pan or wok over a medium-high heat, add the remaining oil and then add the chops, cooking on one side until golden brown, then flipping over and cooking until browned. Reduce the heat to medium and continue cooking for about 10 minutes until they are cooked all the way through. Transfer to a plate and allow to rest for 10 minutes.

While the pork is resting, wipe out any excess oil from your wok and tip in the leftover marinade along with 2 tablespoons of water. Slowly bring to a simmer for 2 minutes, then remove from the heat.

Arrange the rested chops on plates and spoon over the sauce.

CHILLI AND SALT PORK CHOPS

I used to love watching my dad cook this dish; he would use paper bags to help lock in all the flavour while the pork chops were deep-fried. I remember standing in the kitchen stapling the old-style paper bags together to form sealed pockets filled with the marinated pork and spices. These were then slid gently into a pan of hot oil to cook thoroughly while retaining the juicy marinade. The drained bags were then served still sealed and cut open at the table for each guest, releasing their delicious aroma and fresh pool of cooking liquor.

10 MINUTES   **20 MINUTES**   **SERVES 2**

2 tbsp vegetable oil
2 pork chops
1 tbsp Chinese five spice
1 large white onion, finely diced
1 green (bell) pepper, deseeded and finely diced
2 bird's-eye chillies, finely diced
salt
white pepper

Heat 1 tablespoon of the oil in a large non-stick frying pan or wok over a medium heat until shimmering. Add the pork chops, seasoning with a pinch each of salt and pepper. Allow the chops to caramelise on one side for 6–8 minutes, then flip over and repeat on the other side, seasoning again with salt and pepper. Remove from the pan and set to one side to rest. Once rested, slice the chops into bite-sized slices.

In a bowl, mix together the five spice, ½ teaspoon of salt and ¼ teaspoon of pepper and set to one side.

Place a non-stick frying pan or wok over a medium heat and add the remaining oil; once smoking, add the onion and green pepper. Fry for 2 minutes, then add the chillies and fry for a further minute, mixing well.

Turn off the heat, add the sliced pork to the pan along with the mixed seasoning and toss well to cover. Transfer to a plate and enjoy.

CANTONESE-STYLE SWEET AND SOUR PORK

'Life is a pair of chopsticks, serving us sweet, sour, bitter and spicy. Where possible let's make life sweet.'

The original sweet and sour sauce originated in the province of Hunan, China. The sauce was a light vinegar and sugar mixture with very little resemblance to the bright orange dish served in many restaurants today.

10 MINUTES   **8 MINUTES**   **SERVES 2**

groundnut oil, for frying
300g (10½oz) pork loin, chopped into 2cm (¾in) cubes
1 egg, beaten
¼ tsp salt
50g (½ cup) cornflour (cornstarch)

For the sweet and sour sauce
240ml (1 cup) orange juice
2 tbsp sugar
1 tbsp tomato purée (paste)
1 tbsp tomato ketchup
3 tbsp white wine vinegar
½ red (bell) pepper, deseeded and roughly chopped
½ small onion, roughly chopped
handful of pineapple chunks (fresh or canned)
3 tbsp cornflour (cornstarch) mixed with 6 tbsp water

Put all the sauce ingredients, except the cornflour (cornstarch) mixture, into a large saucepan over a medium heat. Bring to the boil, lower the heat and simmer for 5 minutes. Slowly stir the cornflour mixture into the sauce a little at a time, stirring continuously, until thickened to your desired consistency. The sauce should be thick enough to coat the back of a spoon. Leave to one side.

Pour enough oil into a large saucepan for the pork nuggets to float without touching the bottom of the pan and heat to 170°C (340°F).

Place the pork loin in a large bowl, add the beaten egg and salt and mix well, ensuring all the pork is coated. Tip the cornflour into a separate bowl, then add the pork and stir to coat in cornflour, shaking off any excess. Gently lower the coated pork pieces into the oil and fry for around 5 minutes, or until completely cooked. (If you have a food thermometer probe, the internal temperature should be 75°C/170°F.) Remove the pork and drain on a wire rack or a plate lined with kitchen paper.

Arrange the pork on a plate, spoon over your sweet and sour sauce and serve.

CRISPY BELLY PORK

No one, and I mean no one, can cook crispy belly pork like the Chinese. This dish takes a little forward planning but the end result is well worth the effort. Serve with a pot of sugar to transform this dish from 'Mmm, that's nice' to 'OMG, this is sublime!'

12 HOURS   **1 HOUR 50 MINS**   **SERVES 6-8**

900g (2lb) pork belly
2 tbsp Chinese rice wine (Shaoxing wine)
1½ tbsp Chinese five spice
2 tsp salt
1 tsp white pepper
2 tbsp rice vinegar
160g (½ cup) rock salt
sugar, for dipping

The night before you want to cook, pierce the pork skin all over with a corn cob spike or sharp knife, taking care not to puncture the meat underneath. If using a knife, be sure not to cut too deeply. The more holes you can pierce into the skin, the crisper the skin will be. Lay the pork belly skin side-down and massage the rice wine into the meat side only, followed by the five spice, salt and pepper. Now place the pork belly in a dish skin side-up, dry the skin with kitchen paper and place in the fridge, uncovered, overnight.

When you're ready to cook, preheat the oven to 180°C (350°F). Place the pork on a piece of foil, fold the edges up to the pork belly, covering the meat, but not the skin, on all sides. Dry the skin with kitchen paper again and then brush with the rice vinegar. Cover the skin completely with the rock salt, then transfer to the oven to cook for 1 hour.

Remove the salt crust from the pork belly and transfer the pork to a clean baking tray. Return to the oven, uncovered, for a further 30–40 minutes. Remove from the oven and place under a hot grill for 8–10 minutes until the skin is super-crispy but not burnt.

Cut into slices and serve with a bowl of sugar for dipping.

CAPITAL SPARE RIBS

Finger food messiness at its very best! The recipe originates from China's capital – hence the the name – and the sauce combined with the 'twice-fried' process could possibly be the best thing to happen to spare ribs.

2 HOURS +   **10 MINUTES**   **30 MINUTES**   **SERVES 2-4**

350g (12oz) pork ribs
1 litre (4 cups) vegetable oil

For the marinade
2 eggs, beaten
1 tbsp Chinese five spice
2 tsp chilli powder
2 tbsp cornflour (cornstarch)

For the sauce
1 tbsp oyster sauce
6 tbsp tomato ketchup
3 tbsp brown sauce
1 tbsp Worcestershire sauce
2 tbsp sugar
60ml (¼ cup) chicken stock
pinch or ⅛ tsp white pepper

Wash the ribs in cold water, drain and then pat dry with kitchen paper or a clean tea towel. Place the ribs in a bowl along with all the marinade ingredients. Massage the ingredients into the meat and allow to marinate for at least 2 hours or ideally overnight in the fridge.

Add all the sauce ingredients to a saucepan and slowly bring to the boil, then reduce the heat and simmer for 3 minutes or until thickened. Remove from the heat and set to one side.

First fry: Heat the oil in a saucepan or wok to around 160–170°C (320–340°F) and cook the marinated ribs in batches until cooked through, this should take around 5–6 minutes per batch. Transfer to a wire rack or kitchen paper and allow to drain thoroughly.

Second fry: Heat the same oil to 200°C (400°F) and re-fry the ribs until golden brown and crispy. Transfer to a wire rack or kitchen paper and drain again.

Finally, reheat the sauce and, once reheated, toss in the ribs and coat fully. Transfer to a serving plate and tuck in.

PORK RIBS IN CHILLI AND BLACK BEAN SAUCE

A nod to one of the most popular steamed dim sum dishes; the salt and slight pungency of fermented black beans together with the heat of fresh chilli makes the perfect dressing for delicate pork meat.

15 MINUTES   **45 MINUTES**   **SERVES 2-4**

550g (1lb 4oz) pork ribs, cut into 3–4cm (1¼–1½in) pieces

3 tbsp fermented black beans

2 tbsp vegetable oil

2cm (¾in) piece of ginger, peeled and finely chopped

2 garlic cloves, roughly chopped

1–2 tsp fresh chilli, finely chopped (add as much or as little as you like)

1 onion, finely diced

1 green (bell) pepper, deseeded and finely diced

250ml (1 cup) chicken stock

1 tsp dark soy sauce

1 tbsp light soy sauce

1 tsp sugar

1 tbsp Chinese rice wine (Shaoxing wine)

1 tbsp cornflour (cornstarch) mixed with 2 tbsp water

1 tsp sesame oil

Boil the ribs in a large saucepan of water for 30–35 minutes, stirring occasionally until they are tender. Drain and set to one side.

While the ribs are boiling, prepare the fermented black beans. First, rinse in warm water to remove any grit, then in a small bowl, add 1 tablespoon of warm water to the beans and, using your fingers or the back of a spoon, mush the beans to break them up slightly.

Once the ribs have cooled, place a wok over a medium-high heat and add the vegetable oil along with the ginger and garlic and fry for 15 seconds until aromatic. Next, add the chilli, black beans and diced onion and stir-fry for 1 minute before adding the diced pepper and cooked ribs. Give everything a good mix, then add the stock, dark and light soy sauces and sugar. Bring to the boil and turn down to a simmer for 2–3 minutes. Stir in the rice wine, then give the cornflour (cornstarch) mixture a mix and slowly add to the sauce, stirring constantly. Switch off the heat and drizzle in the sesame oil. Transfer to a serving bowl; it's time to eat!

PEKING-STYLE PORK CHOPS

Tender bites of pork lavishly tossed in a smoky, sweet and darkly tart Peking-style sauce.

2 HOURS + **10 MINUTES** **15 MINUTES** **SERVES 2**

450g (1lb) thin-cut pork chops, each cut into 2–3 pieces

1 litre (4 cups) vegetable oil

100g (1 cup) cornflour (cornstarch), plus 1 tbsp mixed with 2 tbsp water

60ml (¼ cup) pineapple juice

125ml (½ cup) water

1 tsp chilli flakes

1 tbsp hoisin sauce (page 342 or use shop-bought)

1 tbsp Chinese black vinegar

2 tbsp Worcestershire sauce

2 tbsp honey

1 tbsp tomato purée (paste)

3 tbsp tomato ketchup

For the marinade

1 tbsp Chinese rice wine (Shaoxing wine)

1 tbsp oyster sauce

¼ tsp Chinese five spice

1 egg, beaten

Place the pork chops in a bowl along with all the marinade ingredients except the egg, massage into the meat and set to one side for at least 2 hours or ideally overnight in the fridge.

Heat the oil to 180°C (350°F) in a wok or large saucepan.

Add the beaten egg to the marinated pork and mix well. Place the dry cornflour (cornstarch) in another large bowl and dust the pork in it, banging off any excess. Carefully fry the coated pork in batches for 3–5 minutes per batch, or until cooked through and golden brown. A food probe should show an internal temperature of at least 70–75°C (158–167°F). Remove the pork and drain on a wire rack or kitchen paper.

Place a wok over a medium-high heat and add the pineapple juice, water, chilli flakes, hoisin sauce, vinegar, Worcestershire sauce, honey, tomato purée (paste) and ketchup, mix well and bring to the boil. Give the cornflour mixture a mix and slowly add to the sauce, stirring constantly. If the sauce is a little thin, turn the heat down to a simmer and allow to reduce by a third. Once you are happy with the consistency, turn off the heat and add the pork chops, thoroughly coating each piece in the sauce. Transfer to a serving plate and enjoy.

CHINESE ROAST BBQ PORK

In Hong Kong, char siu is usually purchased from a Siu Mei establishment, which specialises in meat dishes – char siu (BBQ pork), soy-sauce chicken, roast goose, crispy belly pork. These shops usually display their merchandise by hanging them in the window and, as a result, char siu is often eaten with one of these other meat dishes in a 'rice box' meal.

2 HOURS +　　**5 MINUTES**　　**1 HOUR**　　**SERVES 4**

800g (1lb 12oz) pork shoulder or loin

1 tbsp Chinese five spice

2 tbsp Chinese rice wine (Shaoxing wine)

2 slices of ginger

2 garlic cloves, crushed

3 tbsp yellow bean sauce

3 tbsp hoisin sauce (page 342 or use shop-bought)

3 tbsp white sugar

2 star anise

1 cinnamon stick

1 tbsp honey, plus 2 tbsp mixed with 2 tbsp hot water for glazing

Put the pork in a large bowl, add the remaining ingredients, except the honey-water glaze, and massage the ingredients into the pork. Cover, transfer to the fridge and leave to marinate for at least 2 hours or overnight.

The next day, remove the pork from the fridge and allow to come back up to room temperature. Preheat the oven to 180°C (350°F).

Sit the pork on a baking tray (reserving the marinade separately), cover in foil and cook in the oven for 20 minutes. Turn and baste with the reserved marinade, then cook for a further 10 minutes, covered. Check the pork is cooked by inserting a skewer to ensure the juices run clear. Baste the pork with the marinade for a second time and return to the oven to cook, uncovered, for a further 20 minutes. You want the pork to be a deep amber colour and the marinade should be sticky and dry.

Remove the pork from the oven and brush with the honey and water mixture to glaze, then flash under the grill for 2–3 minutes or until the edges have scorched. Leave the pork to cool to room temperature, then slice and serve.

STEAMED HOT DOG BUNS

A truly Western spin on the tasty Chinese treat *lop cheung bao*, these soft, fluffy steamed buns with a central core of smoky hot dog sausage are just crying out to be dunked in ketchup and mustard!

40 MINUTES　　**15 MINUTES**　　**SERVES 4-8**

8 meat or veggie hot dog sausages

For the bao
560g (1lb 4oz) plain (all-purpose) flour, plus extra for dusting
11g (¼oz) instant dried yeast
½ tsp salt
1 tsp baking powder
30g (1oz) caster (superfine) sugar
30g (1oz) vegetable oil, plus extra for greasing
320g (11¼oz) whole milk (use soy or almond milk for a vegan option)

Place all of the bao ingredients in a large bowl and bring together to form a soft dough. Turn out on to a lightly floured worktop and knead for 6 minutes.

Bring the mixture together to form a ball and place in a lightly greased bowl, cover and leave to stand for 2 hours, or until doubled in size.

On a lightly floured worktop, turn out the dough, gently flatten and roll into a long sausage, dividing the sausage into 8 equal pieces (depending on how large you'd like your bao to be!). Roll each piece into a long strip around 25cm (10in) and wrap each strip around a hot dog sausage so the dough overlaps. Tuck in the loose ends and place on non-stick paper. Loosely cover with a damp tea towel to prevent the prepared buns from drying out and allow to rest for 20 minutes while you heat the steamer.

Place the rested buns into the hot steamer for 10 minutes, then remove the steamer basket from above the water, ensuring you do not remove the lid and place on the worktop to rest for 5 minutes; this will prevent your buns from sinking.

Serve and enjoy with ketchup and a blob of mustard.

Kwoklyn's tip
Weight measures have been used in this recipe to provide greater accuracy in achieving perfectly fluffy steamed buns.

HOISIN BONELESS SPARE RIBS

The luscious red of this marinade is synonymous with Chinese takeaway-style ribs and the boneless strips of meat make this an almost mess-free meal, unless of course you 'want' to get your hands in there!

2 HOURS +   **10 MINUTES**   **45 MINUTES**   **SERVES 4**

½ tbsp Chinese five spice

3 garlic cloves, minced

60ml (¼ cup) Chinese rice wine (Shaoxing wine)

125ml (½ cup) hoisin sauce (page 342 or use shop-bought)

2 tbsp dark soy sauce

1 tbsp sugar

1–2 drops of red food colouring (optional)

750g (1lb 10oz) pork (you can use loin, shoulder, or butt), cut into 10cm (4in) strips

Mix all the ingredients except the pork together in a large bowl and then add the sliced pork and massage the marinade into the meat. Cover and leave in the fridge for at least 2 hours but ideally overnight.

Preheat the oven to 170°C (340°F) while you transfer the pork to a baking tray, reserving any leftover marinade. Roast the pork in the oven for 40–45 minutes, basting at least 2–3 times with all of the reserved marinade during cooking.

Finally, place the cooked pork under a preheated grill for 1–2 minutes to caramelise and char slightly. Serve and enjoy with a bowl of Golden Fried Rice (page 277) or Fine Egg Noodles with Beansprouts (page 324).

CHINESE ROAST PORK CHOP SUEY

There are many stories of the origins of the humble chop suey. One account claims it was invented by a Chinese American working on the Transcontinental Railroad in the nineteenth century. Created wherever and by whoever, you'll most likely find this dish on EVERY Chinese restaurant menu. The pinch of pepper is essential as it totally changes the flavour of the dish.

10 MINUTES   **8 MINUTES**   **SERVES 2**

1 tbsp groundnut oil
200g (7oz) Chinese Roast BBQ Pork (see page 193)
1 small onion, thinly sliced
2 handfuls of beansprouts
1 small carrot, sliced into slivers
pinch of salt
pinch of granulated sugar
60ml (¼ cup) water
2 spring onions (scallions), halved and sliced into slivers
½ tbsp dark soy sauce
pinch of white pepper
1 tbsp cornflour (cornstarch) mixed with 2 tbsp water
1 tsp sesame oil

Heat the groundnut oil in a non-stick wok and fry the pork for 2 minutes. Add the onion and stir-fry for a further minute, then add the beansprouts, carrot, salt, sugar and water and bring to the boil. Now add the spring onions (scallions), soy sauce and white pepper and mix thoroughly – ensure the heat is high. Check the seasoning and adjust if necessary. Pour in just enough of the cornflour (cornstarch) mixture to thicken the sauce, stirring the ingredients the entire time. Remove from the heat, stir in the sesame oil and serve straightaway.

SLICED PORK IN CHILLI BEAN SAUCE

Tender pork loin served with crisp Chinese leaf and the distinctively powerful tang of doubanjiang.

40 MINUTES   **6 MINUTES**   **SERVES 2**

350g (12oz) pork loin, cut into very thin slices
1 tbsp light soy sauce
3 tbsp fermented chilli bean paste (doubanjiang)
1 tsp sugar
125ml (½ cup) water
2 tbsp vegetable oil
2 garlic cloves, roughly chopped
1–2 tsp chilli flakes
280g (10oz) Chinese leaf (Napa cabbage), cut into bite-sized pieces
1 tsp cornflour (cornstarch) mixed with 2 tsp water

For the marinade
½ tbsp Chinese rice wine (Shaoxing wine)
1 tsp dark soy sauce
½ tbsp fermented chilli bean paste (doubanjiang)
1 tsp cornflour (cornstarch)

Place the pork slices in a bowl along with the marinade ingredients. Massage the marinade ingredients into the meat and set to one side for 30 minutes.

While the pork is marinating, in another bowl, combine the light soy sauce, chilli bean paste, sugar and water and set to one side.

Place a wok over a medium-high heat and, once hot, add the oil and marinated pork and stir-fry for 1 minute. Add the garlic and chilli flakes, fry for 45 seconds and then pour in the sauce mixture, giving everything a good stir. Add the cabbage and continue to stir-fry for a further 1–2 minutes. Give the cornflour (cornstarch) mixture a mix and slowly add to the sauce, stirring constantly. Once your sauce has thickened, remove from the heat and transfer to a serving plate.

SWEET AND SOUR MINI RIBS

Mini ribs simmered to tender perfection and tossed in sticky sweet and sour sauce.

---

10 MINUTES   **45 MINUTES**   **SERVES 2-4**

3 tbsp light soy sauce

2 tbsp dark soy sauce

3 tbsp rice vinegar

2 tbsp Chinese rice wine (Shaoxing wine)

3 tbsp sugar

350–400g (12–14oz) pork ribs, cut into 2.5cm (1in) pieces

2 tbsp vegetable oil

3 thin slices of ginger

250ml (1 cup) pineapple juice

250ml (1 cup) water

In a large bowl, combine the light soy, dark soy, rice vinegar, rice wine and sugar. Mix well and set to one side.

Blanch the ribs in boiling water for 3–5 minutes; this will not only partially cook the ribs but also cook out any impurities in the meat. Drain and set to one side.

Place a wok that has a lid over a medium-high heat, add the oil, ginger and drained ribs and cook, tossing regularly to caramelise on all sides for 5–6 minutes. Then give the sauce mixture a stir and add to the wok, mixing well. Cook for a further 2 minutes and then pour in the pineapple juice and water, bringing it all back to the boil and then turning down the heat to a very low simmer. Place the lid on the wok and cook over a low heat for 30 minutes.

Remove the lid, turn the heat back up to high and continue to cook for 3–4 minutes until the sauce becomes sticky. Transfer to a serving plate and enjoy.

AROMATIC PORK CHOPS

Pork is a popular meat in China and is prepared in many different ways, from being served in hotpots or on skewers to spiced with Sichuan peppercorns, deep-fried and roasted. My recipe for this versatile meat uses a Cantonese marinade which subtly flavours the pork.

2 HOURS +   **10 MINUTES**   **6 MINUTES**   **SERVES 4**

5 spring onions (scallions)
5cm (2in) cube of ginger, peeled
5 garlic cloves
3 tbsp vegetable oil, plus a little extra
   for roasting
3 tbsp light soy sauce
1 tbsp sugar
8 thin pork chops
1 tsp salt
1 tsp ground black pepper

Place all the ingredients into a blender, except the pork, salt and black pepper, and blitz to a paste. Rub the marinade into each pork chop and once the pork is completely coated, cover with clingfilm (plastic wrap) or foil and allow to marinate for at least 2 hours or overnight in the fridge.

Preheat a griddle pan over a medium-high heat, drizzle the chops (both sides) with a little oil and sprinkle with the salt and pepper. Cook the pork for 2–3 minutes on each side, or until cooked to your liking.

VEGETABLES

MOCK DUCK WITH PANCAKES

Why miss out on the absolute deliciousness of duck and pancakes when you can enjoy all of the taste, and a surprisingly similar texture, completely feather free!

This is thought to be a creation of Buddhist monks for entertaining guests from the outside world, such as patrons, visiting pilgrims and potential benefactors, who would normally have eaten meat but would only eat vegetarian food when visiting a monastery.

10 MINUTES   **10 MINUTES**   **SERVES 4**

1 x 280g (10oz) can of mock duck
2 tbsp vegetable oil
1 x pack of Chinese pancakes (about 10)
3 spring onions (scallions), cut into 3cm (1¼in) lengths and then shredded
½ cucumber, cut into thin 3cm (1¼in) batons
3 tbsp hoisin sauce (page 342 or use shop-bought) mixed with 1 tbsp water

Open the can of mock duck and drain all of the water, then use kitchen paper to pat dry and cut into 2cm (¾in) strips.

Place a wok over a medium-high heat and, once smoking hot, add the oil followed by the mock duck and fry for 3–4 minutes until crispy. Transfer to kitchen paper or a wire rack to drain.

Steam the Chinese pancakes for 8 minutes and take to the table in the warm steamer basket to keep them fresh. Place the chopped spring onions (scallions) and cucumber on a plate along with a small bowl of the hoisin sauce. Transfer the crispy mock duck to a serving plate and start building.

Place a single pancake on your plate, add 1 teaspoon of hoisin sauce and spread all over the pancake, then add slices of spring onion and cucumber and a few slices of mock duck. Roll the pancake into a cylinder and enjoy.

SPICY HOISIN
MIXED VEGETABLES

Chunky vegetables stir-fried in a rich, sticky sweet, aromatic sauce, with a hint of chilli and served with creamy cashew nuts; it's no wonder that, once tried, this dish is cooked time and time again. Everything happens in your wok so washing up is a doddle afterwards too.

10 MINUTES   **5 MINUTES**   **SERVES 2**

1 tbsp groundnut oil

4 garlic cloves, finely chopped

1 tsp grated ginger

1 onion, diced

1 carrot, diced

30g (¼ cup) canned water chestnuts, drained

3 baby corn cobs, halved lengthways

35g (¼ cup) canned straw mushrooms, drained

60g (1 cup) button mushrooms, cut into bite-sized pieces

30g (¼ cup) canned bamboo shoots, drained

1 tbsp rice vinegar

1 tbsp light soy sauce

125ml (½ cup) hoisin sauce (page 342 or use shop-bought)

½ tsp chilli flakes

1 tbsp cornflour (cornstarch) mixed with 2 tbsp water

1 tsp sesame oil

30g (¼ cup) unsalted roasted cashew nuts (if you have salted cashew nuts, rinse under cold water and pat dry)

Place a wok over a medium-high heat. When hot, add the oil, garlic and ginger and fry until fragrant, about 15 seconds. Add the onion and carrot and fry for 2 minutes, then add the water chestnuts, baby corn, straw mushrooms, button mushrooms and bamboo shoots and stir-fry for a further 2 minutes. Turn the heat down to medium, add the rice vinegar, soy sauce, hoisin sauce and chilli flakes and stir-fry for a further 2–3 minutes.

Gradually add the cornflour (cornstarch) mixture, stirring constantly to thicken the sauce. Remove from the heat, add the sesame oil and cashew nuts and mix well. Transfer to a serving dish and tuck in.

HOISIN-GLAZED TEMPEH

Tempeh has an amazing texture; it's much firmer than tofu as it's made using the entire soya bean. Once fried, the tempeh becomes crispy, and when added to a sauce, it absorbs it like a sponge. The rich hoisin sauce is perfect for this dish – the tempeh becomes sweet, savoury and spicy with a crisp outside, but then give it a sprinkle of sesame seeds and the flavour dimensions really soar.

5 MINUTES   **10 MINUTES**   **SERVES 2-3**

1 x 340g (12oz) block of tempeh
3 tbsp oil (vegetable or groundnut)
2 garlic cloves, finely chopped
1 tbsp grated ginger
75ml (⅓ cup) hoisin sauce (page 342 or use shop-bought)
1 tsp sesame oil
1 tbsp sesame seeds, toasted
2 spring onions (scallions), thinly sliced

Cut the tempeh into bite-sized pieces and pat dry on kitchen paper.

Heat 2 tablespoons of the oil in a non-stick frying pan over a medium-high heat and fry the tempeh until golden brown on all sides. Transfer to kitchen paper to drain.

Heat your wok over a medium-high heat, add the remaining tablespoon of oil along with the garlic and ginger and cook for 20–30 seconds until fragrant. Add the cooked tempeh and hoisin sauce and stir-fry for 3 minutes. Transfer to a serving bowl, drizzle with the sesame oil and sprinkle with the toasted sesame seeds and sliced spring onions (scallions).

BAKED MUSHROOMS WITH A FIVE-SPICE CRUST

Served with noodles, rice, salad or even in a freshly steamed bao, these juicy and aromatic mushrooms with a crispy crumb pretty much work with everything.

5 MINUTES   **20 MINUTES**   **SERVES 2-4**

4 large mushrooms (flat or portobello)
2 tbsp oil (vegetable, groundnut or coconut)
1 tbsp salt
½ tsp white pepper
1 onion, finely diced
50g (1 cup) fresh breadcrumbs
1 tbsp Chinese five spice
1 tbsp garlic powder

Clean the mushrooms and remove the stalks. Gently rub in 1 tablespoon of the oil and sprinkle with a little of the salt and pepper and set to one side.

Heat a large non-stick wok or frying pan over a medium-high heat, add the remaining 1 tablespoon of oil and fry the onion for 2 minutes. Add the breadcrumbs, five spice, garlic powder and the remaining salt and pepper and continue to fry for a further 2 minutes, making sure the ingredients are well mixed. Remove from the heat.

Preheat the oven to 200°C (400°F).

Using a spoon, fill each of the mushrooms with the breadcrumb mixture. Place filled-side up on a baking tray and bake in the oven for 20 minutes. Remove from the oven and serve.

BRAISED TOFU

Buying 'pre-fried' is a mid-week game changer when it comes to cooking with tofu (bean curd); you get that light crust on the outside while still retaining the delicate inner texture and all without the messy fuss of having to fry it yourself! In as little time as it takes to steam a pot of rice, you'll be ladling out plump hunks of tofu and crisp veggies in this flavourful aromatic sauce.

5 MINUTES **10 MINUTES** **SERVES 2**

2 tbsp vegetable oil

3 slices of ginger

2 garlic cloves, minced

5 fresh shiitake (poku) mushrooms, destalked and sliced

1 carrot, thinly sliced

80g (½ cup) canned sliced bamboo shoots, drained

275ml (1½ cups) chicken or vegetable stock

2 tbsp Mushroom Stir-fry Sauce (page 343) or oyster sauce

1 tbsp light soy sauce

1 tsp dark soy sauce

1 tsp sugar

270g (9½oz) pre-fried tofu

1 tbsp Chinese rice wine (Shaoxing wine)

1 tbsp cornflour (cornstarch) mixed with 2 tbsp water

1 tsp sesame oil

Place a wok over a medium-high heat, then add the oil along with the ginger and garlic and stir-fry for 15 seconds until fragrant. Add the sliced mushrooms and stir-fry for 1 minute, then add the sliced carrot and bamboo shoots. Stir to combine the ingredients, then add the stock along with the Mushroom Stir-fry Sauce, light and dark soy sauces, sugar and pre-fried tofu. Give it all a good mix and bring to the boil, then reduce the heat and allow to simmer for 2–3 minutes.

Stir in the rice wine, then give the cornflour (cornstarch) mixture a mix and slowly add to the sauce, stirring constantly. Continue cooking for 1–1½ minutes until the sauce is velvety and clinging to all of the ingredients. Switch off the heat and drizzle with the sesame oil. Transfer to a serving plate and enjoy with your favourite rice dish.

GARLIC BROCCOLI

More than just a simple side to your meal, this garlic-enriched sauce will elevate a head of green broccoli into a full-blown dish in its own right.

5 MINUTES   **10 MINUTES**   **SERVES 2**

450g (1lb) broccoli, cut into bite-sized pieces
2 tbsp vegetable oil
5 garlic cloves, roughly chopped
3 thin slices of ginger
250ml (1 cup) chicken stock
1 tsp dark soy sauce
2 tbsp oyster sauce or Mushroom Stir-fry Sauce (page 343)
⅛ tsp or a pinch of white pepper
2 tsp sugar
2 tbsp Chinese rice wine (Shaoxing wine)
1 tbsp cornflour (cornstarch) mixed with 2 tbsp water
1 tsp sesame oil

Bring a saucepan of water to the boil, add the broccoli, cook for 1 minute and then drain.

Place a wok over a medium-high heat, add the oil, garlic and ginger and fry for 20 seconds until fragrant, then add the pre-cooked broccoli and stir-fry for 1 minute. Now add the stock, dark soy sauce, oyster sauce, white pepper and sugar and bring to the boil, then turn the heat down and allow to simmer for a further 2 minutes. Turn the heat back up and stir in the rice wine, then give the cornflour (cornstarch) mixture a mix and slowly add to the sauce, stirring constantly until thickened to your desired consistency. Switch off the heat and drizzle with the sesame oil. Transfer to a serving plate and enjoy.

VEGETABLE MOO SHU SERVED IN PANCAKES

A vegan homage to the original moo shu pork of northern China, these freshly tossed veggies in hoisin sauce wrapped in chewy Chinese pancakes will be sure to have you questioning whether you really could/should start eating less meat!

5 MINUTES   **12 MINUTES**   **SERVES 4**

3 tbsp vegetable oil

150g (5oz) firm tofu (spiced if you can buy it), cut into thin batons

3 garlic cloves, minced

6 fresh shiitake (poku) mushrooms, destalked and thinly sliced

3 celery sticks, cut into 5cm (2in) matchsticks

2 carrots, cleaned or peeled and cut into 5cm (2in) matchsticks

1 red (bell) pepper, deseeded and thinly sliced

5 spring onions (scallions), cut into 5cm (2in) lengths

3 tbsp hoisin sauce (page 342 or use shop-bought)

1 tbsp Chinese rice wine (Shaoxing wine)

1 tsp sesame oil

1 x pack of Chinese pancakes (about 10)

Place a wok over a medium-high heat, add 2 tablespoons of the oil and fry the tofu for 5–6 minutes until golden brown. Transfer to a wire rack or plate lined with kitchen paper to drain.

Add the remaining 1 tablespoon of oil to the same wok, along with the garlic and fry for 15 seconds, then add the shiitake mushrooms and stir-fry for 1 minute, followed by the celery, carrots and sliced pepper. After a further minute of cooking, add the spring onions (scallions), give everything a really good mix and then add 2 tablespoons of the hoisin sauce and the rice wine. Once all the vegetables are well coated and heated through, switch off the heat and stir in the fried tofu, being careful not to break it up. Drizzle with the sesame oil and transfer to a serving plate.

Steam the Chinese pancakes for 8 minutes and serve alongside the vegetable moo shu with the remaining hoisin sauce.

KATSU CAULIFLOWER WITH TONKATSU SAUCE

Panko breadcrumbs are super crispy even before you fry them, and they bring a crunch to a dish that standard breadcrumbs just can't deliver. As you cut into this cauliflower steak, you'll instantly release the aromatics; as they waft up your nose and trigger your taste buds, this is when your mouth will begin to water uncontrollably. Then you dip into the rich, sweet and sour BBQ sauce and it's game over.

20 MINUTES　　**25 MINUTES**　　**SERVES 2-3**

1 large head of cauliflower
200ml (¾ cup) almond or soya milk
½ tsp garlic powder
½ tsp onion powder
½ tbsp cornflour (cornstarch)
½ tsp salt
100g (¾ cup) plain (all-purpose) flour
100g (2 cups) panko breadcrumbs
oil (vegetable, groundnut or coconut),
　for deep-frying

For the sauce
1 tbsp light soy sauce
¼ tsp garlic powder
100ml (½ cup) tomato ketchup
3 tbsp Worcestershire sauce
2 tbsp white or brown sugar

In a large bowl, mix together all the sauce ingredients and set to one side.

Remove the outer leaves and stalk from the cauliflower, then slice the head into steaks 4cm (1½in) thick. In a large bowl, mix together the almond or soya milk, garlic powder, onion powder, cornflour (cornstarch), salt and plain (all-purpose) flour and mix well to create a smooth, pouring-consistency batter. Spread out the panko breadcrumbs on a large plate. Dip the cauliflower steaks into the batter and then coat with panko breadcrumbs, pressing down to ensure the crumbs stick.

Pour enough oil to deep-fry the cauliflower steaks into a large saucepan and heat to 170°C (340°F). Carefully lower in the cauliflower steaks and fry for 5 minutes on each side, or until tender and golden brown. Transfer to a wire rack or kitchen paper to drain.

Slice each steak into slices and serve with the Tonkatsu sauce.

STIR-FRIED AUBERGINE WITH SESAME SEEDS

Toasted sesame seeds always add an extra special something to a dish; not only do they offer little nibbles of crunch, but they also pack a punch of distinctly nutty flavour that is totally unique to these tiny morsels. Here we have soft aubergine stir-fried in a rich, dark, aromatic sauce with a subtle sour note and rich umami taste, amped to the next level by a liberal sprinkling of sesame seeds.

10 MINUTES　　**15 MINUTES**　　**SERVES 2-3**

2 tbsp sesame seeds
1 tbsp light soy sauce
½ tbsp dark soy sauce
1 tbsp rice vinegar
1 tbsp Chinese rice wine (Shaoxing wine)
½ tbsp sugar
1 tsp cornflour (cornstarch)
2 tbsp oil (vegetable or groundnut)
2 garlic cloves, roughly chopped
1 tbsp grated ginger
2 spring onions (scallions), halved and thinly sliced lengthways
1 green bird's-eye chilli, thinly sliced
2 large aubergines (eggplants), cut into bite-sized pieces
4 tbsp water
1 tsp sesame oil

Heat a dry, non-stick pan over a medium-high heat and toast the sesame seeds until lightly browned and fragrant. Transfer to a bowl and set to one side.

In a bowl, combine the light and dark soy sauces, rice vinegar, rice wine, sugar and cornflour (cornstarch) and mix well. Set to one side.

Heat a wok over a medium-high heat and add the oil, garlic, ginger and spring onions (scallions) and fry for 30 seconds until fragrant. Add the chilli and fry for a further 30 seconds before adding the aubergines (eggplants) and frying for another minute. Add the water and turn the heat down to a simmer. After 10 minutes of simmering, increase the heat, add the soy sauce mixture and combine well. Continue cooking over a medium-high heat to reduce the liquid by half.

Transfer to a serving plate, drizzle with the sesame oil and sprinkle with the toasted sesame seeds.

BEANSPROUTS WITH GARLIC AND ONION

The trick to making this dish taste like it was bought from a Chinese takeaway is the white pepper; the subtle background heat transforms the dish, giving it a further depth of flavour. Simple, wholesome and totally moreish.

5 MINUTES　　　**8 MINUTES**　　　**SERVES 2-3**

1 tbsp oil (vegetable, groundnut or coconut)

2 garlic cloves, roughly chopped

3 spring onions (scallions), halved and then thinly sliced lengthways

1 large onion, sliced

500g (1lb 2oz) beansprouts

2 tbsp Mushroom Stir-fry Sauce (page 343 or use shop-bought)

¼ tsp white pepper

¼ tsp salt (or to taste)

1 tsp sugar

1 tbsp light soy sauce

1 tsp dark soy sauce

125ml (½ cup) vegetable stock

1 tbsp cornflour (cornstarch) mixed with 2 tbsp water

1 tsp sesame oil

Pour the oil into a wok, place over a medium-high heat and fry the garlic and spring onions (scallions) for 30 seconds, or until fragrant. Add the onion and cook for a further minute, then toss in the beansprouts and continue cooking for another minute.

Add the Mushroom Stir-fry Sauce, pepper, salt, sugar, light and dark soy sauces and vegetable stock and heat thoroughly for 2–3 minutes.

Slowly add the cornflour (cornstarch) mixture to the beansprouts, stirring continuously to thicken the sauce. Remove from the heat, stir in the sesame oil and serve.

CHILLI STIR-FRIED LETTUCE

The quick cooking of this dish shocks the lettuce into becoming even more vibrant and green. A very simple, yet ever so tasty recipe that will get you scratching your head as to why you haven't tried stir-frying iceberg lettuce before.

5 MINUTES   **5 MINUTES**   **SERVES 2-3**

1 large iceberg lettuce
2 tbsp oil (vegetable, groundnut or coconut)
3 garlic cloves, very thinly sliced
1 green bird's-eye chilli, thinly sliced
3 tbsp Mushroom Stir-fry Sauce (page 343 or use shop-bought)
sesame oil, to serve

Remove the core from the lettuce, rinse and drain well. Halve the lettuce and cut the leaves into large bite-sized pieces, as they will wilt when cooked.

Heat the oil in a wok over a high heat and add the garlic and chilli, keeping them moving so they don't burn. After 20–30 seconds, add the lettuce and the Mushroom Stir-fry Sauce and cook for about 2 minutes until the leaves wilt. Turn off the heat, add a splash of sesame oil and serve immediately.

CRISPY FRIED TOFU IN A HOT AND SOUR SAUCE

Chinese food is traditionally categorised into five flavours – salty, spicy, sour, sweet, and bitter – and there is a proverb that says, '*One must learn to blend the flavours harmoniously to truly master Chinese cookery.*' This crispy tofu smothered in a tangy, spicy sauce is a quick, simple dish that will make your taste buds sing.

10 MINUTES   10 MINUTES   SERVES 2

1 tbsp sesame seeds
2 tbsp groundnut oil
225g (8oz) firm tofu, cut into 2cm (¾in) cubes
2 spring onions (scallions), finely sliced
1 tsp sesame oil

For the hot and sour sauce
2 tbsp Chinese rice wine (Shaoxing wine)
1½ tbsp dark soy sauce
2 tbsp rice vinegar
160ml (⅔ cup) vegetable stock
1 tbsp tomato purée (paste)
2 tsp chilli bean sauce
½ tsp white pepper
2 tsp granulated sugar

Ensure your wok is completely dry by wiping with kitchen paper before you start. Place it over a medium-low heat, then tip in the sesame seeds and slowly toast for 2–3 minutes, or until they turn golden brown. Transfer to a plate and leave to cool.

Heat the oil in the wok over a medium heat and fry the tofu cubes for 2–3 minutes on each side until they are golden brown. They should be crispy on the outside but soft inside. Transfer to a plate lined with kitchen paper to drain.

Add all the hot and sour sauce ingredients to the wok over a medium-high heat. Bring the sauce to the boil, then lower the heat and simmer for 3–5 minutes. Add the tofu cubes and stir to coat with the sauce and reheat them.

Transfer to a serving dish and sprinkle over the spring onions (scallions), toasted sesame seeds and sesame oil. Serve hot.

RED BRAISED AUBERGINE

Cooked in the common style of braising known as 'red cooking' or *hong shao*, originally from the Shanghai region, the classic ingredients of the sauce bring a deep red-brown colour and rich caramelised flavour to these sumptuously tender chunks of aubergine.

10 MINUTES   **15 MINUTES**   **SERVES 4**

3 tbsp vegetable oil

450g (1lb) aubergines (eggplant), cut into bite-sized pieces

1 tsp Chinese five spice

2 slices of ginger, cut into matchsticks

2 spring onions (scallions), whites cut into 5cm (2in) lengths and shredded, greens finely chopped

2 tbsp Chinese rice wine (Shaoxing wine)

250ml (1 cup) water

2 tbsp light soy sauce

½ tbsp dark soy sauce

½ tbsp sugar

salt, to taste

½ tbsp cornflour (cornstarch) mixed with 1 tbsp water

drizzle of sesame oil

Place a wok over a medium-high heat and, once hot, add the oil followed by the aubergine (eggplant) and fry for 2–3 minutes, stirring continuously. Next, add the five spice, ginger and spring onion (scallion) whites, and after 45 seconds, add the rice wine and give everything a good mix. Now add the water, light and dark soy sauces and sugar, bring to the boil and then turn down to a simmer. Cover and cook for 6–8 minutes before checking for seasoning and adding salt if required.

Give the cornflour (cornstarch) mixture a mix and slowly add to the sauce, stirring constantly. Once the sauce has thickened, remove from the heat, drizzle with sesame oil and serve topped with the spring onion greens.

CHINESE BROCCOLI
IN GARLIC SAUCE

A very 'potent' childhood memory of this dish is of Dad always putting so much garlic in when he cooked it at home that he would literally sweat garlic the next day! For taste and the health benefits that garlic brings, the more garlic the better, but be prepared to be short on company the morning after!

5 MINUTES   **5 MINUTES**   **SERVES 2**

1 tbsp groundnut oil

2 garlic cloves, crushed

400g (14oz) Chinese broccoli (gai lan) or tenderstem broccoli, stems chopped and leaves separated

1 onion, cut into strips

1 tbsp Chinese rice wine (Shaoxing wine)

2 tbsp oyster sauce (or vegetarian oyster sauce)

½ tbsp dark soy sauce

½ tbsp light soy sauce

120ml (½ cup) vegetable stock

¼ tsp salt

¼ tsp white pepper

½ tsp granulated sugar

1 tbsp cornflour (cornstarch) mixed with 2 tbsp water

½ tsp sesame oil

Place a wok over a medium-high heat, add the oil and the garlic and fry for 15 seconds until fragrant. Add the broccoli stems and onion and stir-fry for 2 minutes, followed by the broccoli leaves, frying for a further minute.

Add the remaining ingredients, except the cornflour (cornstarch) mixture and sesame oil, and bring to the boil. As soon as the sauce boils, slowly pour the cornflour mixture into the sauce, stirring continuously, to thicken it. Remove from the heat, stir in the sesame oil and serve straightaway.

CHINESE LEAF WITH MUSHROOM SAUCE

This is a great dish – simple to prepare and cook and has heaps of flavour. The rich mushroom sauce clings to the leaves, and every mouthful is juicy and salty, with that umami smoothness we all crave.

5 MINUTES   **5 MINUTES**   **SERVES 2-3**

2 tbsp oil (vegetable, groundnut or coconut)

1 medium Chinese leaf (Napa cabbage), cored and sliced

1 medium portobello mushroom, thinly sliced

3 tbsp Mushroom Stir-fry Sauce (page 343 or use shop-bought)

1 tbsp light soy sauce

1 tsp sesame oil

Heat the oil in a non-stick frying pan over a medium heat and, once hot, fry the cabbage for 2–3 minutes. Add the sliced mushroom and cook for a further minute, before stirring through the Mushroom Stir-fry Sauce and soy sauce. Once completely combined, transfer to a serving plate, drizzle with the sesame oil and enjoy.

HONEY RICE WINE BROCCOLI STEMS

Get your wok super-hot as this dish only takes a few minutes to cook, leaving the broccoli stems crisp and succulent to eat. The fermented rice wine complements the sweet sticky honey, which helps the sauce cling to the broccoli stems.

5 MINUTES   **5 MINUTES**   **SERVES 2**

340g (12oz) tenderstem broccoli
1 tbsp oil (vegetable, groundnut or coconut)
2 tbsp Chinese rice wine (Shaoxing wine)
1½ tbsp honey (vegan option: use agave syrup, maple syrup, brown rice syrup or molasses)
¼ tsp salt (or to taste)

Trim the broccoli so that each piece is roughly the same length.

Place a non-stick wok over a medium-high heat and, once hot, add the oil. Add the broccoli and fry for 1 minute, then add a splash of water to create some steam and quickly toss the broccoli in the wok. Pour in the rice wine and honey and add salt to taste, then cook over a high heat for 1–2 minutes, or until the liquid has reduced by half. Serve hot.

KUNG PO CAULIFLOWER

This is the spicy cousin of sweet and sour; you know the one... cooler than you could ever imagine, the one that breaks all the rules and not only gets away with it, but they are celebrated for it too. Preparation is key to making this dish all it can be. You want to serve this as fast as possible once the cauliflower comes out of the fryer so that the light batter remains crispy as you chow down.

15 MINUTES   **25 MINUTES**   **SERVES 2-3**

1 head of cauliflower

50g (½ cup) cornflour (cornstarch)

1 egg, beaten (vegan option: use ¼ cup silken tofu blended until completely smooth)

¼ tsp salt

groundnut oil, for deep-frying, plus 1 tbsp

1 garlic clove, roughly crushed

½ small onion, roughly chopped

½ red (bell) pepper, deseeded and roughly chopped

30g (¼ cup) canned bamboo shoots, drained and cut into small cubes

30g (¼ cup) canned water chestnuts, drained and sliced

1 green bird's-eye chilli, finely chopped

30g (¼ cup) roasted cashew nuts

For the kung po sauce

125ml (½ cup) water

2 tbsp hoisin sauce (page 342 or use shop-bought)

2 tbsp sugar

½ tbsp tomato purée (paste)

1 tbsp tomato ketchup

2 tbsp rice vinegar

1 tbsp cornflour (cornstarch) mixed with 2 tbsp water

For the sauce, place a large saucepan over a medium heat and add the water, hoisin sauce, sugar, tomato purée (paste), ketchup and rice vinegar. Bring to the boil and then simmer for 5 minutes. Slowly pour the cornflour (cornstarch) mixture into the sauce, stirring continuously until smooth enough to coat the back of a spoon – don't worry if you don't need to use it all, thicken the sauce to your own personal preference. Leave to one side.

Cut the hard core and stalk from the cauliflower and separate into bite-sized florets. Coat each floret in cornflour, then place into a large bowl with the beaten egg, seasoned with the ¼ teaspoon of salt (or use blended silken tofu) and gently fold through, coating each piece thoroughly. On a separate plate, coat the dipped cauliflower again with cornflour and tap off the excess.

Pour enough oil for deep-frying into a deep-sided wok or saucepan and heat to 180°C (350°F). Carefully drop the coated cauliflower florets into the oil in batches and fry until crispy. Remove and drain on a wire rack or kitchen paper.

Place a wok over a medium-high heat, add the 1 tablespoon of oil and fry the garlic for 15 seconds. Add the onion and red pepper and fry for a further minute. Add the bamboo shoots, water chestnuts and chilli and stir-fry for another minute. Now add the prepared sauce and reheat thoroughly, before turning off the heat and finally adding the cooked cauliflower and cashew nuts. Stir gently to coat in the sauce and transfer to a serving plate.

ASPARAGUS WITH GINGER SOY

Juicy, crisp asparagus and mangetout are served in a rich umami soy sauce with the underlying heat of ginger.

---

5 MINUTES   **15 MINUTES**   **SERVES 2-4**

1 tbsp vegetable oil
100g (¾ cup) raw cashew nuts
thumb-sized piece of ginger, peeled and cut into thin matchsticks
1 garlic clove, finely chopped
2 bunches of asparagus
150g (5oz) mangetout (snowpeas), trimmed
1 tbsp soy sauce
1 tbsp rice wine vinegar
1 tbsp sesame oil

Heat half the oil in a wok over a medium heat. Once the wok is hot, add the cashew nuts and stir-fry for 1–2 minutes until toasted. Transfer to a plate lined with kitchen paper.

Pour the remaining oil into the wok and place over a medium-high heat. Add the ginger and garlic and stir-fry for 30 seconds until fragrant. Add the asparagus and mangetout (snowpeas) and stir-fry for a further 2 minutes until tender. Pour in the soy sauce and rice wine vinegar and stir-fry for 1 minute, or until heated through. Remove from the heat, drizzle with the sesame oil and sprinkle with the toasted cashew nuts. Serve.

Kwoklyn's tip
The best-tasting asparagus are always the ones that are super-fresh. Asparagus tips have the best flavour, so make sure they are firm and not wilting. The stalks should be plump and firm, and the tips should be tightly closed. When you buy your asparagus, store it standing upright in fresh cold water.

CHINESE ORANGE TOFU WITH PEPPERS AND PINEAPPLE

Developed to cater for Western taste buds, this dish is a play on the much-loved and ever-popular sweet and sour dish we see in all Chinese takeaways and restaurants. It's made with fresh orange juice, for a natural sweetness, zest for some twang, and a hint of garlic and ginger for that aromatic note. If you love sweet and sour, you're going to love this dish.

10 MINUTES   **15 MINUTES**   **SERVES 2**

500ml (2 cups) oil (vegetable, groundnut or coconut), for shallow-frying
340g (12oz) firm tofu

For the sauce
1 tbsp oil (vegetable, groundnut or coconut)
1 green (bell) pepper, deseeded and roughly chopped
1 small carrot, cut into bite-sized slices
½ tsp grated ginger
½ tsp grated garlic
1 tsp grated orange zest
250ml (1 cup) orange juice
2 tbsp sugar
2 tbsp tomato purée (paste)
3 tbsp rice vinegar or white wine vinegar
handful of pineapple chunks
2 tbsp cornflour (cornstarch) mixed with 4 tbsp water

Heat the oil for shallow-frying in a large saucepan to 180°C (350°F). The oil needs to be deep enough for the tofu to float without touching the bottom of the pan. Cut the tofu into bite-sized pieces and pat dry with kitchen paper, then gently add the tofu to the oil in batches and fry until golden brown. Drain on kitchen paper and set to one side.

Heat the oil for the sauce in a wok or frying pan and gently fry the green pepper and carrot over a medium-low heat until softened, then add the ginger, garlic and orange zest and fry until fragrant. Transfer to a bowl and set to one side.

Put the orange juice, sugar, tomato purée (paste) and rice vinegar into a large saucepan and place over a medium heat. Bring to the boil, then add the softened vegetables along with the pineapple and allow to simmer for a further 5 minutes. Give the cornflour (cornstarch) mixture a stir and slowly pour into the sauce, a little at a time, stirring constantly until thickened to your desired consistency. Stir the tofu through the sauce to gently reheat and serve immediately.

CAULIFLOWER STEAK WITH A RICH CHINESE GRAVY

I love a big pile of rice smothered in gravy; for me it is comfort on a plate. This recipe is quite simply, 'food for your soul'. A huge Cantonese marinated cauliflower steak that is juicy on the inside and deliciously crispy on the outside, smothered in a rich, dark, aromatic gravy – it's a win-win dish.

10 MINUTES   **25 MINUTES**   **SERVES 3-4**

½ tsp salt
½ tsp black pepper
½ tsp garlic powder
½ tsp onion powder
½ tsp Chinese five spice
1 large head of cauliflower
2 tbsp groundnut oil
2 tsp sesame oil

For the gravy
2 tbsp Mushroom Stir-fry Sauce (page 343 or use shop-bought)
1 tbsp Chinese rice wine (Shaoxing wine)
1 tsp dark soy sauce
pinch of white pepper
250ml (1 cup) vegetable stock
1 tsp cornflour (cornstarch)
1 tsp groundnut oil
2 garlic cloves, roughly chopped

Preheat the oven to 200°C (400°F). Combine the salt, black pepper, garlic powder, onion powder and five spice in a large bowl and set to one side.

Remove the outer leaves and tough stalk from the cauliflower, then slice the head into 4cm (1½in) thick steaks. Rub groundnut oil into both sides of the cauliflower steak and sprinkle liberally with the seasoning mixture, then place the steaks on a lined baking tray and tightly cover with foil. Bake in the oven for 8 minutes, then remove the foil and continue to roast for a further 8 minutes.

While the cauliflower is roasting, make the gravy. Combine the stir-fry sauce, rice wine, dark soy sauce, white pepper, vegetable stock and cornflour (cornstarch) in a bowl and mix well. Heat a wok over a medium-high heat. Add the groundnut oil and fry the garlic until fragrant, then add the stock mixture and bring to the boil. Turn down to a simmer for 2 minutes, then remove from the heat and set to one side.

Remove the roasted cauliflower from the oven and transfer to a hot frying pan. Fry the cauliflower steaks on both sides to form a rich, dark golden crust. Transfer to your serving plate, drizzle with the sesame oil and pour over the gravy.

MOCK CHAR SIU BAO WITH PICKLED CHINESE VEGETABLES

Soft, fluffy steamed buns – check. Firm tempeh patty filling, marinated in a rich, aromatically smoky, sweet Chinese BBQ sauce – check. Topping of tangy, sour, crunchy, pickled vegetables – check. A combination that will no doubt get your taste buds tingling.

2 HOURS 20 MINS   **20 MINUTES**   **SERVES 4**

For the bao

560g (4¾ cups) plain (all-purpose) flour, plus extra for dusting

11g (⅓oz) instant dried yeast

½ tsp salt

1 tsp baking powder

30g (1oz) caster (superfine) sugar

2 tbsp vegetable oil, plus extra for greasing

320ml (1¼ cups) whole milk (for a vegan option use soya or almond milk)

For the filling

125ml (½ cup) hoisin sauce (page 342 or use shop-bought)

1 tbsp Chinese five spice

1 tbsp Chinese rice wine (Shaoxing wine)

2 tbsp sugar

1 tbsp oil (vegetable or groundnut)

1 x 340g (12oz) block of tempeh, cut into 2cm (¾in) thick patties

4 tbsp Chinese Pickled Vegetables (page 270)

Put all of the bao ingredients in a large bowl and bring together to form a soft and springy dough. Turn out on to a clean lightly floured worktop and knead for 6 minutes, then bring the mixture together to form a ball. Place in a lightly greased bowl, cover and leave to stand for 2 hours, or until the dough has doubled in size.

Turn out the dough on to a lightly floured worktop, lightly flatten and roll into a long sausage shape, then divide into 8–12 equal pieces (depending on how large you'd like your bao to be). Roll each piece into a short sausage shape and flatten, then fold in half to create a soft clam shape. Place the sealed dough balls on to a sheet of perforated baking paper in a bamboo steamer with a lid, leaving about 2cm (¾in) between each one, as they will grow as they steam. Steam over a high heat for 8–10 minutes. Be careful when you remove the lid, as the escaping steam will billow around your hand. Remove from the basket and enjoy warm.

Meanwhile, for the filling, preheat the oven to 190°C (375°F). Combine the hoisin sauce, five spice, rice wine and sugar in a large bowl.

Line a baking tray with foil and brush with the oil, then place the tempeh patties on the foil and brush over half of the marinade. Bake in the oven for 10 minutes, or until they have formed a crust, then turn the patties over, brush on the remaining marinade and cook for a further 10 minutes.

Take a steamed bao and carefully pull it open (you may need to cut it with a knife). Place a tempeh patty in the middle, top with some pickled vegetables and tuck in.

SICHUAN-STYLE CRISPY TOFU WITH CHILLI AND SALT

Who knew tofu could taste this good? Here you have delicious crispy nuggets coated with the taste of the Sichuan province.

10 MINUTES   **10 MINUTES**   **SERVES 2**

½ tbsp salt
½ tbsp Sichuan peppercorns, ground
½ tbsp freshly ground black pepper
groundnut oil, for deep-frying,
   plus 1 tbsp
100g (1 cup) cornflour (cornstarch)
1 egg
225g (8oz) firm tofu, cut into 2cm (¾in)
   cubes
1 small onion, finely diced
½ green (bell) pepper, deseeded and
   finely diced
½ tbsp chilli flakes
2 garlic cloves, thinly sliced
2 tbsp water
1 tsp sesame oil

Mix the salt, ground Sichuan peppercorns and black pepper in a small bowl and set to one side.

Pour enough oil to deep-fry the tofu cubes in a wok or deep-sided saucepan and heat to 180°C (350°F).

Tip the cornflour (cornstarch) on to a plate and beat the egg in a shallow bowl. Coat each cube of tofu first with cornflour, shaking off the excess, then with egg and then back into the cornflour. Gently lower the tofu into the hot oil in batches and deep-fry for around 3 minutes, turning once or twice to allow each piece to brown and cook evenly. Transfer to a wire rack or a plate lined with kitchen paper to drain.

Heat the 1 tablespoon of oil in a separate wok or frying pan and wait until the oil just begins to smoke. Add the onion, green pepper and chilli flakes and stir-fry for 30 seconds over a high heat, then add the garlic and mix thoroughly. Add the crispy tofu and evenly sprinkle with the Sichuan pepper mixture. Quickly toss the ingredients, add the water and quickly toss again, coating each piece. Turn off the heat, drizzle with the sesame oil and serve immediately.

LO HON MIXED VEGETABLES (BUDDHA'S DELIGHT)

A mix of Chinese vegetables cooked until tender in a rich, aromatic umami sauce, this is a popular dish eaten by Buddhist monks which has found its way on to many menus across the world as a vegetarian option. Made with mung bean starch, Chinese vermicelli are also known as mung bean noodles, glass noodles and cellophane noodles.

10 MINUTES   **7 MINUTES**   **SERVES 4**

1 nest of dried mung bean (glass) noodles

2 tbsp groundnut oil

3cm (1¼in) cube of ginger, peeled and sliced

2 garlic cloves, thinly sliced

2 spring onions (scallions), halved then sliced lengthways

1 onion, diced

5 dried Chinese mushrooms, rehydrated in hot water, drained and sliced into strips

50g dried wood ear mushrooms, rehydrated in hot water, drained and sliced into strips

60g (½ cup) canned straw mushrooms

2 bok choy, cut into bite-sized pieces

1 carrot, sliced

60g (½ cup) canned bamboo shoots

6 baby corn cobs, halved lengthways

2 tbsp rice wine

2 tbsp oyster sauce (or vegetarian oyster sauce)

1 tbsp light soy sauce

½ tbsp dark soy sauce

1 tsp granulated sugar

240ml (1 cup) vegetable stock

2 tbsp cornflour (cornstarch) mixed with 4 tbsp water

1 tsp sesame oil

Place the noodles in a bowl and pour over boiling water. Soak for 3 minutes, then drain and set to one side.

Place a wok over a medium-high heat, add the oil, ginger, garlic and spring onions (scallions) and stir-fry for 30 seconds, until fragrant. Add the onion and stir-fry for a further minute. Add all the mushrooms, bok choy, carrot, bamboo shoots and baby corn and fry for a further 3 minutes.

Add the remaining ingredients, except the noodles, cornflour (cornstarch) mixture and sesame oil, and bring to the boil. Lower the heat and simmer for 2 minutes, then slowly pour the cornflour mixture into the sauce, stirring continuously, to thicken. Remove from the heat, stir in the noodles and sesame oil, and serve.

TOFU WITH CHINESE MUSHROOMS

Meaty Chinese mushrooms swimming in a rich aromatic sauce with tofu and juicy Chinese broccoli. Also called tofu bubbles, the tofu used in this dish is deep-fried to create a golden surface and a light, fluffy texture within. Use vegetarian oyster sauce if you prefer.

10 MINUTES   **6 MINUTES**   **SERVES 2**

2 tbsp groundnut oil

3cm (1¼in) piece of ginger, peeled and sliced

1 garlic clove, thinly sliced

8 large Chinese dried mushrooms, rehydrated in hot water, drained and cut into bite-sized pieces

200g (7oz) ready-fried tofu puffs

120g (4oz) Chinese broccoli (gai lan) or tenderstem broccoli, stems and leaves separated, cut into bite-sized pieces

½ tbsp light soy sauce

1 tsp dark soy sauce

1 tbsp oyster sauce (or vegetarian oyster sauce)

120ml (½ cup) vegetable stock

¼ tsp granulated sugar

¼ tsp salt

¼ tsp white pepper

1 tbsp cornflour (cornstarch) mixed with 2 tbsp water

1 tsp sesame oil

Place a wok over a medium-high heat, add the oil, ginger and garlic and fry for 30 seconds. Add the mushrooms and tofu and stir-fry for 2 minutes. Add the broccoli stems, together with the soy sauces, oyster sauce, stock, sugar, salt and pepper, and bring to the boil.

Turn down the heat to a simmer, then add the broccoli leaves and cook for 1 minute. Slowly pour in the cornflour (cornstarch) mixture, stirring continuously, to thicken the sauce. Remove from the heat, add the sesame oil and serve straightaway.

MANGETOUT, MUSHROOMS AND BAMBOO SHOOTS

This super quick stir-fry of juicy mushrooms and crispy mangetout makes a perfect lunchtime snack or works well served on top of a bed of rice for a healthy meat-free dinner.

5 MINUTES   **8 MINUTES**   **SERVES 2**

2 tbsp vegetable oil

2 tbsp ginger, minced

200g (3 cups) fresh shiitake (poku) mushrooms, destalked and sliced

300g (10oz) mangetout (snowpeas)

150g (1 cup) canned sliced bamboo shoots, drained

2 tbsp hoisin sauce (page 342 or use shop-bought)

1 tbsp light soy sauce

½ tbsp Chinese rice wine (Shaoxing wine)

2 tsp sugar

4 tbsp roasted unsalted cashew nuts

Place a wok over a medium-high heat, add the oil and minced ginger and fry for around 15 seconds until fragrant. Add the sliced mushrooms and stir-fry for 1 minute followed by the mangetout (snowpeas). After a further minute of cooking, add the bamboo shoots along with the hoisin sauce, soy sauce, rice wine and sugar. Stir to combine all the ingredients, and if the dish is a little dry, you can add a splash of water at this point.

Once all the ingredients are piping hot, switch off the heat and stir through the cashew nuts. Transfer to a serving plate and enjoy.

SICHUAN CRISP CAULIFLOWER

Succulent pieces of cauliflower covered in a crispy coating and drenched in a rich velvety sauce that is sweet, a little sour, spicy, pleasantly aromatic and silky smooth, thanks to a glug of dark soy sauce. There's so much happening in this dish that your taste buds are going to party for quite a while after you devour each mouthful.

10 MINUTES   **15 MINUTES**   **SERVES 2**

1 head of cauliflower
50g (½ cup) cornflour (cornstarch)
1 tbsp garlic salt
1 tbsp Chinese five spice
1 egg, beaten (vegan option: use ¼ cup silken tofu blended until completely smooth)
groundnut oil, for deep-frying, plus 1 tbsp
2 garlic cloves, roughly chopped
8 whole dried red chillies
½ tbsp grated ginger
1 onion, sliced
½ tsp salt
½ tsp ground black pepper

For the sauce
1 tbsp chilli flakes
2 garlic cloves, finely chopped
1 tbsp light soy sauce
½ tbsp dark soy sauce
1 tsp Chinese black vinegar (or use a good balsamic vinegar)
2 tsp cornflour (cornstarch)
75ml (⅓ cup) vegetable stock

Place a large saucepan over a medium heat and add all the sauce ingredients. Bring to the boil and then simmer for 2 minutes. Remove from the heat and set to one side.

Cut the hard core and stalk from the cauliflower and separate the head into bite-sized florets. In a large bowl, combine the cornflour (cornstarch), garlic salt and five spice. Coat each floret in the cornflour mixture, then place into a large bowl with the beaten egg (or blended silken tofu) and gently fold through, coating each piece thoroughly. Cover the coated cauliflower with more of the cornflour mixture and dust off any excess.

Pour enough oil to deep-fry the cauliflower into a large saucepan and heat to 180°C (350°F). Carefully drop the cauliflower into the oil in batches and fry until crisp. Remove and drain on a wire rack or kitchen paper.

Place a wok over a medium-high heat, add the tablespoon of oil along with the garlic, dried red chillies and ginger and fry for 20 seconds until fragrant. Add the onion, salt and black pepper and fry for another minute, then add the prepared sauce and simmer until thickened. Turn off the heat, add the crispy cauliflower and toss to combine.

Serve hot.

AUBERGINE IN
SPICY GARLIC SAUCE

As the world's top producer and consumer of aubergine (eggplant), it's no wonder that throughout China you'll find so many dishes 'tastifying' these spongy little veggies as they absorb the flavours they are dressed in.

10 MINUTES   **10 MINUTES**   **SERVES 2**

60ml (¼ cup) chicken or vegetable stock
1 tbsp light soy sauce
1 tsp dark soy sauce
1 tsp cornflour (cornstarch)
1 tbsp Mushroom Stir-fry Sauce (page 343) or oyster sauce
2 tbsp vegetable oil
2 tbsp minced ginger
4 garlic cloves, minced
450g (1lb) aubergines (eggplants), cut into bite-sized pieces
2 tsp chilli flakes
2 spring onions (scallions), finely chopped

Combine the stock, light and dark soy sauces, cornflour (cornstarch) and Mushroom Stir-fry Sauce in a bowl. Place to one side.

Place a wok over a medium-high heat, add the oil, ginger and garlic and stir-fry for 20 seconds until fragrant. Next, add the aubergine (eggplant) and stir-fry for 2–3 minutes, then add the chilli flakes and mix well. Pour in the sauce mixture, bring to a simmer and cook for a couple more minutes until the aubergine is tender. Switch off the heat, transfer to a serving plate and garnish with the chopped spring onions (scallions).

CHILLI GINGER CRISPY TOFU

For those of you who love sweet, spicy and crispy in a single mouthful, this dish will have your taste buds singing. The crispy fried tofu drinks up all of that lovely tangy sweet and spicy sauce as it is tossed through the wok.

5 MINUTES   **15 MINUTES**   **SERVES 2**

300ml (1¼ cups) vegetable oil,
   plus 1 tbsp
340g (12oz) firm tofu, cut into bite-sized
   pieces
2 tbsp grated ginger
4 garlic cloves, finely chopped or grated
3 tbsp chilli flakes
3 tbsp light soy sauce
4 tbsp rice vinegar
2 tbsp sugar

Preheat the 300ml (1¼ cups) oil to 175°C (347°F) in a saucepan and carefully lower in the tofu pieces. Fry for 6–8 minutes until golden brown. Drain on kitchen paper and set to one side.

Place a wok over a medium heat, add the 1 tablespoon of oil and gently fry the ginger and garlic until fragrant, taking care not to burn them. After 1 minute, add the chilli flakes and fry for another minute. Add the soy sauce, rice vinegar and sugar and continue to cook until the sauce has thickened. Toss in the cooked tofu, turn to coat evenly and serve.

BOK CHOY WITH MUSHROOM STIR-FRY SAUCE

Bok choy (also known as pak choi) literally translates as 'small white vegetable'. This type of Chinese cabbage, with its dark leaves and bulbous white bottom or stem, is used extensively in Cantonese and Chinese cookery. This simple dish cooks in minutes and delivers a clean, fresh, aromatic taste.

5 MINUTES   **6 MINUTES**   **SERVES 2**

400g (14oz) bok choy
2 tbsp groundnut oil
1 tsp grated ginger
1 garlic clove, roughly chopped
1 tbsp Chinese rice wine (Shaoxing wine)
3 tbsp Mushroom Stir-fry Sauce (page 343 or use shop-bought)
1 tsp sesame oil

Rinse the bok choy and cut lengthways into quarters.

Heat a wok over a medium-high heat and add the oil, then the ginger and garlic and fry for 30 seconds until fragrant. Add the quartered bok choy and stir-fry for 2 minutes, then add the rice wine and cook for a further 2 minutes. Add the Mushroom Stir-fry Sauce, mix well and transfer the saucy bok choy to a plate. Drizzle with the sesame oil and serve.

PURPLE SPROUTING BROCCOLI AND PEANUT SATAY SAUCE

Satay sauce varies from region to region; it originates from Indonesia but was widely adopted by the Chinese for their love of peanuts – this sauce has lots of them. Young tender broccoli stems are lightly steamed and smothered in a rich, spicy–sour peanut sauce. Delicious simplicity on your plate.

5 MINUTES   **10 MINUTES**   **SERVES 2-3**

1 tbsp sesame seeds (optional)
3 tbsp chunky peanut butter
1 tbsp rice vinegar
2 tbsp light soy sauce
1 tsp chilli flakes (optional)
280g (9oz) purple sprouting broccoli

Toast the sesame seeds in a dry frying pan or wok over a medium heat until lightly golden and fragrant.

Combine the peanut butter, vinegar, soy sauce and chilli flakes (if using) in a small saucepan over a low heat, stirring until warmed and combined.

Trim the broccoli stems and cut them into bite-sized pieces, then place in a steamer basket and steam for 4–5 minutes, or until tender. Remove the broccoli from the steamer and arrange on a serving plate, then pour over the satay sauce and sprinkle with the toasted sesame seeds (if using).

CHINESE MUSHROOMS WITH OYSTER SAUCE

Most Chinese supermarkets stock a vegetarian oyster sauce which is made from soya beans, yeast extract and wheat flour, if you want to make this dish completely vegetarian. It definitely replicates the rich depth of flavour real oyster sauce brings to the dish.

5 MINUTES   **7 MINUTES**   **SERVES 4**

340g (12oz) shiitake (poku) or portobello mushrooms
1 tbsp groundnut oil
1 tbsp crushed garlic
½ tsp finely chopped ginger
2 tbsp oyster sauce (or vegetarian oyster sauce)
1 tbsp dark soy sauce
1 tsp brown sugar
¼ tsp salt
¼ tsp white pepper
80ml (⅓ cup) vegetable stock
1 tbsp cornflour (cornstarch) mixed with 2 tbsp water
1 tsp sesame oil

Cut the mushrooms into bite-sized pieces if they're large.

Place a wok over a medium-high heat, add the oil, garlic and ginger and fry for about 30 seconds until fragrant. Add the mushrooms and stir-fry for 1–2 minutes, then add the oyster sauce, soy sauce, sugar, salt, pepper and vegetable stock and mix well.

Bring to the boil and let it bubble away for 2 minutes to reduce the sauce a little. Pour in the cornflour (cornstarch) mixture, stirring continuously, to thicken the sauce, then remove from the heat and drizzle with the sesame oil. Transfer to a serving dish and enjoy.

CHINESE-STYLE SALT AND PEPPER CHIPS

There's something truly special about a bag of chips from the local Chinese takeaway; you all know what I'm talking about... they just have 'that' taste don't they? While you may not be able to recreate that truly authentic fried flavour that we all know and love, my Chinese-style salt and pepper seasoning will have your taste buds singing a most welcome and familiar tune!

5 MINUTES   **15 MINUTES**   **SERVES 2**

1 litre (4 cups) vegetable oil, plus 1 tbsp
400g (14oz) frozen thick-cut chips
1 onion, finely diced
2 garlic cloves, roughly chopped
½ green or red (bell) pepper, deseeded and finely diced
1 tsp Chinese five spice
2 tsp salt
1 tsp coarsely ground black pepper
2 tsp chilli flakes

Heat the vegetable oil to around 180–200°C (350–400°F) in a deep wok or saucepan, or fryer, add the chips and cook for 7–9 minutes, or according to the packet instructions, until cooked all the way through and crispy. Drain and set to one side.

Place a wok over a medium-high heat and add the 1 tablespoon of oil along with the onion and garlic and fry for 1–1½ minutes until softened. Add the diced pepper and continue to cook for a further 1–2 minutes, then toss in the cooked chips and sprinkle over the five spice, salt, black pepper and chilli flakes. Give everything a really good mix and serve immediately.

CHILLI BEAN TOFU AND VEGETABLE SKEWERS

What is it about eating food with your hands? It must be a primal thing but somehow I find that it always tastes better. These tofu vegetable skewers are one such dish that I especially enjoy eating with my hands.

10 MINUTES   **10 MINUTES**   **SERVES 4**

2 tbsp chilli bean sauce

2 tbsp vegetable oil

1 tbsp tomato purée (paste)

1 tbsp sugar

2 tbsp light soy sauce

340g (12oz) firm tofu, cut into 3cm (1¼in) cubes

6 fresh baby corn, cut in half

1 red (bell) pepper, deseeded and cut into bite-sized cubes

If using wooden skewers, it's a good idea to soak them in warm water for about 10 minutes before cooking to stop them from burning.

Combine the chilli bean sauce, oil, tomato purée (paste), sugar and soy sauce in a bowl.

Preheat your grill (broiler) to medium-high. Thread the tofu, baby corn and red pepper cubes on to the skewers and brush with the chilli bean sauce mixture. I'd recommend 2 skewers per person. Lay on a baking tray and place under the grill for 8–10 minutes, turning frequently and brushing with more sauce (this will build up a tasty layer).

Once browned all over, tender and covered in sauce, transfer the skewers to a serving plate.

Kwoklyn's tip
These are great cooked on a barbecue, as the smoky flavour really adds to the already tasty skewers.

TERIYAKI BOWL

Sometimes all we want is a big bowl of love, something simple to make that isn't going to create an explosion of pots and pans to wash up afterwards. A mountain of yummy vegetables in a rich, aromatic, velvety umami sweet chilli sauce, served over noodles or steamed rice, is just the ticket for moments like these.

10 MINUTES   **10 MINUTES**   **SERVES 2**

1 tbsp oil (vegetable or groundnut)

1 onion, roughly diced

1 tsp grated garlic

2 tsp grated ginger

1 red (bell) pepper, deseeded and roughly diced

1 courgette (zucchini), cut into bite-sized pieces

60g (2oz) tenderstem broccoli, cut into small florets

6–8 baby corn cobs

1 medium aubergine (eggplant), cut into bite-sized pieces

For the sauce

125ml (½ cup) light soy sauce

3 tbsp brown sugar

2 tsp chilli flakes

1 tbsp honey (vegan option: use agave or maple syrup)

Combine all the sauce ingredients in a bowl, mix well and set to one side.

Heat the oil in a wok over a medium-high heat, add the onion, garlic and ginger and fry until fragrant and the onion is translucent. Add the remaining vegetables and stir-fry for 3–4 minutes. Add the sauce, bring to the boil and simmer for 3 minutes.

Serve on top of freshly steamed rice or springy noodles.

FRIED POTATO BIRDS' NESTS

I can still hear the customers 'Ooooos' and 'Aaaaahs' as Dad would serve their favourite dishes in a potato birds' nest. The juices would seep into the crispy fried potato and, for me, the best part of the dish was tearing off chunks to eat along with my steamed rice. If you are looking to wow your guests, then you have got to give these a go.

15 MINUTES　　**30 MINUTES**　　**MAKES 3-4**

2 large waxy potatoes, cut into very fine
　matchsticks
1 litre (4 cups) vegetable oil
pinch of sea salt

Begin by washing the potato matchsticks in cold water to remove any excess starch, then drain and pat dry with a clean tea towel.

Place some potato into a metal sieve that will fit comfortably in your wok or saucepan for cooking. Make sure the potato fans out across all of the sieve and then place a second sieve directly on top of the potato, pressing it down to ensure the nest maintains its shape while cooking.

Heat the oil to 180–200°C (350–400°F); the oil needs to be deep enough to totally submerge the sieves holding the potato birds' nest.

Carefully lower the sieves into the oil and fry for 5–10 minutes until golden brown. Carefully remove the nest from the sieve moulds and transfer to a wire rack to drain. Once cooled, season with a pinch of salt.

Repeat with the remaining potato. Place the birds' nests on to a serving plate and fill with your favourite Chinese dish, the saucier the better.

SEARED AUBERGINE WITH MISO AND SESAME SEEDS

Aubergines have the ability to absorb all the flavours from their surrounding ingredients, so when you add garlic, the rich intense umami flavour of miso paste and nutty toasted sesame seeds, you know you're on to a winner.

10 MINUTES   **12 MINUTES**   **SERVES 2**

2 tbsp sesame seeds
2 tbsp oil (vegetable or groundnut)
2 garlic cloves, finely chopped or grated
2 large aubergines (eggplants), cut into
  bite-sized pieces
4 tbsp water
2 tbsp red miso paste
2 tbsp Chinese rice wine (Shaoxing
  wine)
1 tsp sugar
½ tsp salt
¼ tsp white pepper
2 tbsp light soy sauce

Place a non-stick pan over a medium-high heat, wipe completely dry with kitchen paper and then add the sesame seeds and toast until lightly browned and fragrant. Transfer to a bowl and set to one side.

Place a wok over a medium heat, add the oil and gently fry the garlic until fragrant. Add the aubergine (eggplant) and fry for a further minute, then add the water, turn down to a simmer and cover with a lid. Cook for 6–8 minutes.

Once the aubergine has softened, remove the lid. Add the miso paste, rice wine, sugar, salt, pepper and soy sauce, combine well and continue cooking until the liquid has reduced by half.

Transfer to a serving plate, sprinkle over the toasted sesame seeds and enjoy.

SICHUAN PEPPER MUSHROOMS

These mushrooms are packed full of wondrous flavour as they are infused with the Holy Trinity of Cantonese cooking – garlic, ginger and spring onion – but this recipe also borrows ingredients from the Sichuan province. The taste is often described as aromatic, pungent (from the rice wine) and mouth-numbingly spicy.

10 MINUTES   **20 MINUTES**   **SERVES 2-3**

1 tsp Sichuan peppercorns
1 tbsp vegetable oil
2 garlic cloves, finely chopped
1 tbsp grated ginger
2 spring onions (scallions), thinly sliced
2 large dried chillies, thinly sliced
1 onion, thinly sliced
3 large portobello mushrooms, quartered (they will shrink when cooked)
125ml (½ cup) Chinese rice wine (Shaoxing wine)
500ml (2 cups) vegetable stock
2 tbsp light soy sauce

Place the Sichuan peppercorns in a dry wok or heavy-based frying pan over a medium-low heat. Heat the peppercorns, shaking the pan occasionally until they begin to darken and become fragrant, then set to one side to cool. When cooled, lightly bruise (not crush) the toasted peppercorns using a mortar and pestle or rolling pin.

Heat the oil in a wok, add the garlic, ginger and spring onions (scallions) and fry until fragrant. Add the Sichuan peppercorns and dried chillies and stir-fry for 20 seconds, then add the onion and mushrooms and fry for another minute. Pour in the rice wine and cook until the liquor has been absorbed. Add the vegetable stock and soy sauce and bring to the boil, then turn down the heat to medium and simmer for 10–15 minutes, or until the mushrooms are tender and the sauce is syrupy (keep an eye on the pan, to avoid burning the sauce). Stir and serve.

AUBERGINE FRITTERS WITH HOISIN DIP

My juicy and crispy aubergine fritters make a perfect late-night snack. Curl up on the sofa, pop on your favourite film and scoff away; sounds like heaven to me!

5 MINUTES   **10 MINUTES**   **SERVES 2-4**

500ml (2 cups) vegetable oil
180g (1½ cups) plain (all-purpose) flour
¼ tsp baking powder
½ tsp salt
600ml (2½ cups) sparkling water
1 large aubergine (eggplant), cut into 5mm (¼in) slices
4 tbsp hoisin sauce (page 342 or use shop-bought)

Pour the oil into a large saucepan and heat to 175°C (350°F).

In a large bowl, combine the flour, baking powder and salt. Add the sparkling water and use a fork to mix everything together. It is perfectly fine to have small lumps of flour in your mixture; it's more important not to overwork the mixture, as this will build up the gluten in the flour and make your batter doughy.

One slice at a time, dip the aubergine (eggplant) into the batter and then carefully lower into the oil. Fry in small batches for 3–5 minutes, turning occasionally for even cooking and colour. Drain on kitchen paper and serve hot with the hoisin sauce for dipping.

CRISPY TOFU WITH SPRING ONIONS

With just a few basic ingredients, you really can create a dish that your family and friends will think you've spent days preparing. Aromatic spring onions and crispy tofu are served with a rich, tasty, fermented chilli bean sauce. This is traditional Chinese cooking at its simplest.

5 MINUTES   **10 MINUTES**   **SERVES 3-4**

340g (12oz) firm tofu
2 tbsp groundnut oil
300g (10½oz) spring onions (scallions),
    cut into 2.5cm (1in) lengths
2 tsp fermented chilli bean paste
    (doubanjiang)
½ tsp sugar
1 tsp light soy sauce

Slice the tofu into 2cm (¾in) cubes and pat dry with kitchen paper. Heat a non-stick wok with half the oil and fry the tofu cubes until golden brown on all sides. Remove and drain on kitchen paper.

Heat the remaining oil in the wok over a medium heat, then add the spring onions (scallions) and fry for 1 minute. Return the fried tofu to the pan with the chilli bean paste, sugar and soy sauce. Fry for a further 1–2 minutes and serve hot.

Kwoklyn's tip
If you are able to buy pre-fried tofu, then you can use this instead of firm tofu to make this recipe even speedier.

SICHUAN-STYLE AUBERGINE AND TOFU

Crispy coated bites of tender aubergine and springy tofu in a spicy, slightly malty flavoured sauce. A perfect vegan topping to ladle over steamed rice or toss through wide rice stick noodles.

10 MINUTES   **25 MINUTES**   **SERVES 2-4**

500ml (2 cups) vegetable oil, plus 1 tbsp

450g (1lb) aubergines (eggplants), cut into 2–3cm (¾–1¼in) cubes

250g (9oz) firm tofu, cut into 2cm (¾in) cubes

4 tbsp cornflour (cornstarch)

2 garlic cloves, minced

1 tbsp ginger, minced

1 chilli, finely chopped

3 spring onions (scallions), cut into 3cm (1¼in) lengths and green and white parts separated

1 tsp sugar

1 tsp dark soy sauce

2½ tbsp Mushroom Stir-fry Sauce (page 343) or oyster sauce

1 tsp Chinese black vinegar

175ml (¾ cup) vegetable stock (you might need a little more if the sauce is too thick)

Place the oil in a saucepan or wok and heat to around 180°C (350°F).

Coat the aubergine (eggplant) and tofu in the cornflour (cornstarch), bang off any excess and fry them separately in batches until golden brown. Transfer to a wire rack or plate lined with kitchen paper to drain.

In a clean wok, add the 1 tablespoon of oil and fry the garlic, ginger, chilli and the spring onion (scallion) whites for 20 seconds until fragrant. Then add the cooked aubergine, the spring onion greens, sugar, dark soy sauce, Mushroom Stir-fry Sauce, black vinegar and stock. Bring to the boil and add the cooked tofu. The sauce should thicken from the cornflour on the aubergine and tofu, but if the sauce is too thin to begin with, continue to reduce slightly until it thickens; if the sauce is too thick, add a little more stock. Once you have reached your desired consistency, remove from the heat and serve.

CHINESE PICKLED VEGETABLES

This is a great side to rich or spicy dishes as it acts as a palate cleanser as you eat. It is especially good with Chinese-style curries or on top of a tofu burger – not only does it introduce a sour–sweet note, but the vegetables are still crunchy, adding another texture dimension to each bite.

10 MINUTES   **5 MINUTES**   **SERVES 3-4**   **2 HOURS +**

250ml (1 cup) rice vinegar
65g (⅓ cup) granulated sugar
1½ tsp salt
¼ white cabbage, shredded
¼ red cabbage, shredded
2 carrots, cut into thin matchsticks
½ cucumber, deseeded and cut into batons

Put the rice vinegar, sugar and salt into a saucepan over a medium-low heat to gently dissolve the sugar and salt. Once dissolved, remove from the heat.

Put the vegetables into a large sterilised glass container and pour over the vinegar liquid, ensuring that all the vegetables are submerged. Cover and place in the fridge, removing after 1 hour to give the vegetables a good mix. Re-cover and return to the fridge. The vegetables will be ready to eat after 2 hours but they will be better if left overnight. Eat within 1 week.

RICE & NOODLES

PERFECT STEAMED RICE

This method is a foolproof way to cook perfect steamed rice EVERY time and there is no fluffier grain, in my humble opinion, than the long-grain Thai fragrant rice. The smell that fills the kitchen as this rice steams is quite simply heavenly.

5 MINUTES   **25 MINUTES**   **SERVES 4**

360g (2 cups) long-grain rice

Tip the rice into a medium saucepan and fill the pan with warm water. Wash the rice with your hands, rubbing the grains together, then carefully drain the water. Repeat with warm water at least three times, as this process removes some of the starch.

Cover the washed rice with water so there is 2.5cm (1in) water above the rice. Turn the heat on to full and bring to the boil – it is important that you DO NOT stir. You must pay FULL ATTENTION to the pan now as the water boils. Once the water has been absorbed and tiny craters appear in the rice (10–15 minutes), turn the heat down to its lowest setting and place the lid firmly on the saucepan, sealing in the steam.

Leave for 3 minutes and then switch off the heat – it is very important that you DO NOT remove the lid (no peeking!). Leave to steam in the residual heat for a further 10 minutes.

Remove the lid and stir the rice with a spoon to loosen the grains. You'll have perfect fluffy rice ready to serve immediately.

Kwoklyn's tip
Where possible, boil your rice the day before you want to use it in a fried rice recipe. (See opposite and page 278.) Let the rice cool fully, cover and pop in the fridge as soon as possible. Cooked rice will keep refrigerated in an airtight container for up to 3 days and you can then fry it cold straight from the fridge.

EGG FRIED RICE

Rice is the staple food of more than half of the world's population – incredibly, more than 3.5 billion people depend on rice for more than 20% of their daily calories. The Chinese have never liked to waste food, so they came up with this ingenious way to use up any leftover rice from previous meals. It has become more popular, especially in the Western world, than its older sibling, steamed rice.

10 MINUTES   **10 MINUTES**   **SERVES 2**

1 tbsp groundnut oil
550g (1lb 4oz) cold steamed rice
  (see opposite)
pinch of salt
1 tbsp light soy sauce
2 tbsp oyster sauce
1 egg, beaten
1 tsp sesame oil

Suggested additions:
prawns (shrimp) and king prawns
  (jumbo shrimp)
shredded chicken
chopped onion
chopped (bell) peppers
pineapple chunks
peas
sweetcorn and baby corn
bamboo shoots
water chestnuts

Heat the groundnut oil in a non-stick wok until hot, then add the rice and cook for 2 minutes. Remember, this is fried rice, so your wok needs to be hot, hot, hot and you should be able to hear the rice sizzling as you cook.

Add the salt, soy sauce and oyster sauce and keep stir-frying until the rice is completely heated through. Check the seasoning and add a little more salt if required. Create a well in the centre of the rice and pour in the beaten egg. Cook until the egg is set and then mix it through the rice. Turn off the heat, drizzle over the sesame oil and serve hot.

This recipe can easily be upgraded to **Wok 'U' Like Fried Rice** by the simple addition of as many or as few ingredients as you prefer; simply add any raw vegetables and meat to the heated groundnut oil, stir-frying until the veg has softened or the meat is sealed and cooked through before continuing with the seasoning as above.

The beauty of this fried rice is that you can add whatever you have available and customise it to your taste. As well as using boiled, steamed rice, you can also use the microwaveable rice found in many supermarkets, but make sure you use ready-cooked rice that you can cook straight from the packet.

GOLDEN FRIED RICE

The golden egg yolks coating the grains of rice give this dish its name and luxurious colour as well as a distinctly rich, eggy aroma, while the extra pinch of salt for seasoning at the end really brings out the flavour.

5 MINUTES **8 MINUTES** **SERVES 2**

250g (2 cups) cooled Perfect Steamed Rice (page 274 or you can use pre-cooked packet rice for ease)
4 egg yolks
¼ tsp ground turmeric
1 tsp Chinese rice wine (Shaoxing wine)
pinch of salt, to taste
pinch of white pepper, to taste
2 tbsp vegetable oil
2 spring onions (scallions), finely chopped
drizzle of sesame oil

In a large bowl, combine the rice, egg yolks, turmeric, rice wine, salt and white pepper. Ensure all of the ingredients are well mixed and the rice has been broken down into individual grains.

Place a wok over a medium-high heat and, once smoking, add the oil followed by the rice mixture. Stir-fry for 2–3 minutes and then add the chopped spring onions (scallions). Continue to fry for another minute and then check the seasoning, adding a little more salt and pepper if required. Switch off the heat and drizzle with sesame oil. Transfer to a serving plate and enjoy.

Kwoklyn's tip
Make sure your wok is smoking before adding the oil and don't overload the pan with rice, as you need to keep the temperature high so that the rice can fry and not sweat. Listen for the popping sound of the rice cooking; if it isn't popping, it isn't frying!

EIGHT TREASURE FRIED RICE

Since the Western Zhou dynasty in ancient China, around 2,000 years ago, eight treasure fried rice has been traditionally served during Chinese New Year. 'Why eight?' I hear you ask? Well, in China the word for eight is *ba* which sounds like *fa*, which means fortune.

---

5 MINUTES   **10 MINUTES**   **SERVES 4**

1½ tbsp oil (vegetable, groundnut or coconut)

1 small onion, diced

1 small carrot, diced

30g (¼ cup) canned bamboo shoots, drained and sliced

35g (¼ cup) canned straw mushrooms, drained

½ red (bell) pepper, deseeded and diced

¼ cup canned sweetcorn

30g (¼ cup) peas

3 spring onions (scallions), sliced, plus extra to serve

250g (9oz) cooked steamed rice, cold (page 274 or use pre-cooked packets of rice)

1 tbsp light soy sauce

½ tbsp dark soy sauce

2 tbsp Mushroom Stir-fry Sauce (page 343 or use shop-bought)

salt, to taste

1 tsp sesame oil

Pour the oil into a wok and place over a medium-high heat, then add the onion and carrot and stir-fry for 1 minute. Add the remaining vegetables and cook for a further 1–2 minutes, or until any liquid has been evaporated.

Add the rice and cook for 2–3 minutes – remember, this is fried rice so your wok needs to be hot, hot, hot and you should be able to hear the ingredients sizzling as you cook. Add the light and dark soy sauces, Mushroom Stir-fry Sauce and salt to taste. Continue frying until the rice is completely heated through and is piping hot. Remove from the heat, stir in the sesame oil, sprinkle with extra spring onions (scallions), serve and enjoy.

CURRY SEAFOOD FRIED RICE

Rustling up a bowl of something fast doesn't mean we have to skimp on flavour or quality! Perfectly seasoned rice with a generous helping of your favourite seafood titbits makes this the perfect bowl of 'grab and go'!

2 MINUTES   **8 MINUTES**   **SERVES 2**

2 tbsp vegetable oil

2 eggs, beaten

250g (2 cups) cooled Perfect Steamed Rice (page 274 or you can use pre-cooked packet rice for ease)

250g (2 cups) cooked mixed seafood of your choice, such as prawns (shrimp), squid, mussels, fish and/or fish sticks

1 tbsp curry powder

½ tsp ground turmeric

1 tsp chilli powder

½ tsp paprika

pinch of salt, to taste

pinch of white pepper, to taste

2 spring onions (scallions), finely chopped

60g (½ cup) peas

drizzle of sesame oil

Place a wok over a medium-high heat and, once smoking, add the oil and beaten eggs and allow them to lightly set. Once the eggs have cooked, add the rice, stir quickly and leave to fry for 1–2 minutes. Next, add the cooked seafood along with the curry powder, turmeric, chilli powder, paprika, salt and pepper and continue to cook for a further 2–3 minutes.

Add the chopped spring onions (scallions) and peas, continue to fry for another minute and then check the seasoning, adding a little more salt and pepper if required. Switch off the heat and drizzle with sesame oil before transferring to a serving plate.

JASMINE RICE

These long-grain rice kernels have a fragrance reminiscent of jasmine and popcorn. Jasmine rice is slightly sweeter in taste than traditional long-grain rice, and stickier, so the grains will cling together.

5 MINUTES   25 MINUTES   SERVES 4

360g (2 cups) jasmine rice
1 tsp salt

Put the rice into a medium saucepan and fill with warm water. Rubbing your hands together, wash the rice in the pan, then carefully drain away the water. Repeat this process at least three times, as this helps to remove some of the starch. Cover the washed rice with cold water so the water level sits 2.5cm (1in) above the rice, then add the salt. Place over a high heat and bring to the boil – it is important you **do not** stir and you must give your full attention to the pan. As soon as the water has been absorbed and tiny craters appear in the rice (10–15 minutes), turn the heat down to its lowest setting and place the lid firmly on to the saucepan (sealing in the steam). Leave for 2 minutes and then switch off the heat – don't be tempted to remove the lid (no peeking) as you want to keep the steam in the pan. Leave to steam in the residual heat for a further 10 minutes.

Remove the lid and stir the rice with a spoon to loosen the grains. Serve your perfect fluffy jasmine rice immediately.

COCONUT RICE

This creamy, sticky rice can be served as a dish all on its own; it's packed full of flavour with Cantonese aromatics and the rich creamy taste of coconut. It's also a fantastic side dish to any sweet recipe, as the creamy flavour cuts through the sweetness, balancing the entire meal.

5 MINUTES   **25 MINUTES**   **SERVES 4**

360g (2 cups) long-grain rice
½ tbsp oil (vegetable, groundnut or coconut)
1 small onion, finely diced
1 garlic clove, finely chopped
500ml (2 cups) coconut milk
500ml (2 cups) vegetable stock (this may vary depending on the size of your saucepan)

Wash the rice under warm water to remove the excess starch, then drain and set to one side.

Heat the oil in a medium saucepan and fry the onion and garlic for 2 minutes. Turn the heat down to low and add the washed rice, stirring until it is all mixed through. Add the coconut milk and enough of the vegetable stock so that the top of the liquid sits 2.5cm (1in) above the top of the rice. Increase the heat to high and bring to the boil – it is important you do not stir. As soon as the liquid has been absorbed and tiny craters appear in the rice (10–15 minutes), turn the heat down to its lowest setting and place the lid firmly on to the saucepan (sealing in the steam). Leave for 2 minutes and then switch off the heat – don't be tempted to remove the lid, not even for a sneaky peek. Leave to steam in the residual heat for a further 10 minutes.

Serve alone or accompanied – let your taste buds decide.

YEUNG CHOW (YANGZHOU) SPECIAL FRIED RICE

The earliest recorded history of fried rice dates back to around 13,500 years ago (wow!).

This particular dish was invented during the Qing Dynasty and named after the city of its creation, Yangzhou. There are two methods for cooking the egg, as 'silver covered gold' where the egg is scrambled before mixing into the rice or as 'gold covered silver' where the egg is poured into the pan and stirred into the rice during cooking, thereby coating the rice and other ingredients. I always go with the 'gold covered silver' method for my rice!

10 MINUTES   **10 MINUTES**   **SERVES 2**

1 tbsp groundnut oil
40g (1½oz) char siu pork (see page 193), cut into small cubes
35g (1¼oz) cooked prawns (shrimp)
550g (1lb 4oz) cold steamed rice (see page 274)
2 tbsp oyster sauce
1 tbsp light soy sauce
30g (¼ cup) peas
pinch of salt, to taste
1 egg, beaten
1 tsp sesame oil

Heat the groundnut oil in a non-stick wok, add the pork and cook for 1 minute, then add the prawns (shrimp) and the rice. Cook for 2 minutes – remember this is fried rice so your wok needs to be hot, hot, hot and you should be able to hear the ingredients sizzling as you cook.

Add the oyster sauce, soy sauce and the peas. Keep stir-frying until the rice is completely heated through. Check the seasoning and add a small pinch of salt if required.

Create a well in the centre of the rice and pour in the egg, cook until it is set, then mix it through the rice. Turn off the heat, drizzle over the sesame oil and serve hot.

LAP CHEUNG STICKY RICE

A classic dim sum dish often served wrapped and steamed in lotus leaves (*lo mai gai*), this sticky rice with sweet cured Chinese sausage, soft shiitake mushrooms and crunchy peanuts can be used as a stuffing or simply served as a glorious bowl of sumptuous stickiness.

10 MINUTES   **30 MINUTES**   **SERVES 2-4**

6 dried scallops (optional)
300g (10½oz) glutinous rice
2 tbsp vegetable oil
3 fresh shiitake (poku) mushrooms, destalked and thinly sliced
1 small onion, finely diced
3 Chinese sausage, cut into 5mm (¼in) dice
1 tsp chicken powder
2 tbsp light soy sauce
1 tsp dark soy sauce
1 tbsp Chinese rice wine (Shaoxing wine)
30g (¼ cup) peas
80g (½ cup) roasted unsalted peanuts
2 tsp sesame oil

Begin by breaking up the dried scallops and rinsing in cold water, then drain and place to one side. Now wash the glutinous rice three times in lukewarm water, drain through a sieve and leave to one side.

Place a wok over a medium-high heat and, once smoking, add the oil, followed by the sliced mushrooms and diced onion. Fry for 1–2 minutes, then add the Chinese sausage and scallops, stir and turn the heat down to medium-low. Add the chicken powder, 1 tablespoon of the light soy sauce, the dark soy sauce and rice wine. Stir again to combine the ingredients and remove from the heat.

Place the rice in a rice cooker or a saucepan with a lid and add enough water so that it sits 2.5cm (1in) above the top of the rice. Switch the rice cooker on to cook and place the lid firmly on top. Once all of the water has been absorbed, add the Chinese sausage filling and replace the lid, leaving the rice cooker switched on to complete its cooking cycle.

(If you are boiling the rice in a saucepan on the hob, turn the heat up to full without the lid on and, once the water has been absorbed, switch off the heat, add the Chinese sausage filling and then place the lid on the rice.)

Allow the rice to steam in the residual heat for 15 minutes. Once the rice has cooked, add the peas, peanuts, sesame oil and remaining 1 tablespoon of light soy sauce. Give everything a good mix and then place the lid back on your rice for a further 10 minutes. Best served hot.

SEASONED GLUTINOUS RICE

Despite its name this rice dish doesn't actually contain any gluten at all and refers only to its texture; in Hong Kong and China it is referred to as sticky rice and made with grains that are very short and almost round. Seasoned or steamed, little can compare to the flavour; it's aromatic yet a little pungent and really does taste outstanding.

2 HOURS 5 MINS   **30 MINUTES**   **SERVES 4**

450g (2½ cups) glutinous rice
2 tbsp light soy sauce
⅛ tsp white pepper
½ tsp Chinese five spice
250ml (1 cup) water
½ tbsp oil (vegetable, groundnut or coconut)
½ tbsp sesame oil

Place the rice in a large bowl and wash under cold water, then rinse. Repeat this at least three times to remove some of the starch. Cover with cold water and allow to soak for 2 hours.

Drain the soaked rice, then add all the remaining ingredients and mix well. Transfer the rice to a heatproof bowl, place into a steamer and steam for 30 minutes.

Serve piping hot.

CHINESE BAKED RICE

This dish is very popular in Hong Kong cafés; a bed of fried rice is topped with crispy-coated marinated mushrooms, then smothered in a rich aromatic tomato sauce and finally layered with oozing melted mozzarella. Asian-Italian fusion at its simplest.

35 MINUTES   **40 MINUTES**   **SERVES 4**

For the fried rice

1½ tbsp oil (vegetable, groundnut or coconut)

250g (9oz) cooked steamed rice, cold (page 274 or use pre-cooked packets of rice)

1 tbsp light soy sauce

½ tbsp dark soy sauce

2 tbsp Mushroom Stir-fry Sauce (page 343 or use shop-bought)

½ tsp salt

1 tsp sesame oil

For the topping

1 tbsp Chinese rice wine (Shaoxing wine)

2 tbsp light soy sauce

½ tsp salt

½ tsp sugar

¼ tsp white pepper

3 large portobello mushrooms

4 tbsp plain (all-purpose) flour

4 tbsp oil (vegetable, groundnut or coconut)

2 garlic cloves, finely chopped

1 onion, sliced

1 x 400g (14oz) can of chopped tomatoes

4 tbsp tomato ketchup

65g (½ cup) grated mozzarella (omit if vegan)

First make the fried rice. Heat the oil in a wok over a medium-high heat, add the rice and cook for 2–3 minutes (remember this is fried rice so your wok needs to be hot enough that you can hear the ingredients sizzling as you cook). Add the light and dark soy sauces, Mushroom Stir-fry Sauce and salt and continue frying until the rice is completely heated through and piping hot. Remove from the heat, stir in the sesame oil, remove from the wok and set to one side to cool.

Combine the rice wine, soy sauce, salt, sugar and white pepper in a large bowl and mix well. Marinate the mushrooms in the mixture for 30 minutes.

In a large bowl, coat the marinated mushrooms thoroughly in the flour, banging off any excess. Heat a large non-stick frying pan over a medium-high heat, add 3 tablespoons of the oil and fry the mushrooms on both sides for 3–4 minutes until crispy and golden brown. Remove from the pan and drain on kitchen paper.

Preheat the oven to 200°C (400°F).

Place the wok back over a medium-high heat and add the remaining oil, the garlic and onion and fry for 3–4 minutes, or until caramelised. Add the canned tomatoes and ketchup, bring to the boil and then turn down to a simmer, covering loosely and cooking for 5–10 minutes, or until the sauce has reduced by half.

In a baking tray or ovenproof dish, spread out the fried rice evenly and place the fried mushrooms on top. Pour over the sauce, ensuring all of the mushrooms and rice are covered. Lastly sprinkle with mozzarella (if using) and bake in the oven for 15 minutes, or until piping hot and bubbling. Serve immediately.

STICKY RICE PARCELS

Glutinous rice, wrapped in a lotus leaf and bursting with marinated trinkets of yumminess. In the days when weary travellers made the journey along the Old Silk Road, small resting houses, or tea houses, were established, offering refreshments and sustenance. In Chinese they were referred to as yum cha houses, translated as 'the act of drinking tea'.

2½ HOURS   **1½ HOURS**   **SERVES 2-4**

360g (2 cups) glutinous rice
2–3 dried lotus leaves
3 tsp vegetable oil
1 shallot, finely diced
3 spring onions (scallions), thinly sliced
2 garlic cloves, finely chopped
1 tbsp Chinese rice wine (Shaoxing wine)
½ tbsp sesame oil
½ tbsp Mushroom Stir-fry Sauce (page 343 or use shop-bought)
2 tsp dark soy sauce, plus extra to serve

For the marinated mushrooms
35g (2 cups) dried Chinese mushrooms
½ tsp cornflour (cornstarch)
1 tsp vegetable oil
1 tsp oyster sauce
½ tsp Chinese rice wine (Shaoxing wine)
1 tsp dark soy sauce
¼ tsp sugar
¼ tsp ground white pepper
½ tsp salt

Place the sticky rice in a large bowl and cover completely with water. Let stand at room temperature for at least 2 hours or overnight.

Rinse the dried mushrooms under warm water and put into a large bowl. Cover with boiling water and soak for 15 minutes until soft, then gently squeeze the excess water out of the mushrooms. Remove and discard the stalks and cut the mushrooms into 6 slices. Mix the sliced mushrooms with the remaining marinade ingredients until thoroughly combined and let stand in the fridge for at least 2 hours.

Cut each lotus leaf in half down the middle. Place the leaves in a large bowl or container and cover with water, weighing the leaves down with a plate if necessary to keep them submerged. Leave to soak for 1 hour.

Drain the sticky rice well and transfer to a large bowl.

Heat 2 teaspoons of the oil in a wok over a high heat until shimmering. Add the shallot, spring onions (scallions) and garlic and cook for about 2 minutes until softened. Add the mixture into the bowl of soaked sticky rice along with the rice wine, sesame oil, Mushroom Stir-fry Sauce and dark soy sauce and combine well. In the same wok, heat the remaining teaspoon of oil over a high heat until shimmering. Add the marinated mushrooms and stir-fry for 2 minutes. Transfer to a plate.

Drain the lotus leaves, pat them dry with kitchen paper and spread out on a worktop. Place 2–3 tablespoons of sticky rice mixture into the centre of each lotus leaf, then add 1–2 tablespoons of mushroom mixture followed by another 2–3 tablespoons of sticky rice mixture.

Wrap each parcel by folding the end closest to you over the rice and then folding the left and right edges over the top, then rolling the rest of the leaf to form a tight package. Using kitchen string, tie up each package, making sure that all the leaves are securely wrapped.

Place the rice parcels into a steamer for 1½ hours; keep an eye on the water level, topping up with more boiling water if needed to prevent the steamer from boiling dry.

Remove from the steamer and allow to rest for a few minutes before serving in the leaf with a drizzle of soy sauce.

HONG KONG-STYLE NOODLE SOUP WITH TOFU AND CHINESE VEGETABLES

The cooked egg noodles should still be springy and chewy so don't be scared to slightly undercook them; once you add them to the hot soup they'll continue to cook a little longer. I like to eat my noodles with a dash of chilli sauce or chilli oil to ramp up the flavour. This is a very traditional and widely eaten dish across China, Hong Kong and the world.

5 MINUTES   **10 MINUTES**   **SERVES 2**

1 litre (4 cups) vegetable stock
¼ tsp white pepper
thumb-sized piece of ginger, sliced
½ tbsp light soy sauce
1 nest of fresh egg noodles (vegan option: use dried rice noodles/vermicelli)
200g (7oz) firm tofu, cut into bite-sized pieces
2 handfuls of your chosen Chinese vegetable (choy sum, bok choy, gai lan/Chinese broccoli or Chinese leaf/Napa cabbage), cut into bite-sized pieces
1 tsp sesame oil
1 spring onion (scallion), thinly sliced
salt, to taste

Put the stock, white pepper, ginger and soy sauce into a saucepan, place over a medium heat and bring to a gentle simmer. Taste for seasoning.

Bring another saucepan of water to the boil, add the noodles and cook for 1 minute until tender but still springy (cook rice noodles for a little longer). Drain and place into 2 serving bowls.

Add the tofu and vegetables to your soup and return to the boil. Once boiling, remove the soup from the heat and gently pour over the noodles. Add a splash of sesame oil and a sprinkle of sliced spring onion (scallion) and eat it while it's hot.

CHILLI TOFU RAMEN

For those of you who have a sweet tooth but enjoy a hint of heat, this dish is definitely one for you. Soft curly noodles, sitting in a fiery, aromatic broth, topped with crispy, chewy tofu and lavishly smothered in a sweet chilli sauce.

10 MINUTES   10 MINUTES   SERVES 2

½ tsp oil (vegetable, groundnut or coconut)

2 garlic cloves, crushed

2 slices of ginger

750ml (3 cups) vegetable stock

3 tbsp light soy sauce

¼ tsp chilli powder

2 nests of dried ramen noodles

2 tbsp sesame seeds, toasted

2 spring onions (scallions), finely chopped

For the tofu

280g (9oz) firm tofu, cut into bite-sized pieces

2 tbsp cornflour (cornstarch)

1½ tbsp oil (vegetable or groundnut)

2 garlic cloves, finely chopped

6 tbsp sweet chilli sauce

To prepare the tofu, dry the cubes on kitchen paper, then put into a bowl and coat with the cornflour (cornstarch). Heat a non-stick frying pan over a medium-high heat, add the oil and fry the tofu until golden brown. Add the garlic and fry for 30 seconds until fragrant, then stir in the sweet chilli sauce. Once all the ingredients are combined, remove from the heat.

Heat the ½ teaspoon of oil in a large saucepan over a medium-high heat, add the garlic and ginger and fry for 30 seconds. Add the stock, soy sauce and chilli powder. Bring to the boil, then turn down to a simmer while you cook the noodles.

Cook the ramen noodles in a saucepan of boiling water for 3 minutes until tender; drain and transfer to serving bowls. Pour the soup over your noodles, arrange the chilli tofu pieces on top and finally sprinkle with the sesame seeds and spring onions (scallions).

PLAIN CHOW MEIN

Hand-pulled fresh egg noodles are made by mixing beaten eggs with flour and, instead of kneading the dough, a noodle master compresses the dough under a bamboo pole, which makes the noodles denser and more springy. Their dried counterparts, however, are prepared by laying out in sheet form and then cutting to the desired shape. Dried noodles hold their shape longer than fresh noodles, making them ideal for chow mein dishes as they can withstand more wok tossing.

5 MINUTES   **10 MINUTES**   **SERVES 2**

2 nests of dried egg noodles
1½ tbsp groundnut oil
1 small onion, thinly sliced
handful of beansprouts
pinch of white pepper
pinch of salt
pinch of sugar
2 spring onions (scallions), halved then
   sliced lengthways
2 tbsp dark soy sauce
1 tsp sesame oil

Cook the dried egg noodles in a pan of boiling water for around 3 minutes or until soft, drain and allow to cool.

Heat the groundnut oil in a non-stick wok over a medium-high heat and fry the onion for 2 minutes until soft. Add the beansprouts, white pepper, salt and sugar, and stir for a further minute or two. Add the drained noodles and half of the spring onions (scallions) and stir thoroughly, turning the heat to high. Stir-fry for 2 minutes, ensuring you keep the ingredients moving, then add the soy sauce and mix well. Remove from the heat, add the sesame oil, garnish with the remaining spring onions and serve straightaway.

SINGAPORE CHOW MEIN

This dish still makes me chuckle when I think about making it. On a busy night there would be three of us cooking in the kitchen, all standing in a row in front of the Chinese range, which basically was five flame-throwing holes with woks sitting on the top. Because of the sheer heat these cookers would produce, as soon as we added the dried chillies and the curry powder, the air would instantly fill with hot spices, making it virtually impossible to breathe. All three of us would be coughing, sneezing and choking on the fumes. Good times!

---

10 MINUTES   **10 MINUTES**   **SERVES 4**

2 nests of dried egg noodles
2 tbsp groundnut oil
1 tbsp finely grated ginger
1 red chilli, deseeded and finely chopped
2 tbsp medium curry powder (see page 317 for home-made)
1 red (bell) pepper, deseeded and sliced
1 carrot, halved then cut into matchsticks
handful of beansprouts
100g (3½oz) cooked chicken breast, shredded
30g (1oz) Chinese Roast BBQ Pork (see page 193)
100g (3½oz) cooked prawns (shrimp)
1 tsp chilli flakes
2 tbsp light soy sauce
2 tbsp oyster sauce
1 tbsp rice vinegar
½ tsp sesame oil
2 spring onions (scallions), thinly sliced lengthways

Cook the dried egg noodles in a pan of boiling water for around 3 minutes or until soft, drain and allow to cool.

Heat the oil in a wok and stir-fry the ginger, chilli and curry powder for a few seconds. Add the pepper, carrot and beansprouts and cook for another minute, then add the cooked chicken, pork and prawns (shrimp) and stir well to combine.

Add the drained noodles and stir-fry, mixing the ingredients thoroughly. After 2 minutes, season with the chilli flakes, soy sauce, oyster sauce and vinegar and stir to combine.

Remove from the heat, drizzle in the sesame oil and mix together. Transfer to a serving plate, sprinkle over the sliced spring onions (scallions), and serve immediately.

DICED HOISIN CHICKEN HO FUN

This dish will certainly put your chopstick skills to the test as you wrestle the slippery, wide, flat noodles to your mouth, so take the advice of a seasoned pro when I tell you that the ONLY way to eat ho fun is 'bowl up, head down and slurp...' Added to which, the delectable aromats in the sauce will be all that much closer to inhale!

10 MINUTES   **10 MINUTES**   **SERVES 4**

240g (8¾oz) dried wide flat rice noodles
60ml (¼ cup) chicken stock
3 tbsp hoisin sauce (page 342 or use shop-bought)
¼ tsp Chinese five spice
1 tsp sugar
1 tbsp Chinese rice wine (Shaoxing wine)
3 tbsp vegetable oil
200g (7oz) chicken breast, cut into small dice
1 garlic clove, roughly chopped
3 spring onions (scallions), cut into 5cm (2in) lengths
1 onion, cut into thin slices
1 carrot, cleaned or peeled and cut into thin matchsticks
drizzle of sesame oil

Place the rice noodles into a saucepan of boiling water and cook for 2–3 minutes. Once softened, strain through a sieve and set aside to cool.

In a bowl, combine the chicken stock, hoisin sauce, five spice, sugar and rice wine, mix well and set to one side.

Place a wok over a medium-high heat and, once smoking, add the oil along with the diced chicken, garlic and half the spring onions (scallions). Stir-fry for 2 minutes, then add the sliced onion and continue cooking for another minute. Now add the drained rice noodles, which should still be a little warm. Stir to combine the ingredients, pour over the sauce mix and toss in the carrot. Give it all another stir and continue to cook for a further minute, then turn off the heat and add the remaining spring onions followed by a drizzle of sesame oil. Mix well and serve.

HONG KONG CRISPY NOODLES WITH MIXED VEGETABLES

I order this dish every time we eat at a Chinese restaurant; the crispy noodles soften under the rich aromatic gravy flecked with garlic. The vegetables are crunchy, as they have been cooked quickly to retain their bright vibrant colours. The combination of textures from crispy noodles to crunchy vegetables is simply sensational.

10 MINUTES　　**10 MINUTES**　　**SERVES 2**

1 nest of dried fine egg noodles (vegan option: use dried rice noodles/ vermicelli)
250ml (1 cup) oil (vegetable, groundnut or coconut), for shallow-frying, plus 1 tbsp
2 slices of ginger
1 garlic clove, finely chopped
1 onion, sliced
1 carrot, sliced
30g (¼ cup) canned bamboo shoots, drained and sliced
3 baby corn cobs, halved lengthways
25g (¼ cup) mangetout (snowpeas)
35g (¼ cup) canned straw mushrooms, drained and halved
handful of beansprouts
2 spring onions (scallions), halved and then sliced lengthways
1 tbsp dark soy sauce
1 tbsp light soy sauce
½ tsp white pepper
½ tsp salt
½ tsp sugar
2 tbsp Mushroom Stir-fry Sauce (page 343 or use shop-bought)
75ml (⅓ cup) vegetable stock
1 tbsp cornflour (cornstarch) mixed with 2 tbsp water
2 tsp sesame oil

Put the egg noodles into a bowl, cover with boiling water and leave for 2 minutes, or until soft, then drain and allow to cool.

Pour the oil for shallow-frying into a wok and place over a medium–high heat; once the oil begins to shimmer, carefully lower the drained noodles into the oil so they cover the entire bottom of the wok. Once golden brown and crispy, flip them over to brown the other side. Transfer to a wire rack or kitchen paper to drain.

Heat the tablespoon of oil in a wok and add the ginger and garlic, frying until fragrant. Add the onion and cook until translucent, followed by the carrot, bamboo shoots, baby corn, mangetout (snowpeas) and straw mushrooms. Fry for 1 minute, then add the beansprouts and spring onions (scallions) and mix well. Add the dark and light soy sauces, white pepper, salt, sugar, Mushroom Stir-fry Sauce and vegetable stock and bring to the boil. Slowly pour in the cornflour (cornstarch) mixture, stirring constantly until the sauce reaches your desired consistency. Remove from the heat and stir in the sesame oil.

Place the crispy noodles on to a large plate and, using a pair of scissors, cut the noodle nest into quarters. Pour the vegetables over the noodles and serve.

TOFU, PICKLED CABBAGE AND BLACK BEANS ON RICE NOODLES

This is traditional Cantonese cooking at its very best. It combines a rich garlic and black bean sauce with pickled cabbage and crispy tofu, sitting on top of firm rice noodles in an aromatic ginger-spiced soup, seasoned with nutty sesame oil.

10 MINUTES   **15 MINUTES**   **SERVES 2**

2 nests of dried rice noodles (vermicelli)
2 tbsp oil (vegetable, groundnut or coconut)
200g (7oz) firm tofu, cut into small bite-sized pieces
thumb-sized piece of ginger, peeled and sliced
4 garlic cloves, roughly chopped
3 tbsp fermented black beans
1 small can Chinese pickled vegetables, drained
1 tbsp dark soy sauce
1 tbsp light soy sauce
125ml (½ cup) vegetable stock
1 tbsp cornflour (cornstarch) mixed with 2 tbsp water
1 tsp sesame oil

For the soup
3cm (1¼in) piece of fresh ginger, sliced
1 tbsp light soy sauce
800ml (3¼ cups) vegetable stock
½ tsp white pepper
1 tsp salt

Soak the rice noodles in a large bowl of boiling water for 10 minutes, then drain and set to one side.

Heat 1 tablespoon of the oil in a wok and fry the tofu pieces over a medium heat until golden brown on all sides, then drain on kitchen paper and set to one side.

For the soup, put the ginger, soy sauce, vegetable stock, white pepper and salt into a large saucepan and bring to the boil, then turn down to a simmer.

Place your wok over a medium-high heat, add the remaining tablespoon of oil along with the ginger and garlic and fry for 30 seconds until fragrant. Add the black beans and fried tofu and fry for a minute before adding the pickled vegetables, dark and light soy sauces and vegetable stock. Bring to the boil, then turn down the heat and simmer for 3 minutes. Increase the heat to high and slowly add the cornflour (cornstarch) mixture, stirring constantly to thicken the sauce. Remove from the heat.

Place the cooked rice noodles into serving bowls and pour over the soup so that the noodles are completely covered. Spoon over the tofu and black bean topping and finally drizzle with the sesame oil.

CHILLI BEAN KING PRAWN NOODLES

Juicy king prawns are smothered in a classic Chinese fermented chilli bean paste and served with chewy noodles and crunchy beansprouts. From kitchen to bowl in less than 15 minutes! Give it a go – you won't be disappointed.

5 MINUTES   **9 MINUTES**   **SERVES 2**

1 bunch of spring onions (scallions)
2 nests of dried egg noodles
2 tbsp vegetable oil
340g (12oz) raw king prawns (jumbo shrimp), peeled and deveined
50g (1 cup) beansprouts
3 tbsp fermented chilli bean paste (doubanjiang)

Prepare the spring onions (scallions) by slicing the green ends into 5cm (2in) lengths and chopping the white parts into thin rings.

Soak the noodle nests in boiling water for 5 minutes until soft, then drain and set to one side.

Heat the oil in a large non-stick frying pan or wok, add the spring onion greens and half the whites and fry for about 30 seconds until fragrant. Add the prawns (shrimp) and fry until pink, then add the beansprouts and continue to fry for a further 2 minutes.

Add the chilli bean paste along with the drained noodles and stir to combine with the other ingredients. Continue to fry for a further 3 minutes.

Transfer to a warm serving plate and garnish with the remaining spring onion whites.

SWEET CHILLI SALMON WITH SOBA NOODLES

If you're looking for a dish that's simple to cook but delivers on taste and texture, looks stunning and will satisfy your hunger, then look no further. Here crispy, flaky salmon, juicy broccoli stems and chewy noodles are all richly drizzled in a sweet chilli sauce.

5 MINUTES   **25 MINUTES**   **SERVES 2**

2 portions of soba noodles
1 tbsp vegetable oil
2 salmon steaks
9 tbsp sweet chilli sauce
200g (7oz) tenderstem broccoli
2 tbsp rice vinegar
salt
white pepper

Bring a medium saucepan filled with water to the boil; once boiling, add the soba noodles and cook for 5 minutes, then drain and set to one side, reserving the cooking liquid.

Heat the oil in a non-stick frying pan over a medium heat. Place the salmon steaks into the pan skin-side down, season with a pinch of salt and white pepper and fry for 5 minutes. Turn the salmon steaks over, season again with salt and pepper and fry the other side for 5 minutes. Turn the salmon steaks one last time and drizzle each with 2 tablespoons of the sweet chilli sauce, then fry for a further 2–3 minutes. Remove from the pan, loosely cover with foil and leave to rest.

Add 250ml (2 cups) of noodle water to the same frying pan and add the broccoli, allowing it to bubble in the noodle water for 2–3 minutes; add more water if needed. Add the remaining 5 tablespoons of sweet chilli sauce, along with the rice vinegar, and mix well. Then add the noodles and cook for 1 minute.

Remove the pan from the heat and use a pair of tongs or chopsticks to divide the noodles and broccoli between 2 serving plates and place a salmon fillet on to each pile of noodles. Drizzle with a little of the sauce and serve.

SRIRACHA LO MEIN

Lo mein is cooked ever so slightly differently to chow mein; chow mein is stir-fried until the noodles are crispy whereas lo mein is stir-fried with a sauce so that they remain soft. Sriracha is a delicious sauce originating from Thailand and works well with vegetables and noodles.

10 MINUTES   **8 MINUTES**   **SERVES 2**

3 tbsp Sriracha chilli sauce
2 tbsp light soy sauce
1 tsp sugar
2 nests of fresh lo mein egg noodles
2 tbsp vegetable oil
1 red (bell) pepper, deseeded and cut into strips
8 fresh baby corn, halved lengthways
175g (3½ cups) beansprouts
pinch of salt

Combine the Sriracha sauce, soy sauce and sugar in a bowl and set to one side.

Loosen the noodles in a bowl of warm water, then drain and set aside.

Place a wok over a medium-high heat, add the oil and fry the red pepper and baby corn for 1 minute. Add the beansprouts and fry for a further minute, then add the loosened noodles along with the sauce mix and continue to fry until all the ingredients are combined and warmed through. Taste for seasoning and add salt if required. Serve immediately.

UDON NOODLE CURRY SOUP

We all love a good curry, and this dish combines the authentic Chinese curry taste with a soup. Served on top of soft noodles, crunchy beansprouts and meaty mushrooms, it's sure to satisfy those curry cravings.

10 MINUTES   **20 MINUTES**   **SERVES 2**

2 tbsp oil (vegetable, groundnut or coconut)

1 medium white onion, sliced

1 medium carrot, cut into matchsticks

50g (½ cup) beansprouts

½ large portobello mushroom, cut into thin strips

750ml (3 cups) vegetable stock

250ml (1 cup) curry sauce (see below)

1 tbsp light soy sauce

¼ tsp salt (or to taste)

2 nests (170g/6oz) fresh udon noodles

2 spring onions (scallions), thinly sliced

For the curry sauce

1 tbsp oil (vegetable, groundnut or coconut)

2 onions, finely diced

5 garlic cloves, finely chopped

2 carrots, finely diced

1 celery stick, finely diced

2 tbsp plain (all-purpose) flour

1½ tbsp curry powder (use your favourite: mild, medium or hot)

600ml (2½ cups) vegetable stock

½ tbsp honey

1½ tbsp light soy sauce

1 bay leaf

1 tsp garam masala

For the curry sauce, heat the oil in a saucepan, then add the onions and garlic and cook until softened. Stir in the carrots and celery and cook over a low heat for 10–12 minutes. Add the flour and curry powder and cook for 1 minute. Gradually pour in the stock, stirring constantly until combined, then add the honey, soy sauce and bay leaf. Slowly bring to the boil. Simmer for 15 minutes, or until the sauce thickens but is still of pouring consistency. If your sauce is too thick, add a splash of water to loosen it. Stir in the garam masala, then strain the curry sauce through a sieve and set to one side. (Any leftover sauce can be frozen in a sealed container for up to 3 months or stored in a sealed container in the fridge for up to 1 week.)

Heat the oil in a saucepan over a medium-high heat, add the onion and carrot and fry until lightly browned. Add the beansprouts and mushroom and fry for another minute.

Add the stock, curry sauce and soy sauce and mix well until smoothly combined. Bring to the boil, then turn down the heat to a low simmer. Taste for seasoning and add salt if needed.

Bring a large saucepan of water to the boil, add the fresh noodles and cook for about 1½ minutes. Drain and place into serving bowls. Pour over your curry soup, garnish with the spring onions (scallions) and serve.

STIR-FRIED HO FUN

Noodles are an essential ingredient and a staple of the Chinese diet; widely produced across Hong Kong and China, they come in many forms. Ho fun is a type of noodle made with rice flour and is often served with vegetables in Cantonese restaurants. The noodles in this recipe are fried alongside a mix of crunchy and soft vegetables in a traditional Cantonese-style sauce.

10 MINUTES   **10 MINUTES**   **SERVES 2**

1 packet fresh ho fun (rice stick) noodles (360–450g/12–14oz depending on the brand available)
1 tbsp oil (vegetable, groundnut or coconut)
3 slices of ginger
2 garlic cloves, finely chopped
1 onion, sliced
1 carrot, sliced
5 baby corn cobs, halved lengthways
30g (¼ cup) bamboo shoots, drained
35g (¼ cup) canned straw mushrooms, drained
3 tbsp Mushroom Stir-fry Sauce (page 343 or use shop-bought)
1 tbsp light soy sauce
pinch of white pepper
1 tsp sugar
4 tbsp vegetable stock
1 bok choy, quartered
1 tsp sesame oil
salt, to taste

Place the ho fun noodles in a large bowl of warm water and carefully separate the noodles, then drain and set to one side.

Heat the oil in a wok over a medium-high heat. Add the ginger and garlic and after 30 seconds, add the onion and fry until translucent. Add the carrot, baby corn, bamboo shoots and straw mushrooms and fry for a further 2–3 minutes.

Add the drained noodles to the wok and mix well. After 2 minutes of cooking, add the Mushroom Stir-fry Sauce, soy sauce, pepper, sugar, vegetable stock and bok choy. Stir gently to combine and heat thoroughly; check the seasoning and add salt if required.

Remove from the heat, drizzle with the sesame oil and stir through before serving.

MUSHROOM TERIYAKI
WITH SOBA NOODLES

This dish is a perfect combination of meaty portobello mushrooms pan-seared with sweet chilli sauce. With its crispy crust, springy soba noodles, and sweet honey and sour vinegar teriyaki sauce, it is utterly irresistible.

5 MINUTES   **15 MINUTES**   **SERVES 2**

120g (4½oz) soba noodles
1 tbsp oil (vegetable, groundnut or coconut)
2 large portobello mushrooms, destalked and cleaned
2 tbsp sweet chilli sauce
3 tbsp honey (vegan option: use agave or maple syrup)
3 tbsp rice vinegar
1½ tbsp light soy sauce
handful of tenderstem broccoli
1 red chilli, finely diced
1 tbsp sesame seeds, toasted
salt, to taste

Put the noodles into a deep saucepan, pour over boiling water and allow to gently simmer over a low heat for about 5–6 minutes while you are cooking the mushrooms.

Heat the oil in a large wok, add the portobello mushrooms and cook over a medium-high heat for 4–5 minutes on one side until browned, then turn, sprinkle with salt and the sweet chilli sauce and cook for a further 4–5 minutes until browned on the other side. Remove from the pan and set to one side.

Add 125ml (½ cup) of the soba noodle cooking water to the same wok along with the honey, vinegar and soy sauce. Now add the broccoli along with half the chopped chilli. Cook over a medium-high heat for 6 minutes; if the sauce starts to look dry, add a little more noodle water.

Once the broccoli is tender, drain the noodles and add them to the wok, stirring through to ensure the noodles are well coated with the sauce. Sprinkle over the remaining chilli and transfer to serving plates. Slice the cooked mushrooms and arrange over the top of the noodles. Sprinkle with the toasted sesame seeds and enjoy.

CHICKEN CHOW MEIN

Chow mein appears on many Cantonese restaurant menus and is one of the top 10 most popular dishes ordered in the UK and the USA. Noodles were widely eaten along the old Silk Road, the trading route forged from China into and through Tibet, the Middle East and Europe. A popular and inexpensive dish served in China, pedlars would walk through the street serving them to passers-by.

10 MINUTES **10 MINUTES** **SERVES 2**

2 nests of dried egg noodles
1½ tbsp groundnut oil
200g (7oz) chicken breast fillet, thinly sliced
1 small onion, thinly sliced
handful of beansprouts
pinch of white pepper
pinch of salt
pinch of sugar
2 spring onions (scallions), halved then sliced lengthways
2 tbsp dark soy sauce
1 tsp sesame oil

Cook the dried egg noodles in a pan of boiling water for around 3 minutes or until soft, drain and allow to cool.

Heat ½ tablespoon of the groundnut oil in a non-stick wok and fry the chicken. Once thoroughly cooked, tip on to a plate lined with kitchen paper to drain.

Wipe the wok clean with kitchen paper, add the remaining oil and fry the onion for 2 minutes over a medium heat until soft. Add the chicken, beansprouts, white pepper, salt and sugar, and stir-fry for a further minute or two.

Add the drained noodles and half of the spring onions (scallions) and mix thoroughly, turning the heat to high. Stir-fry for 2 minutes, ensuring you keep the ingredients moving, then add the soy sauce and mix well. Remove from the heat, drizzle over the sesame oil and garnish with the remaining spring onions. Serve straightaway.

BARBECUE KING PRAWNS WITH UDON NOODLES

Udon noodles are quite different to the ones I grew up with in the restaurant; they're thicker and chewier, which creates a completely unique mouth-feel. Mixed with a classic Chinese BBQ sauce, crisp mangetout and juicy king prawns, this dish is simply delicious and will have you going back for seconds and maybe even thirds.

30 MINUTES   **10 MINUTES**   **SERVES 2**

16 large raw king prawns (jumbo shrimp), peeled
5 tbsp Chinese BBQ Sauce (page 344 or use shop-bought)
2 tbsp vegetable oil
175g (3½ cups) beansprouts
100g (3½oz) mangetout (snowpeas)
300g (10½oz) straight-to-wok udon noodles
2 tbsp light soy sauce
1 tsp sugar
4 tbsp water

Carefully cut a slit along the back of each prawn (shrimp) and remove the digestive tracts. Rinse under cold water, then pat dry with kitchen paper and add to a large bowl. Add 2 tablespoons of the Chinese BBQ Sauce and massage into the king prawns. Allow to marinate for 20 minutes.

Heat a non-stick griddle pan over a medium-high heat, add 1 tablespoon of the vegetable oil and cook the prawns for 2 minutes on each side; transfer to a warmed plate.

Place a wok over a medium-high heat and add the remaining vegetable oil along with the beansprouts and mangetout (snowpeas). Stir-fry for 1 minute, then add the noodles and continue to stir-fry for a further 3 minutes. Add the remaining BBQ sauce, the light soy sauce, sugar and water and mix well until piping hot. Serve in warmed bowls and enjoy.

SINGAPORE RICE NOODLES

Although technically not a Chinese or Cantonese recipe, this dish can be found on many menus across the world and fuels the nation's love of a 'Ruby Murray' (curry). Here, rice noodles are flavoured with spices, creating that perfect mouthful of hot and spicy.

10 MINUTES **10 MINUTES** **SERVES 4**

250g (9oz) dried rice noodles (vermicelli)

2 tbsp groundnut oil

1 tbsp finely grated ginger

1 red chilli, deseeded and finely chopped

2 tbsp medium curry powder (see below)

1 red (bell) pepper, deseeded and sliced

1 carrot, halved then cut into matchsticks

handful of beansprouts

100g (3½oz) cooked chicken breast, shredded

100g (3½oz) cooked prawns (shrimp)

1 tsp chilli flakes

2 tbsp light soy sauce

2 tbsp oyster sauce

1 tbsp rice vinegar

1 egg, beaten

½ tsp sesame oil

2 spring onions (scallions), thinly sliced lengthways

Make your own curry powder:

4½ tsp ground coriander

2 tsp ground turmeric

1½ tsp cumin seeds

½ tsp whole black peppercorns

½ tsp chilli flakes

½ tsp cardamom seeds

1cm (½in) cinnamon stick

¼ tsp cloves

¼ tsp ground ginger

Pour boiling water over the rice noodles in a large bowl, leave for 10 minutes, then drain and allow to cool.

Heat the oil in a wok, add the ginger, chilli and curry powder and stir-fry for a few seconds. Add the pepper, carrot and beansprouts and cook for another minute, then add the cooked chicken and prawns (shrimp) and stir well to combine.

Add the noodles and stir-fry for 2 minutes, mixing everything thoroughly. Season with the chilli flakes, soy sauce, oyster sauce and vinegar and stir to combine.

Create a well in the centre of your wok by pushing the noodles up the sides, then add the beaten egg, stirring gently until the egg is cooked through. Combine with the rest of the ingredients in the pan. Remove from the heat, drizzle in the sesame oil and mix together.

Transfer to a serving plate, sprinkle over the spring onions (scallions), and serve immediately.

Make your own curry powder:
Grind all the ingredients in a blender or pestle and mortar until you have a fine powder. This quantity will make at least 3 tablespoons of curry powder (more than enough for the above noodle recipe) but can easily be multiplied to make a larger batch and stored in an airtight jar for use within a month.

BRAISED BELLY PORK ON YELLOW BEAN NOODLES

Braising is a very popular cooking technique of in China. The slow cooking process makes the meat tender and any fat literally melts in the mouth. As the meat gently cooks away in the pot, it takes on all of those lovely flavours you've added. Served on top of sweet aromatic noodles, this dish ticks all the boxes.

5 MINUTES   **1 HOUR 5 MINS**   **SERVES 2**

2 tbsp dark soy sauce
6 tbsp light soy sauce
4 tbsp yellow bean sauce
2 tbsp Chinese rice wine (Shaoxing wine)
1½ tbsp vegetable oil
350g (12oz) piece of belly pork
pinch of salt
pinch of white pepper
1 tbsp sugar
300g (10½oz) straight-to-wok noodles (use your favourite)

Mix the dark soy sauce, light soy sauce, 2 tablespoons of the yellow bean sauce and the rice wine together in a bowl and set to one side.

Place a saucepan that has a tight-fitting lid over a medium-low heat and add ½ tablespoon of the oil. Season the pork belly with a pinch of salt and white pepper, then add to the pan and cook for 6 minutes, turning frequently. Sprinkle in the sugar and continue to cook for a further 2 minutes. Pour in the soy sauce mixture and cook for a further 1–2 minutes, then pour in 500ml (2 cups) water and mix well. Bring to a very gentle simmer, cover with the lid and cook slowly for 40 minutes. After 40 minutes, remove the lid and continue cooking until the sauce has almost gone. Remove the pan from the heat and set to one side.

Place a wok over a medium-high heat, add the remaining oil along with your noodles and cook for 2 minutes. Once the noodles have loosened and softened, add the remaining 2 tablespoons of yellow bean sauce along with 3 tablespoons of water and mix well. Once fully coated, transfer to serving bowls or plates. Cut the rested pork belly into slices and arrange over the noodles, drizzling with the leftover cooking sauce.

MUSHROOM LO MEIN

Unlike chow mein, in which noodles are fried to crispiness, lo mein is cooked in a sauce to keep them soft. You'll be surprised how much flavour they take on, providing you with a great comforting bowl of savoury, noodle-y delight.

10 MINUTES   **6 MINUTES**   **SERVES 2-3**

1 tbsp Chinese rice wine (Shaoxing wine)

3 tbsp Mushroom Stir-fry Sauce (page 343 or use shop-bought)

2 tbsp light soy sauce

2 tsp sugar

1 tsp Chinese five spice

1 tbsp rice vinegar

¼ tsp white pepper

2 nests of fresh lo mein egg noodles (vegan option: use fresh udon noodles)

2 tbsp oil (vegetable, groundnut or coconut)

1 garlic clove, finely chopped

2 spring onions (scallions), cut in half and then into thin strips

1 carrot, cut into matchsticks

1 large portobello mushroom, cut into bite-sized pieces

6–8 baby corn cobs, quartered lengthways

30g (¼ cup) canned water chestnuts, drained and sliced

½ tbsp sesame oil

Combine the rice wine, Mushroom Stir-fry Sauce, soy sauce, sugar, five spice, rice vinegar and white pepper in a bowl. Set to one side.

Loosen the noodles by soaking in a bowl of warm water, drain and set to one side.

Place a wok over a medium-high heat and add the oil, garlic and spring onions (scallions) and fry for around 20 seconds until fragrant. Add the carrot and mushrooms and fry for a further 2 minutes, then add the baby corn, water chestnuts and the loosened noodles. Fry for a further 2 minutes, add the sauce mixture and continue to fry until all the ingredients are combined well and warmed through. Remove from the heat, stir in the sesame oil and transfer to serving bowls.

SATAY CHICKEN UDON NOODLES

Even I was surprised at just how quick this dish was to cook; no sooner had I started the dish, than it was on my plate and being scoffed. Washing up consisted of just my wok and the wooden spoon I used. Chewy noodles, juicy chicken, crunchy onions and peppers smothered in a rich spicy satay sauce. Lovely!

10 MINUTES **8 MINUTES** **SERVES 2**

2 tbsp oil (vegetable, groundnut or coconut)

2 chicken breasts, cut into bite-sized pieces

1 white onion, cut into strips

1 green (bell) pepper, deseeded and cut into strips

1 tsp salt

pinch of white pepper

4 tbsp satay dipping sauce (or use 2–3 tbsp satay paste, to taste)

300g (10½oz) straight-to-wok udon noodles

Heat a large non-stick wok over a medium-high heat and add the oil. Add the chicken and allow to brown on one side, then stir in the onion and green pepper for 1–2 minutes to soften.

Season with the salt and pepper, then stir in the satay dipping sauce, along with 250ml (1 cup) water. Once all the ingredients are well combined in the sauce, add the noodles and cook for 2 minutes, stirring frequently to separate the noodles. Serve immediately.

Kwoklyn's tip
Add a sprinkle of crushed salted peanuts just before serving to add a lovely crunch.

FINE EGG NOODLES
WITH BEANSPROUTS

Deliciously simple as a noodle dish on their own or as the bed for a saucy topping. Once you master the basics of cooking fried noodles to perfection, there really is no limit to the variety of stir-fried noodle dishes you can create.

5 MINUTES **7 MINUTES** **SERVES 2**

2 nests of dried egg noodles
(size number 2 in your Chinese
supermarket)
2 tbsp vegetable oil
1 small onion, thinly sliced
1 tbsp light soy sauce
½ tbsp dark soy sauce
2 tbsp oyster sauce or you can use
Mushroom Stir-fry Sauce (page 343)
150g (2 cups) beansprouts
1 tsp sesame oil

Place the dried egg noodles into a pan of boiling water for 1 minute. Once softened, strain through a sieve and spread out on a clean tea towel and allow to cool.

Place a wok over a medium-high heat, add the oil and onion and cook for 1 minute. Next, add the cooled noodles and give everything a really good mix, then fry for 3–4 minutes, stirring occasionally. Try to be patient as you cook the noodles as you want to char some of the strands to help recreate the classic Chinese takeaway taste. Now add the light and dark soy sauces, oyster sauce and beansprouts. Give the ingredients a stir to ensure everything is well combined, and once the beansprouts have slightly softened, turn off the heat, add the sesame oil and serve.

LONG LIFE NOODLES

In Chinese culture, long noodles represent longevity so you will always find a heaped serving of Long Life Noodles on the table at a Chinese celebration banquet. Eating noodles also symbolises good luck and prosperity, so next time you tuck into a steaming bowl of noodles, take a moment to feel the good vibes of your own creation.

5 MINUTES   **8 MINUTES**   **SERVES 2**

240g (8¾oz) dried Chinese egg noodles
1 tbsp Chinese rice wine (Shaoxing wine)
1 tsp light soy sauce
1 tsp dark soy sauce
2 tbsp oyster sauce
½ tsp sugar
⅛ tsp or a pinch of white pepper
2 tbsp vegetable oil
60g (1 cup) fresh shiitake (poku) mushrooms, destalked and thinly sliced
3 spring onions (scallions), cut into 5cm (2in) lengths
drizzle of sesame oil

Cook the egg noodles in a saucepan of boiling water for 1–2 minutes and, once softened, strain through a sieve and then lay out on a clean tea towel and allow to cool.

In a bowl, combine the rice wine, light and dark soy sauces, oyster sauce, sugar and pepper, mix well and set to one side.

Place a wok over a medium-high heat and, once smoking, add the oil along with the mushrooms and half the spring onions (scallions). After a minute of stir-frying, add the cooled noodles and continue to stir-fry for another minute. Evenly pour over the sauce mixture and continue to cook for another 2–3 minutes, being careful not to break up the noodles, as long noodles represent prosperity. Finally, add the remaining spring onions, stir gently to combine, then turn off the heat, drizzle with sesame oil and serve.

DESSERTS

CHINESE EGG CUSTARD TARTS

These egg tarts are usually served at the beginning of the meal with Chinese tea as you are ordering the food. Twice as sweet as British egg tarts but so moreish you'll be diving in for seconds and thirds.

45 MINUTES   **30 MINUTES**   **MAKES 8-12**

For the pastry

225g (1¾ cups) plain (all-purpose) flour, plus extra for dusting

30g (3½ tbsp) icing (confectioners') sugar

60g (2oz) salted butter, chilled and grated

65g (2¼oz) lard, chilled and grated

1 egg, beaten

½ tsp vanilla extract

For the filling

50g (¼ cup) caster (superfine) sugar

150ml (⅔ cup) hot water

2 eggs

5 tbsp evaporated milk

½ tsp vanilla extract

Sift the flour and icing (confectioners') sugar into a large mixing bowl. Add the butter and lard and gently rub into the dry ingredients with your fingertips until the mixture resembles fine breadcrumbs.

Add the egg and the vanilla extract and mix with a table knife, drawing the mixture together to form a ball. Cover in clingfilm (plastic wrap) and rest in the fridge for 30 minutes.

Preheat the oven to 200°C (400°F).

Make the custard filling: mix the sugar into the hot water in a bowl until it's completely dissolved. In a large bowl, whisk the eggs with the evaporated milk, then add the sugar water and vanilla extract and mix together well. Strain the mixture through a fine sieve into a jug – this should remove any foam that has formed. Put to one side.

Roll out the dough on a lightly floured worktop to 5mm (¼in) thick (try not to handle it too much), then cut out 12 discs with a cookie cutter slightly wider than your muffin tray holes. Lightly press the pastry discs into each hole using your thumbs, starting from the bottom then up to the sides to make even tart shells.

Carefully pour the egg mixture into each tart shell but don't overfill.

Transfer the tarts to the middle shelf of the preheated oven and bake for 10–15 minutes until the edges are lightly coloured. Reduce the oven temperature to 150°C (300°F) and bake for another 10–15 minutes until the custard is cooked through.

Delicious eaten warm but will keep in the fridge for a day or two. (If you can resist that long!)

NUTELLA MOCHI

Mochi is made by pounding glutinous rice flour to make a sticky, chewy dough. It is then filled with a variety of fillings and eaten as a sweet snack. This is my take on the sweet treat and I hope you agree that it's nothing short of yummy.

---

15 MINUTES   **15 MINUTES**   **SERVES 4**

160g (1 cup) glutinous rice flour
   (see tip below)
180ml (¾ cup) cold water
400g (2 cups) sugar
cornflour (cornstarch), for dusting
3 tbsp Nutella
3 tbsp crunchy peanut butter
35g (¼ cup) sesame seeds, toasted

Put the rice flour, cold water and the sugar into a large microwaveable bowl and mix to combine. Cover the bowl with clingfilm (plastic wrap) and place it into the microwave for 3 minutes on full power. Remove from the microwave and vigorously mix for 3 minutes, then re-cover with clingfilm and return to the microwave for a further 3 minutes on full power. Vigorously mix again for a further 3 minutes.

Dust your worktop generously with cornflour (cornstarch), turn out the mixture and begin to knead vigorously for up to 10 minutes. The mixture should feel very springy and be medium firm. Separate the dough into 12 equal pieces and roll into balls.

Take one ball and flatten into a disc about 7cm (2¾in) in diameter. Put 1 teaspoon of Nutella and 1 teaspoon of peanut butter into the centre of the disc, then fold in the edges to cover the filling and reshape into a smooth ball. Roll the ball into the toasted sesame seeds to evenly cover and set to one side while you finish the rest.

Once all of the mochi have been made, they are ready to serve.

Kwoklyn's tip
Glutinous rice flour is made from sweet white rice that becomes moist and sticky once cooked. You can find glutinous rice flour at your local Chinese supermarket or from online suppliers. You can add any filling you like to mochi, such as red bean paste, black sesame paste, lotus seed paste or even your favourite jam, marmalade or a dollop of frozen ice cream.

LYCHEE AND MANGO PUDDING

My version of an Eton mess without the meringue: sweet, juicy lychee and mango smothered in a sweet, thick cream and flecked with black peppercorns – a little play on that sweet and savoury that we all love.

10 MINUTES   **SERVES 4**

12 lychees (fresh or canned)
1 mango, peeled, stoned and cut into
 bite-sized pieces, or use canned
300ml (1¼ cups) double (heavy) cream
1½ tbsp icing (confectioners') sugar
pinch of salt
½ tsp crushed black peppercorns

If you are using fresh lychees, peel them and remove their stones but try to keep them whole. If you are using canned lychees or mango, drain, chop and set to one side.

Whisk the double (heavy) cream in a large bowl until it has thickened to the same consistency as a thick custard. Sift in the sugar and salt, then add the crushed black peppercorns, lychees and mango and carefully fold through until completely combined. Portion into serving bowls and dive in.

KWOKLYN'S CHILLI ICE CREAM

If you have never tried chilli ice cream, you are missing out! It is creamy, smooth and cool at first and then slowly you begin to feel the warm heat building in your mouth. As the heat develops you realise you need to have another mouthful to cool things down; and so the cycle begins again!

5 MINUTES   **30 MINUTES**   **SERVES 6**

5 Thai red chillies, deseeded and very finely chopped
80ml (⅓ cup) water
2 tbsp sugar
600ml (2½ cups) double (heavy) cream
1 x 397g (14oz) can condensed milk
1 tsp cornflour (cornstarch)
3 drops of chilli extract (optional)

Place a non-stick wok over a medium heat, add the finely chopped chilli and dry-fry gently for 2–3 minutes, then add the water and gently simmer for another 2–3 minutes, allowing the chillies to soften. Add the sugar, combine and continue to cook until you have a syrupy chilli mix. Turn off the heat and allow it to cool for 15 minutes.

Pour the double (heavy) cream into a large bowl and whisk until you have stiff peaks, then add the condensed milk, cornflour (cornstarch), cooled chilli syrup and chilli extract (if using) and continue to whisk until the mixture has thickened.

Transfer to an airtight container and freeze for at least 8 hours.

CHINESE TOFFEE APPLES

I have such clear visions of cooking these little molten toffee balls, so vivid I can smell the caramelised sugar and the hot sesame seeds with the sweet aroma of apples.

10 MINUTES   **15 MINUTES**   **SERVES 4**

groundnut oil, for deep-frying
100g (¾ cup) self-raising (self-rising) flour
1 egg, beaten
about 300ml (1¼ cups) water
4 apples of a firm variety, peeled, cored and cut into 3cm (1¼in) cubes

To finish
8 tbsp granulated sugar
4 tbsp water
1½ tbsp sesame seeds

Pour enough oil to deep-fry the apple cubes into a wok or deep-sided saucepan and heat to 170°C (340°F).

Mix the flour and beaten egg together in a large bowl, then slowly add enough water so you have a medium-thick batter.

Dip each apple cube into the batter and carefully drop into the oil. Fry for around 8–10 minutes, cooking in batches if necessary, until golden brown. Transfer to a wire rack or a plate lined with kitchen paper to drain.

To finish, heat a wok over a medium heat and stir in the sugar and water. After about 3 minutes the sugar should begin to caramelise, so gently add the apples and the sesame seeds. Mix well – being really careful not to splash the molten sugar – ensuring each apple is thoroughly covered. Transfer the apples to a wire rack to cool for 15 minutes before serving.

CHINESE FRIED SESAME BALLS

As a child I always remember Dad ordering these when we first arrived at a restaurant to eat. I've found that many Chinese people tend to have fruit at the end of a meal, so sweet treats like these are eaten at the beginning and could be enjoyed as a little appetiser.

15 MINUTES   **15 MINUTES**   **SERVES 8**

110g (½ cup) soft light brown sugar
160ml (⅔ cup) hot water
250g (1½ cups) glutinous rice flour, plus extra for dusting (see tip below)
6 tbsp sweet lotus seed paste (or use red bean paste or Nutella)
70g (½ cup) sesame seeds
vegetable oil, for deep-frying

In a large jug, mix the brown sugar with the hot water, stirring until completely dissolved.

Put the rice flour in a large bowl and create a well in the middle. Add the sugar water and mix into the flour; continue to mix for 5 minutes until the dough stops sticking to the bowl.

Lightly dust your worktop with rice flour, turn out the dough and knead for 5 minutes until the dough becomes smooth. You can use a little more flour or water to achieve this if required.

Divide the dough into 8 equal pieces, roll into balls and then flatten into discs about 7cm (2¾in) in diameter. Place 2 teaspoons of your chosen paste into the centre of each disc, then fold in the edges to cover the filling and reshape into smooth balls. Roll in the sesame seeds to evenly cover.

Heat the oil in a large, deep saucepan to about 165°C (330°F) – you don't want to fry the balls at too high a temperature. Fill the pan about two-thirds full. Working in batches of 4, gently lower the balls into the oil and fry for 15 minutes. During this time you will need to frequently turn them so they achieve an even golden brown all over. As the balls cook, they will expand and begin to float, so ensure there is plenty of room in the pan and cook in smaller batches if it works better with the pan you are using. Transfer to a wire rack or plate lined with kitchen paper to drain. Allow to cool for 20 minutes before serving.

Kwoklyn's tip
Glutinous rice flour is made from sweet white rice that becomes moist and sticky once cooked. You can find glutinous rice flour at your local Chinese supermarket or from online suppliers.

BANANA FRITTERS

Gooey bananas covered in a fluffy batter and served with a blob of ice cream and oozing golden syrup. Yum!

We often ate this at the end of 'staff dinner' as the head chef had a sweet tooth, and while he was cooking the bananas he'd leave the can of golden syrup in a bowl of warm water to make it extra runny for drizzling over the top.

10 MINUTES   15 MINUTES   SERVES 4

groundnut oil, for deep-frying
260g (2 cups) self-raising (self-rising) flour
½ tsp bicarbonate of soda (baking soda)
360ml (1½ cups) water
4 bananas, peeled and halved
130g (1 cup) plain (all-purpose) flour

To serve
6 tbsp golden (light corn) syrup
4 scoops vanilla ice cream

Pour enough oil into a wok or deep-sided saucepan to deep-fry the bananas and heat to 170°C (340°F).

Sift the self-raising (self-rising) flour into a large bowl, add the bicarbonate of soda (baking soda) and the water and mix to form a smooth batter. Lightly dust the bananas in plain (all-purpose) flour, then dip into the batter to coat and carefully drop into the oil. Deep-fry for around 6–8 minutes until golden brown. Transfer to a wire rack or a plate lined with kitchen paper to drain.

Divide between 4 plates, drizzle over the golden (light corn) syrup and add a scoop of ice cream to serve.

LYCHEE CRUSH

This drink will have you romanticising about sandy beaches, hot summer afternoons and the gentle wash of the sea lapping across the shore. Sweet, juicy and creamy, it's a drink that slips down so smoothly, kicking your taste buds into action on the way through.

2 MINUTES   **SERVES 4**

650ml (2¾ cups) lychee juice
6 tbsp condensed milk (or a vegan alternative)
300ml (1¼ cups) coconut milk
3 cups crushed ice
1 x 420g (15oz) can lychees

Put all the ingredients in a blender, reserving 4 whole lychees for decoration. Blend on full power for 20–30 seconds.

Pour into 4 glasses and top each one with a whole lychee.

HONG KONG-STYLE BUBBLE TEA

Bubble tea is a sweet tea-based drink that is served with chewy tapioca pearls, creating a drink and a meal all in one. It's a fun drink and quite unique. I used to serve this delicious recipe in my bubble-tea bar in Leicester.

15 MINUTES   **3 MINUTES**   **SERVES 4**

150g (1 cup) tapioca pearls
1 litre (4 cups) water
5 teabags
1 x 397g (14oz) can condensed milk
500ml (2 cups) strong black coffee
ice

Cook the tapioca pearls according to the packet instructions. Once fully cooked and softened, drain and set to one side.

Bring the water to the boil in a saucepan, add the teabags and simmer for 2 minutes. Remove from the heat, discard the teabags and add the condensed milk, stirring until completely dissolved, then stir in the coffee. Fill a jug with as much ice as you can and pour the coffee/tea into the jug.

Spoon 3 tablespoons of cooked tapioca pearls into each of 4 glasses and add a couple of ice cubes. Fill with your chilled coffee/tea.

CONDIMENTS

HOISIN SAUCE

A rich, thick and fragrant sauce that sings 'Cantonese' to your taste buds. It's used in many dishes either as a glaze, in marinades or to flavour a sauce in a stir-fry. It's also a fantastic dipping sauce with its hints of Chinese five spice and aromatic garlic.

5 MINUTES **5 MINUTES** **MAKES 1 SMALL JAR**

125g (⅔ cup) demerara sugar
250ml (1 cup) water
⅛ tsp cream of tartar
½ tsp lemon juice
3 tbsp light soy sauce
1 tbsp dark soy sauce
3 tbsp smooth peanut butter
3 tbsp rice vinegar
1 tsp garlic powder
½ tsp Chinese five spice
¼ tsp white pepper
¼ tsp sesame oil

Mix the sugar, water, cream of tartar, lemon juice, light and dark soy sauces, peanut butter, rice vinegar, garlic powder, five spice and pepper together in a saucepan and place over a low heat. Once all of the ingredients have dissolved, slowly bring to the boil and simmer until the sauce has reduced by a third. Remove from the heat and add the sesame oil.

Allow to cool, then store your hoisin sauce in an airtight jar in the fridge for up to a month.

HOT CHILLI DRAGON SAUCE

The aroma from this sauce fills your kitchen like no other; it's aromatic, it's spicy, it's quite simply amazing. I love the sound of the sizzle as you pour the oil into the soy sauce. You won't have tasted anything quite like this dip before, but you will want to use it again and again once you have.

5 MINUTES **5 MINUTES** **SERVES 4**

3–5 green bird's-eye chillies, finely chopped
3 spring onions (scallions), thinly sliced into ringlets
4 tbsp light soy sauce
4 tbsp vegetable oil

Put the chopped chillies and spring onions (scallions) into a heatproof bowl, pour over the soy sauce and mix well.

Heat the oil in a saucepan until it begins to smoke a little, then remove the pan from the heat and slowly and carefully drizzle the oil over the soy sauce mixture. It will sizzle and spit (like a dragon) and it will fill the air with an amazing aroma.

This dip is great with everything.

MUSHROOM STIR-FRY SAUCE

The Chinese have been using mushroom sauce in their cooking for centuries; its savoury flavour is ideal for stir-fries and in noodle dishes, and it is widely used in Western Chinese dishes across the world.

20 MINUTES   **20 MINUTES**   **MAKES 1 SMALL JAR**

4 medium dried shiitake (poku) or Chinese mushrooms
250ml (1 cup) boiling water
½ tbsp oil (vegetable, groundnut or coconut)
1 nori seaweed sheet, ground into a powder
2 tbsp light soy sauce
½ tbsp dark soy sauce
1 tbsp sugar
¼ tsp salt
1 tsp cornflour (cornstarch)

Rinse the mushrooms under warm water and put into a large bowl. Pour over the boiling water and leave to soak for 15 minutes until soft. Gently squeeze the excess water out of the mushrooms, reserving the soaking liquid for later. Remove and discard the stalks from the mushrooms, then cut the caps into 4 slices.

Heat a wok or non-stick frying pan over a medium heat, add the oil and fry the mushroom slices for 3 minutes. Remove and set to one side.

Place the mushroom liquid, powdered nori, fried mushrooms, soy sauces, sugar, salt and cornflour (cornstarch) into a blender and blitz until smooth. Pour the mixture into a small saucepan and gently simmer until the sauce has thickened and reduced by about a third. Remove from the heat and allow to cool.

Store in an airtight container. The sauce can be kept in the fridge for 1 week or in the freezer for up to 3 months.

Kwoklyn's tip
Freeze the sauce in ice-cube trays – once frozen, transfer to a ziplock bag kept in the freezer. Defrost only as much as you need each time.

CHINESE BBQ SAUCE

The epitome of all Chinese sauces and one that many, if not all of us, know and love across the world. This sauce works really well as a marinade; I also enjoy it as a dipping sauce.

15 MINUTES   **SERVES 8**

1 x 400g (14oz) can hoisin barbecue sauce
1 x 400g (14oz) can yellow bean sauce
1½ tbsp Chinese five spice
4 tbsp Chinese rice wine (Shaoxing wine)
1.5 litres (6 cups) vegetable stock
5 tbsp white sugar

Put all the ingredients into a saucepan and slowly bring to a simmer. Simmer for 15 minutes and then remove from the heat.

Once fully cooled, pour the sauce into an airtight container and store in the fridge for up to a week, or pour into individual ice-cube trays and freeze. Once frozen, place the cubes into a ziplock bag and store in the freezer for up to 6 months. Allow 2–3 cubes per portion, reheated from frozen.

CHINESE GRAVY

At some point, we've all known that person who, amidst the list of sesame prawn toast, fried rice and chow mein, will order steak, chips and gravy from their Chinese takeaway. Once you know how to make this tasty gravy though, it's easy to see why anyone would order such a meal!

10 MINUTES   **25 MINUTES**   **SERVES 8-10**

1 tsp chicken powder, dissolved in 350ml (scant 1½ cups) hot water and cooled
1 tsp dark soy sauce
1 tsp light soy sauce
1 tbsp oyster sauce
½ tbsp muscovado sugar
1–2 tsp gravy browning (optional)

For the paste
350ml (scant 1½ cups) vegetable oil
1 large onion, thinly sliced
3 spring onions (scallions), roughly chopped
5 garlic cloves, whole and unpeeled
thumb-sized piece of ginger, unpeeled and roughly chopped
1 bay leaf
½ cinnamon stick
3 star anise
200g (1½ cups) plain (all-purpose) flour

Heat the oil in a wok or deep-sided saucepan to 170–180°C (340–350°F), then add all of the paste ingredients, except the flour. Fry over a medium heat for 8–10 minutes until charred slightly but not burnt, and the oil is infused with flavour. Using a metal sieve, strain the oil into a heatproof jug or pan and, using the back of a wooden spoon or metal ladle, press the ingredients against the sieve, extracting all of the oil.

At this point the oil should still be hot, so pour it back into the wok over a medium heat and add the flour a bit at a time, whisking through the oil to create a thick roux (it should be stir-able but thick). Sometimes you need less flour and sometimes you need a little more depending on how much oil you managed to squeeze from the aromats and the flour you're using. Once you are happy with the thickness of the roux, allow it to cool and store in an airtight container in your cupboard for up to 6 months.

To make the gravy, heat 1½ tablespoons of roux in a wok and, stirring constantly, add the chicken powder water, soy sauces, oyster sauce and sugar. Bring to the boil and then turn down to a simmer, allowing the gravy to thicken. Once you are happy with the thickness of your gravy, add the gravy browning to add colour (if using). Give the gravy a good stir through and pour over your chips, steak, roast chicken or, like me, over rice.

WASABI MAYO

For those of you who haven't made your own mayonnaise before, you won't believe just how simple it is until you've gone ahead and done it. And for those of you who love the idea of a wasabi mayo but don't have the inclination to make your own from scratch, simply mix the wasabi into shop-bought mayonnaise. To make a Sriracha mayo, simply replace the wasabi with the same amount of Sriracha.

5 MINUTES   **SERVES 8–10**

3 egg yolks
300ml (1¼ cups) groundnut oil
2 tbsp wasabi paste
1 tbsp lemon juice
pinch of salt
5 pinches of black pepper

Put your egg yolks into a food processor and begin to blend on medium speed, then very slowly drizzle the oil into the mixture. Once half of the oil has been added, you can begin to add the oil a little quicker, and when all of the oil has been added and thoroughly mixed in, turn off the blender. Add the wasabi paste, lemon juice, salt and black pepper and blend again for 5–10 seconds. Store in an airtight container in the fridge for 3–4 days.

Kwoklyn's tip
If you don't have a food processor, you can use a large bowl and a balloon whisk. Place a folded tea towel on your worktop and put the bowl on top to stop it from slipping around during mixing. Add the egg yolks and begin to whisk, and as you whisk, very slowly drizzle in the oil, a few drops at a time. Once half of the oil has been added, you can begin to add the oil a little quicker, and when all of the oil has been added, you can add the flavourings and whisk again for 5–10 seconds.

TONKATSU SAUCE

This tangy, sweet, aromatic sauce is normally served with deep-fried cutlets, but it really does work with anything. Not too dissimilar to a good BBQ sauce, you can dip a myriad of goodies into this sticky, unctuous condiment.

5 MINUTES   **SERVES 4**

1¼ tsp garlic powder
600ml (2½ cups) tomato ketchup
12 tbsp Worcestershire sauce
5 tbsp light soy sauce
8 tbsp sugar

Put all the ingredients into a small saucepan and gently warm. Once the sugar has completely dissolved, remove from the heat. Be careful not to boil.

Once completely cooled, transfer to an airtight container and store in the fridge for up to 2 weeks. You can also freeze in ice-cube trays for up to 3 months.

INDEX

ACKNOWLEDGEMENTS

FAMILY: where life begins, and LOVE never ends!

My Complete Chinese Takeout Cookbook is a behind the scenes glimpse at my life growing up in Mum and Dad's restaurants and takeaways.

Each recipe is a family member and as I typed, it unlocked the millions of memories I had as a child, surrounded by food; happy, safe, content and full. Maya-Lily and Lola-Rose, my beautiful little Wans, this book is a peek at Daddy's life during the 1970s, 80s, 90s and into the new millennium, the food I ate and what it means to me; how Nanny and Grandad fed me with love and food, and how both are the same.

Maya-Lily and Lola-Rose (my beautiful babies), there are no words that could ever come close to telling you how much I love you. I am so proud of the women you have grown into; you are without question the greatest achievement of my life.

Mum and Dad, where do I start? You have given me so much and taught me that no matter what life throws my way you will ALWAYS be there to pick me up. I am truly blessed to call you Mum and Dad.

Oilen and Babe (Gok), I often wish we could do it all again, life really was as simple as a *Jungle Book* T-shirt and heading to the restaurant for a bowl of noodles. Nurture taught us that family always come first but I didn't need to be taught how to love you.

Jo, well, what can I say? We lived this extraordinary life behind the walls of a fully functioning, disjointed, hectic but exciting Cantonese restaurant that I called HOME. While I was melting in a hot, noisy, frantic kitchen, you were washing up out back in the freezing cold surrounded by what can only be described as a biblical number of plates and bowls, and not forgetting the chopsticks. Do you remember the sound of washing hundreds of pairs of chopsticks as you rubbed them together in the hot soapy water in that huge aluminium washing up bowl? Anyway, what I wanted to say is that I knew I loved you then and I love you even more now.

Clare, you are seriously one hell of an agent. My feet are still running at a million miles an hour since you took the gamble to act for me.

Sarah Lavelle and Quadrille, thank you so much for having the confidence to allow me to become one of your authors.